IMAGINE PUBLISHING

Imagine Publishing Ltd
Richmond House
33 Richmond Hill
Bournemouth
Dorset BH2 6EZ
☎ +44 (0) 1202 586200
Website: www.imagine-publishing.co.uk

Edited by
April Madden

Designed by
Ali Innes

Proofed by
Julie Easton, Colleen Johnson and Rosie Tanner

Editor in Chief
Jo Cole

Group Art Editor
Lora Barnes

Head of Design
Ross Andrews

Printed by
William Gibbons, 26 Planetary Road, Willenhall,
West Midlands, WV13 3XT

Disclaimer
The publisher cannot accept responsibility for any unsolicited material
lost or damaged in the post. All text and layout is the copyright of
Imagine Publishing Ltd. Nothing in this magazine may be reproduced
in whole or part without the written permission of the publisher.
All copyrights are recognised and used specifically for the purpose
of criticism and review. Although the magazine has endeavoured
to ensure all information is correct at time of print, prices and
availability may change. This bookazine is fully independent and
not affiliated in any way with the companies mentioned herein.

Trademark(s) or registered trademark(s) of Corel Corporation and/or its
subsidiaries in Canada, the US and/or other countries. Screenshots
are ©Copyright 2009 Corel Corporation, reprinted by permission

The Complete Guide to Digital Painting © 2009 Imagine Publishing Ltd

ISBN 978-1-906078-22-5

Welcome

This is the second in the series that will help beginners and advanced artists expand your digital painting skills

Welcome to The Complete Guide to Digital Painting Volume 2, the second title in our Complete Guide to Digital Painting series. Whether you're a raw beginner or a fully fledged digital artist, you'll find a wealth of content in these pages to enable you to work from photos and sketches alike to create your very own digital masterpieces. We'll start off with a section on preparation and on some of the top techniques for established art styles, before moving on to a range of inspirational and sometimes experimental tutorials designed to help you take your creative talents in different directions and learn fabulous new techniques to enhance your artwork. We'll take a look at reproducing the look of real media as well as explaining some of the unique tricks native to Corel's Painter software. We'll teach you how to build up a composition, from background detailing and foreground focus to lighting, action, pattern and much more. We'll also take a look at how some of the world's greatest artists painted, and teach you how to re-create their styles. And you'll also find all the source files you need on the accompanying disc. You hold in your hands everything you need to explore and enjoy all aspects of digital art. Happy painting!

Contents

30

24

48

42

58

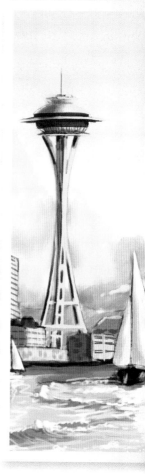

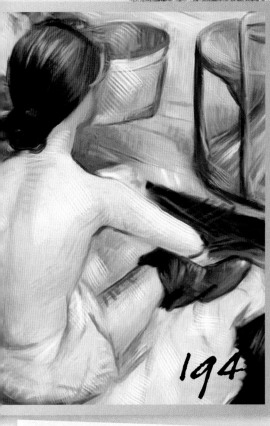

194

96

120

148

Art skills section

242

Prep photos
for painting

Photo editing can dramatically improve your paintings. **David Cole** shows us how

n the Seventies, a high-end hi-fi equipment manufacturer used the expression 'Rubbish In, Rubbish Out' to help sell its expensive equipment. The message was that the music coming out of a hi-fi system could only be as good as the signal first introduced into the system. This pretty much goes for photographic manipulation too; in general, bad photos make bad paintings.

You can, of course, hope to salvage an unexciting photo in the painting process, but it is much easier and much more fun to start painting from a photograph that looks right and stimulates you. You don't want the painting stage to feel like a chore.

While what stimulates us visually is a matter of individual taste, there are a few ways in which photos created or retouched for painting differ, or should differ, from photos made to be seen primarily as photos.

First, and in general, paintings do not have the same level of detail across the image that photos have. Painters use detail creatively so when we manipulate photos for painting, we need to get the best imitation of simplification we can using Painter's selective blurring and sharpening tools. This is important because in painting we also need simple areas where brushstrokes can breathe and be read clearly. This is why Painter X's Smart Blur is a very useful development.

Second, we ought to chew away at the composition until it's right. Of course, photographers are just as concerned with composition as painters, but in photos for painting we need to use cropping in tandem with simplification to get the base image settled. There is no excuse for poor composition in painting where the painter has control over what appears on the canvas.

Thirdly, dynamic range. Paintings have a very wide range of tone and hue and this degree of subtlety is really only seen in HDR (higher dynamic range) photographs. HDR is often produced by combining three photos with different exposure ranges in a composite that looks quite painterly. Painter does not yet have native tools to do this, but you can approximate it using three differently exposed but otherwise identical photos as clone sources for a single painting. If you check out some HDR images, you'll see what can be done. HDR really helps getting a photo ready for painting.

Finally, colour. This is, of course, also related to dynamic range and hue intensity, but in colour cloning it is also about producing colour harmony in the photo to be painted. In Painter, this can be achieved by using two or three versions of the source photo as clone sources, each with a different but harmonious hue. These can then be brushed into the painting. Or you can use the Adjust Selected Color tool to play around with individual colours in your source photo to achieve a colour scheme you like.

So this article is about selecting and editing photos for painting. It will suggest some preparatory steps that you are probably familiar with, but should also give you some ideas you not have tried before.

Getting the composition right

Often, the problem lies within the framing of a photograph

This photo of a duck is poorly framed. The duck is the subject, but it is lost in the picture and the dark waterfall overwhelms it. We need to decide on a better angle of view and the right, tighter crop. Luckily, the image has sufficient resolution that we can choose quite a tight crop if we wish.

Original photo

Cropped photo

In this instance, we are going to crop the photograph just enough to make it clear that the duck is the subject, and to get it to fall on a third node (regarding the rule of thirds). To achieve this, we used the Crop tool from the Tools palette.

Fixing the brightness and contrast

Bring out detail in your shots

The exposure is not bad on this photo but it is a little overdone and the colour is rather bleached. We also need to add some contrast to make it read better.

Reducing the brightness This doesn't require a vast reduction in brightness, enough to make the lighter tones more distinct. We don't want to lose shadow detail.

Adding contrast Contrast can add sparkle and punch to an image by making darks darker and lights lighter. Ideally, strong contrast should be concentrated in the centre of the image but we will add some contrast all over and if necessary, remove it selectively later.

Dodging to lighten selectively We need to lighten the duck's head, around the eyes particularly, using the Dodge tool found in the Photo brush category. This should be done carefully at a very low setting.

Basic editing

Painter has many effects and tools that can be applied pretty easily to help photos before you start to clone them. Broadly, there are tools that change the anatomy and orientation of an image, ones that change the tonal values in an image, ones that change the image's focus and ones that change various aspects of the photo's colours.

When preparing a photo, it's wise to start with the big things – do I like the image? Is the subject too close? Not close enough? Does it need to be cropped? Is the horizon straight (if you want it straight)? Is the subject too central (remember the rule of thirds)? Do you need another tree to the right or some hills to the left to make the composition right? If you do, source them from another photo and paste them in before you start painting. We need to get comfortable with the basic image before we start painting. Take your time over this.

The main tools for changing the physical dimensions and view angles are in the Menu bar's Canvas and Effects drop-down menus. Under Canvas, check out Resize and Canvas Size, under Effects see Orientation and also the Crop tool in the Tools palette.

Having got the basics of the photo the way we want it, the next thing to look at is whether it has the right tonal values. Are the highlights blown? Not bright enough? Are the shadow areas too dark, to the point where they are losing detail? Or are they not dark enough? Is the overall arrangement of light and dark pleasing? Once you have made your assessment of which changes are needed, or if you just want to experiment, you can change darks and lights and the relationship between them in a number of ways.

The easiest way is to change the values is with the Brightness/Contrast function at Effects>Tonal Control>Brightness/Contrast. Brightness determines how bright an image is and Contrast adjusts the difference between light and dark values. We can adjust these parameters to taste and try out a number of different values. A rough rule of thumb is that we want to avoid wherever possible blown-out highlights – very light areas that are so bright, no detail remains in them, and also shadow areas that are so dark there is no detail in them. Broadly, blown highlights and solid black shadows that are like this in the original image cannot be salvaged, and we want to avoid blowing highlights and losing shadow detail when we adjust Brightness and Contrast.

Changing the brightness and contrast will, of course, affect your colours. But we may also want to add colour intensity to the image to make it come alive – this is adding colour saturation. Or

Control the size and angle of your canvas to get the best composition

> "We want to avoid blowing highlights and losing shadow detail when we adjust Brightness/Contrast"

we may want to change the overall nature or hue of the colours, for example, to cool or warm our picture. Painter allows you to change all colours or just one colour, and in this article we will look at the one you will probably use most often – Adjust Colors. This can be found in Painter on the path Effects>Tonal Control>Adjust Colors.

Finally, it is worth mentioning some of the developments in tools for photo preparation since Painter 9. Initially, Painter 9.5 introduced photo-painting palettes and then Painter X improved on that by added an Underpainting palette that includes colour schemes based on various media styles, such as Impressionist, classical, modern, watercolour, sketchbook and chalk drawing. If it suits your needs, you can also choose a colour scheme that matches the colours of any open image. These are very valuable tools when preparing a photo to become a painting and are worth checking out.

It may look odd, but Painter X's automated schemes are great

Enhance the colour
Make your hues sing

Are we happy with the colours, or are they too intense? Not intense enough? Do they fit the subject? In this case, increasing the contrast has already given the colours a push, but we can add impact by increasing the colour saturation. We may also want to adjust individual colours.

01 Adding colour saturation We can add extra colour saturation very easily by going to Effects>Tonal Control> Adjust Colors and choosing Color Saturation . We don't want the colours to be garish but we do want a little more intensity.

02 Changing a specified colour We want to desaturate the sky reflections in the water a little. We select the water so only it is affected, move the cursor over the second tool down on the left in the Tools palette, and pick the right-hand tool that looks like a key ring. We make a selection with this.

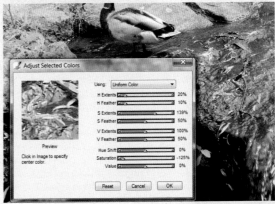

03 Completing the saturation reduction Now we go to Adjust Selected Colors at Effects>Tonal Control>Adjust Selected Colors. We move the cursor in the main picture on some sky's bluish water reflection. The cursor becomes a dropper. Now we click in the reflection area. In the Adjust Selected Colors box, we change the value of S Extents to 139% and lower the bottom Saturation control to -125%. That's it. We deselect the area and we're ready to paint.

Super softening

We used the Super Softener tool to throw the azaleas into relief. We used two versions of the photo to paint – the (slightly sharpened) original and the super-softened one (setting: 50). With both versions open and the original version active, we brushed with the Straight Cloner, then used the softened version as the clone source for the background around the flowers.

Keep the flowers in focus

Soften and blur the background

Put the two together for a stronger impact for your painting

Using focus changes to set up a loose painting

In this walkthrough, we will use the Glass Distortion effect at Effects>Focus>Glass Distortion to prepare a photo for some loose brushwork and a vigorous treatment. Painter has plenty of brushes to help simulate loose brushstrokes, but sometimes it's hard to know where to start. Using Glass Distortion will make the process a little easier by getting the starting photo closer to a loose-brushed treatment.

01 Poppies We duplicate our photo layer, set a Gel composite mode with a value of 52%, then we drop the layer and select Adjust Colors. We set Hue Shift to 0, Saturation to 11% and Value to 7%.

Original photo

Changing focus

In photography, particularly in portraiture and sports, selective focus is used to isolate a subject and draw attention to it. Adjustments in depth of field can blur areas, such as the foreground and the background, of a photograph that the photographer feels are distracting viewers from the main subject. By keeping only the subject in focus – sometimes just the eyes in a portrait – and in full detail, the photographer ensures that the viewer is not distracted by what is happening beyond the subject. This selectivity operates in the same way in painting, except that painters can choose either to create the look of a blur, for example, with a large brush or a palette knife, or actually simplify the detail in an area but keep the boundaries and colours in that area distinct.

Real in-camera simplification – maintaining outlines but simplifying colours and contours – is impossible to achieve, but we can get a good distance towards it in photo-retouching using digital tools. Throughout its advancements, Corel Painter has recognised that this is an important feature, the process enhanced by its Selection tools and Blur effects. Simplification of this sort is rather different to the effect of blurring. Painters may use it because they actually prefer to see their image broken up into a

pattern of shapes with just a few points of detail and one focus of attention. There is just something satisfying to the eye about reduced detail.

Simplification can also help to create the illusion of distance. So, crudely, things that are closer to us are more distinct in that they have sharper outlines. Therefore objects that are miles away in the distance are softer.

Blur can also be used to give the impression of speed in action photos, with motor racing for example. This can be achieved in oils with just a swipe of a palette knife and by photographers by hand-tracking a moving object. It is also straightforward to achieve this with digital tools like Painter where the single movement of a palette knife can be easily simulated.

In Painter, the Focus tools are found at Effects>Focus. There are a range of blurring and sharpening tools. The purpose of Camera Motion Blur and Depth of Field are self-evident; Motion Blur simulates camera shake – moving your hand while taking a photo – and Depth of Field creates a blur similar to the distance from the plane of camera focus in photography. Sharpening Focus heightens contrast by intensifying highlights and shadows. This creates the illusion of greater sharpness. Softening Focus blurs the transition

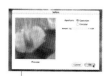

Play with focus using Corel Painter's dedicated tools and options

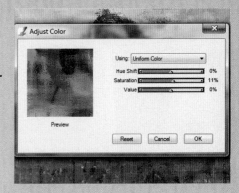

02 Changing the paper texture
We want a paper to interact with Glass Distortion for a heavily textured treatment. We open the Papers palette in the Tools palette and hit Hot Press (this is a smooth paper for watercolour but it will not look like this at all in our treatment).

03 Applying Glass Distortion
We go to Glass Distortion and apply the following: Using to Paper, Softness to 35.9%, Map to Refraction, Quality to Good, Amount to 1.44, Variance to 17.00, Direction to 49 degrees.

04 More colour
We want this to have intense colours so we need to add a little more colour saturation. We go to Effects>Tonal Control>Adjust Colors and increase Saturation to 11%.

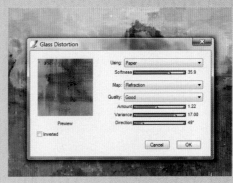

05 Nearly ready
We apply Glass Distortion again to Poppies B. We use the same settings as before, except that we change the Amount to 1.22. This will remove some of the waviness of the previous treatment, and we are now ready to paint.

"By keeping only the subject in focus, the photographer ensures the viewer isn't distracted by what is happening behind"

from one element to another in an image – and Super Soften just does more of it. It takes time but gives you full control over the result. Zoom Blur unsurprisingly creates the effect of zooming in with a zoom lens, basically making a tunnel of blur with an area of distinguishable image at the end. You will notice that a number of these effects offer you different types of effects creation – that is, effects based on Gaussian or Circular Aperture options – just experiment with these.

Painter X has a fine simplification tool. Smart Blur is quite successful in softening and generalising a subject while maintaining its boundaries. It gets closer to real simplification than the other Blur tools and does not stray so far beyond the boundaries of the area you are trying to simplify as the other Painter blurring tools might.

Finally, there is Glass Distortion, which is one of the most interesting focus effects and one used for the main worked-up photograph. It rather unpromisingly offers the effect of images seen through a range of glass between the image and the viewer – like a pebble bathroom window, for example. But in fact, this is a surprisingly useful tool to get a loose painting effect started, which we will explore in a moment.

The Sharpening tool
One of Painter's hidden gems

We use sharpening subtly all the time to make an image more distinct. Here we use the Sharpening tool flat out to create an interesting variation of the contrast effect. The effect makes an image suitable for use as a clone source for a pen-drawing simulation. The settings in the Effects>Focus>Sharpen box are Gaussian, maximum for Amount, Highlight and Shadow, and Red, Green and Blue all checked.

Altering the settings in a photograph can give the composition an entirely different effect

Portraits with impact
Create a classical painting effect

This photo is not a bad starting point for a painting simulation, but it will need some help. There needs to be more focus on the eyes and the background needs to be simplified so as not to distract attention from the face. To achieve this, we will darken the area around the face, the side of the face not facing the light and also simplify the colours.

Original photo

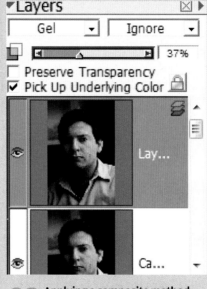

01 Creating a duplicate layer We start by selecting All>Copy>Paste in Place. We make sure that the Pick Up Underlying Color box is checked (it's found near the top of the Layers palette). Pick Up Underlying Color enables the user to see the image below where they erase on the image above.

02 Applying a composite method We need to intensify and slightly darken the overall image, so we now need to set the composite method to Gel . This is rather like the Multiply blending mode in Photoshop. However, the resulting image is too dark and we should reduce the opacity of the layer down to 25% or thereabouts.

03 Lightening the face Now we use the Eraser tool in the Tools palette set to an Opacity of 15% to return to the lighter layer below and cover the right side of the face – the upper cheek and eye – and just a little around the left eye. We need to be gentle and brush evenly.

Create a mood

Create mood with the colour tools as well as Painter X's Underpainting tool

In this section, we will look at how to choose and enhance the mood of a photograph for painting. There are, of course, all sorts of moods that reflect different emotions – happiness, loneliness, anger, innocence, etc – but we will go for a portrait of a young man with the sort of quiet intensity and simplified palette common in Seventeenth Century portraits – for example, see Rembrandt's self-portraits. We will not be using primarily earth colours as he did though, we will allow ourselves a slightly larger range of colours, but we will try to get something of his sense of dramatic light and shade.

Moods are about emotions and it is difficult to create an affecting image with a photo that is lifeless, banal or with very flat lighting. As a starting point, there really needs to be a subject with which we sympathise and to which we respond. So the first point is that the photograph's subject is important. It doesn't have to be a portrait – look at some of Andrew Wyeth's pictures of objects and scenes to see what a brooding quality the everyday can have – but it has to create an atmosphere.

"There really needs to be a subject with which we sympathise and to which we respond"

Once you have a photograph with a suitable subject, you can enhance the mood it creates. Obviously what we do to it depends on the emotion it invokes. The elements to consider are the composition, colour palette, the intensity of the hues and the values – how dark, how light and the sharpness of focus. At the risk of stating the obvious, bright saturated colours from a wide palette will usually be associated with spontaneity, or childhood and happy situations, while dark, mainly unsaturated colours from a limited palette are likely to invoke a sense of brooding, mystery or thoughtfulness. However, dark, warm colours could work well with a positive or romantic subject, and a vibrant colour palette can be associated with war and chaos. So there are no rules here!

The trick is to make sure that the elements of the photograph, and the painting derived from it, are in line with its mood. That way, the emotion carried by the image will be consistent and congruous.

In the walkthrough, we use the tools available up to Painter 9.5. However, we have to note here that within Painter X's Underpainting feature, there is a very useful tool for photo preparation. Indeed, the final result of the photo preparation we will go through can be achieved easier and quicker using the Underpainting tools; the photo colours we will be aiming for can be approximated pretty closely simply by going for the Classical Color Scheme. Such is progress!

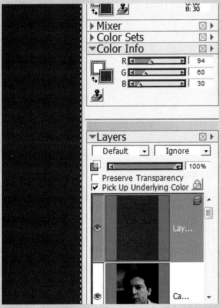

04 Saving the picture
To reduce the two layers to one, we use the Drop All Layers command from Layers. We save it as a TIFF and call it 'Tim1'. Then we close the file and reopen it; the image now has only one layer.

05 Tinting the image
Having opened Tim1, we duplicate its only layer using Select All>Copy>Paste in Place. We double-check that Pick Up Underlying Color is checked, then use the Fill tool from the Tools palette to fill the new layer with a warm, dark brown (R:94, G:60; B:30).

06 Reducing the brown
Next, we're going to need to reduce the opacity of the brown layer until we can see the face below. We use the Eraser at 20% in order to start removing the brown from over the face. We set the composite method to Multiply and the Opacity to 19%.

07 Reducing brightness
We just need to reduce the brightness of the picture a little – this will give it a bit more atmosphere. We first reduce the image to a single layer with the Drop All command. Then we save it as a TIFF, calling it 'Tim2'. Now we close the file and reopen it, reducing the brightness by a smidgen.

08 Sharpening
Nearly there. We'll include a bit of sharpening to add a little bite to the eyes in particular. We could also use a touch more contrast, but need to be careful not to overdo it – we don't want to lighten the left side of the face too much. We save as 'Tim3'.

Create effective portraits

Whether traditional or digital, your portrait needs to deliver impact. **Susi Lawson** shares the techniques needed

Portraits have been one of the most popular visual art forms since the beginning of time. Whether you are painting to honour a world-renowned queen or your adorable nephew, you want the portrait you paint to have an impact on whoever views it. There are certain elements that must be implemented to achieve this, and we are going to present them to you in this tutorial. All portraits must have good light, tonal range, colour balance and, crucially, convey something (like an interest or personality) about the subject. The portrait should be interesting enough that the viewer does not need to know the subject in order for the image to attract their attention and keep it.

The background must be suitable for the foreground and the subject to create compositional unity, and the objects or props in the portrait must convey something about the subject's personality. This can be an occupation, hobby or even a time period. The expression on the face must create an emotion that is compelling, whether it conveys glamour, joy or sadness, and the viewer should be drawn in to feel this. The eyes do not always have to be looking right at the spectator for this connection to happen.

In this portrait, the subject is a 16-year-old girl on the brink of womanhood, and her look seems to convey this longing to grow up. The costume and jewellery convey a certain sophistication; whether pretence or real, it is there. Though this photo was taken only a year ago, the props make this image appear a bit retro. This could be a teenager in the Fifties or now, which gives the portrait a timeless quality. Discover how the image was created in the steps, but also check out the video tutorials on the CD.

Photorealism

All portraits must start with a good image, whether the subject is sitting for the portrait or you are using a reference photo

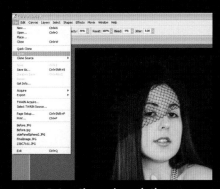

01 Set up the under painting All portraits start with an 'under painting' which can be used as a reference for your 'over painting'. With Corel Painter, cloning is the magic behind the painting! Open your image and go to File>Clone, as shown.

02 Choose Clone Color Ensure that you have selected Clone Color so that you're picking up the colour from your photo. When you want to use your own colour you can go back and unclick this option. This is very easy to overlook, so make sure you keep it in mind.

03 Start cloning We have chosen the Acrylic Capture brush to clone our image. We're using Opacity of around 28% and following the contour of the image as a guide for our brush strokes. The hat net provides a cloning challenge which we will cover on the next page.

Start your portrait

Start painting using traditional art methods combined with digital tools

04 **No more cloning!** We have completed the under painting so unclick Use Clone Color in the Color options. Make two layers for the hair and skin. To paint over the hat net use your colour picker (or Alt+click) to sample the skin and hair colour, and paint directly over the net using the Acrylic Capture brush. (Don't worry, we'll be painting the net back later and fixing the skin.)

05 **Set up layers** We already have the hair and skin layers, so let's add a layer for the eyes, mouth, gloves, bracelet and background. These layers give us security if we make an error and ensure that we can make changes to specific areas if needed. Make sure you have the right layer selected as you work. (To name them, double-click on the layer title.)

06 **Setting up a Color palette** There are many different ways to set up a Color palette, but one way that we like to create an interesting array of colours is to open a picture painted by a great portraitist, such as this one by John Singleton Copley. Just go to your Color Set drop-down menu and choose the Color Set From Image option.

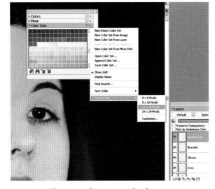

07 **Change the swatch size** The swatch sizes are usually too small, but there is a way to fix this. Go to the drop-down menu again, click on Swatch Size and choose 16 x 16. You will now have larger colour boxes in which to easily choose the colours for your portrait.

08 **Light source and shadows** Look at your image and determine where your light source is coming from. In this image the light is on the right, so our shadows will be to the left. We have chosen the Wet Oily brush at 30% to start applying the facial shadows. We also chose a reddish-brown colour from our Color palette and put a stroke of this on the background to refer back to when needed. But you may prefer to create another layer titled 'Shadows'.

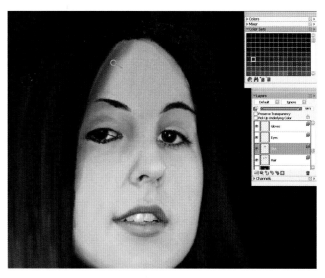

Background effects

The background is essential to any portrait, but each portrait calls for something different and it is important to let the subject tell you what it needs. Sometimes elaborate detail is appropriate with props and dramatic lighting. But with other images, such as this one, a simple black background is all that is needed.

09 **Continue shadows** Continue to paint in the basic shadows of the face, add a darker colour and use a lower opacity. It is better to paint over with low opacities than it is to go too dark. Notice that the shadows further define the cheekbone area.

10 **Deepen shadows** Keep adding the basic shadows going onto the neck and arm area, and adjusting the opacity very low as you go so the shadows appear natural. Define the contour of the arm as you did the face. (Note the small shadows beneath the nose and lower lip.)

11 **Add cheek colour** Choose a pinkish-red colour as shown, and mark this on your background. Now very lightly apply it to both cheeks and across the nose to give a healthy glow to the face (the colour range of the face is always redder in the middle).

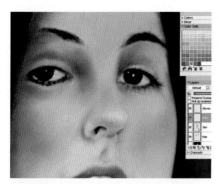

12 **Paint the whites of the eyes** Use your Acrylic Opaque Detail brush at a very low opacity for the eyes. Choose a soft grey colour and paint over the whites of both eyes. But be sure that you're on the Eye layer for this! Now choose a darker grey colour for the shadows beneath the top lids.

13 **Paint the irises** Using the same brush, sample a soft brown colour from the hair and paint in a radiating motion around the iris. Now make the colour lighter and more yellow on the right side, near the light source, to add more life to the eyes. For blue and green eyes, sample from a photo of the subject instead.

14 **Block in the hair** Use the same brush again. Now start blocking in the basic colours of the hair. You can sample the existing colours, but you will want to use the darkest browns near the hat and shadows, and work in lighter colours towards the outer hair adding golden highlights. We will get to the details later, but for now this is a good foundation.

Lighting effects

If your portrait is lacking in light and appears a bit flat, a quick and easy way to add interest and more drama is to check out the lighting effects in the Surface Control tools. Here you can play with the colour tones, light direction and adjust the ambience to exactly what your image needs!

Small details
Mixing freehand with cloning

15 **Create a furry texture** Stay with your acrylic brushes, but this time choose the Acrylic Capture brush. With a dark grey, start brushing upward and out to create a fur effect (be sure you have your Hat layer chosen). To create more depth, go lighter and lighter with your colour, as shown.

16 **Paint the lips** Make a new layer called 'Mouth' and, still using the Acrylic Capture brush, sample the existing lip colour. Take care to resample in the shadows where needed and add a lighter highlight to the bottom lip.

17 **Paint the teeth** Use the same technique on the same layer while painting the teeth, taking care to preserve the shadows and highlights. If your portrait looks too opaque try decreasing the opacity of your layer until it looks more natural.

18 **Paint the jewellery** Go back to the Acrylic Opaque Detail brush and sample the monochrome colour of the beads. Now paint over them. Use a light grey for the highlights on the black beads and a beige-grey for the shadows on the white beads. Remember where your light source is.

Custom brushes

To customise your brush for the work you are doing it's very important to adjust the size of the brush. This can be accomplished quite easily using the left and right bracket keys on your keyboard. It is also essential to play with and vary the opacity (or transparency) of a brush by adjusting it in the Menu bar. These are just a couple of the custom options, but they are the most important ones to remember!

Skin deep

Create more details for a photo-realistic effect

Skin highlights

Be sure the highlights on the face are in the correct place or it can throw the whole portrait off. Highlights generally fall on the bridge and tip of the nose, the outer nostrils, the middle of the bottom lip and top edge. Also you will find them on the top of the forehead, cheekbones and the chin.

19 **Define the shadow details** Use the same brush we used for the basic shadows (Wet Oily brush) and start painting in definite shadows, such as the eye lid crease, around the nose, inside corners of the eyes and the red of the cheeks. Refer to the colours you already used for the basic shadows, making them darker.

20 **Forehead tones** The face is comprised of three main colour temperatures, which are yellow on the forehead, red in the middle (as we have already painted) and a cooler blue towards the chin. Here we are using Yellow Ochre to lightly tint the forehead.

21 **Lower face tones** As we've just discussed, the face has three colour tones. The lower area grows cooler, so let's lightly apply a blue-grey colour using a very low opacity to the chin area (we don't want her to appear like she has a 5 o'clock shadow!).

22 **Contour the lips** By sampling the lip colour and choosing a darker shade, add more contour to the lips by painting dark shadows into the corners and easing them towards the centre. The tops of the lips are always darker than the bottom. (Again, be sure you are on the Mouth layer.)

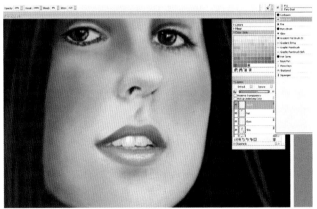

23 **Lip glow** Now we are changing to the Fairy Dust brush found in the F-X category of brushes. Use this with a soft pink (almost white) colour, a small brush tip and a low opacity. Now sprinkle some sparkles onto the lower lip.

24 **Add freckles** Freckles can be a cute addition to a portrait, and this is a good way to add them back if they have been painted over. Go back to the Acrylic category and choose the Opaque Detail brush again. Using a soft reddish-brown, take your stylus pen or brush and make tiny dots varying in size across the nose and cheeks. Now lower the opacity of the layer to make them look more natural.

25 **Eye highlights** The eyes are lacking some spark so go to the Photo category and choose the Dodge brush. Go back and forth across the iris and the white of the eye until a nice highlight appears on both eyes. (Double check that you're on the Eye layer.)

26 **Reduce skin opacity** Now select the Skin layer and decrease the Opacity by about 79%. This will remove any harsh brush strokes and will reveal the hat net, which we can use as a reference to paint back over.

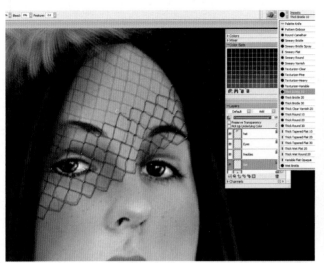

27 Drawing details back in Now choose the Impasto Thick Bristle 10 brush and paint over the net on the skin. Do not paint right over the guidelines as we want this area to serve as the shadow, so stay a bit off line. Use high opacity paint and a tiny brush tip for this. (We will paint this over the hair later.)

28 Paint the background Make one more layer, title it 'Background' and choose the Acrylic Opaque Detail brush again at a high opacity. Even though the background is already black, we want to ensure that there is no 'peek through' from the photo shoot. So paint over the entire background a dense black, which is a nice accent for this charming, sophisticated portrait.

Colour value and tonal range

Make sure you have a wide range of colour values and tonal ranges. This means that your portrait will have very dark to very light tones, ensuring that the image has a convincing form and contour. If you do not have a wide range from dark to light, your image will look flat. This is true no matter what the nationality and overall skin tone of your subject is.

Skin tones | Follow our skin tips

There is no secret palette for painting every face, but there are some basic rules that apply to every portrait when considering light and shadow, colour tones and range. This is true of every skin type and we will explore a few of them. There is really so much variation in skin tones – it is almost impossible to create a 'formula' as so much depends on light and shadows, and even the background can influence the tones of the face as we reflect what is in our surroundings. So take any advice here as a general guide, and use your artist's eye to see the colours present in your subject.

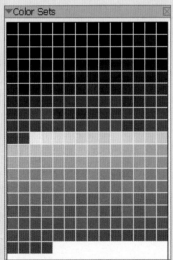

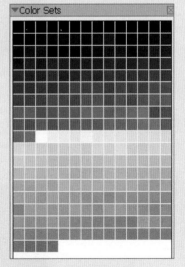

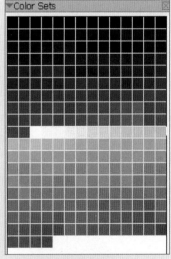

ZONES OF COLOUR

These three zones of colour are present in every face and are as follows: the forehead to the eyebrows tends to show a yellowish cast, then from the brows to the bottom of the nose the face is very warm with lots of reds, and from the bottom of the nose to the chin the colour turns cool towards blues and purples. This colour range is more pronounced in males, so ensure this is softer when painting females. (The neck should be more neutral.)

CHOOSING COLOURS FOR AFRICAN SKIN

The best way to create a palette for dark skin is to scan a portrait and create a palette (you can name and save your Color Set by using the arrow to the right). For very dark skin tones we can mix a Burnt Umber and Burnt Sienna to create a good mass tone for painting brown skin. The darker the skin, the more it will contrast with the highlights. A small amount of Cerulean blue added to the highlights will make them convincing.

CHOOSING COLOURS FOR ASIAN SKIN

You can exchange Burnt Sienna in the previous tone with Yellow Ochre as this will give you a good mass tone for many Asian skin tones. And a little Viridian may be added to the Yellow Ochre if desired.

Notice how both the African and Asian flesh tones show less differentiation between the forehead, cheek and jaw areas that we saw in our lighter skinned lesson earlier.

CHOOSING COLOURS FOR INDIAN SKIN

For Indian skin tones the colours will be a similar combination of the palette for Asian skin tones, but will include many more concentrated oranges and reds to the skin. Keep in mind though, that the ears, cheeks and nose have much thinner skin and ample blood supply, which will make these areas seem redder on everyone. Also remember that the whites of the eyes are never actually pure white!

Brush techniques | Use a hair brush

The texture and look of the hair is all in the brush that you choose and the way that you use it. A Wacom tablet is highly recommended, as it is much more natural to use the stylus pen for the free flowing locks you will want to create!

FOR BABY HAIR AND FINE HAIR

For fine soft hair, such as a baby's, it is best to use a very soft brush (like the Soft Airbrush 20) and allow it to curve softly as you draw the lines. This gives the impression of fine, floaty, downy hair. Build it up from dark to light tones at under 20% Opacity.

FOR BEARDS OR VERY TIGHT CURLS

The best technique for thick beards and extremely curly or fuzzy hair is to go to the Sponge category and experiment. Here we are using the Glazing Sponge 60 brush and it's quite effective, as you can see! You will need to layer over and over to build up density.

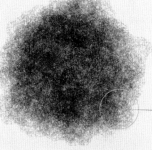

FOR THICK AND STRAIGHT HAIR

The Acrylic Captured brush is the best default brush for thick, straight hair. Lay in the base colour with a wide tip and then lower the opacity as you build up highlights on top, until you achieve the best look. (This is the look we used in this lesson.)

FOR THICK WAVY HAIR

Once again the Acrylic Captured brush is the best default brush to use for this hair texture. You will be using the same technique that was used with straight hair, only you will squiggle your brush as you stroke downward. Start with a straight base and add the squiggles in the highlights.

Hair raising
Hair plays a big part in creating a successful portrait

29 Block in the hair shadows Hair, like the face, has shadows and highlights – and we must show this for the hair to have depth and movement. First, if you are happy with your work so far, flatten all the layers and create a duplicate. The Acrylic Capture brush is a great brush for hair so choose this brush and start painting in the shadows under the hat, near the neck, and any areas where the light source does not quite reach.

30 Hair highlights All hair has highlights, no matter how dark! This defines the hair and creates a nice depth so it doesn't look like a wig, and shows the light source reflecting and giving a shine to the hair. Let's keep the same brush, vary the opacity and thickness, and choose lighter amber and beige colours from the palette. Brush the hair as you would with a real hair brush.

31 Hair details Now reduce the brush tip and add life to the hair by creating smaller hair strands that are not so tidy and tight to the head. This gives more movement and life to the image, and adds interest and visual appeal. Vary the opacity for this to get the best effect.

32 Eyelashes Now give your sophisticated lady some luscious lashes! We found that it looks better to add lashes on the image rather than on the model, as it is a much cleaner look. Here we are using the Soft Airbrush 20 at a low opacity. Apply lightly with a flick of the hand, in much the same way as you would make a check mark. Make sure you don't overdo it though!

Bring the portrait together
Attend to all the small details

33 Eyebrows Now go back to the Acrylic Capture brush and make the eyebrows look more natural. Use a low opacity and brush upwards towards the centre, and then outwards towards the edge of the face – going with the natural arch of the brow.

34 Finish hat details Now that you have the hair completed return to the Impasto Thick Bristle 10 brush and complete the netting across the left and right side of the hair. Use a small brush tip at 77% Opacity and paint the net by using zig zag strokes that connect to one another.

35 Wavy hair If you would like to experiment and see what your model would look like with wavy hair it really is quite simple! First make a new layer so you can delete it if you don't like the results. Using the Acrylic Capture brush, follow the same technique you used for straight hair – but this time as you stroke the brush downward just add a squiggle all over the hair, and viola! She has wavy hair!

Adding movement to the hair

If you want your portrait to really come alive you must remember that the hair is almost as important as the face! If your hair looks like a helmet or a wig then it will kill the whole portrait. To add a feeling of freedom and zest, use a smaller brush and add tiny strands of hair that swing out from the face into the background. Keep this technique to a fine balance as you don't want 'bed head' – you want a real-life look and a bit of a breezy style! Opacity is very important here – be sure it is very low and varied.

Background colours | What works best?

One of the first questions that will come to your mind when painting a portrait is, "What colour should I paint the background"? The answer is usually in the face of the subject. If it's a child then the props and background will be very different from an adult's portrait, and a lot of choosing a great background is just intuition. You have to develop a good understanding of what colours work well together. For example, in this image the basic colours of the clothing are black and white so our first thought was blue as it works well with black and white. But the best way to find out is to make a new layer and experiment with different colours. Blue does work quite well, but when we looked at the black background we decided that it worked best because it expresses more sophistication.

36 Tear ducts Tear ducts are easily overlooked as they are a tiny pink tissue in the corner of the eye, near the nose. But if you skip this step the eye doesn't look right. It is important to note that this area is red, so use the Acrylic Detail brush and paint in this area on both eyes.

37 Lower lid detail Look in the mirror and you will notice that on the flesh of the lower eyelid, where the lashes grow from, you can see an edge of lighter coloured flesh. It is important to include this for a more natural eye. Again, use the Acrylic Detail brush as we used above. If you overdo this and it looks too harsh, go to Edit>Fade for a more subtle appearance.

Balance highlights and shadows

You must have a good idea of your light source before adding the highlights to the hair. Usually the hair is darker at the top and around the neck, but this may change if your light source changes. Adding highlights defines the hair strands and separates them, really making the hair look real and also adding a shine. Always start with the darker colour as a base and work lighter towards the surface of the hair, and even brighter where the light is creating a glow. The highlights should be the same colour as the hair base, but varied in tones. Brown can have a lot of warm highlights such as gold, amber and auburn.

Finishing touches

Details, details! Explore your portrait to see if any are missing

38 **Hair body** Add some more body to the straight hair by going back to the Acrylic Captured Bristle brush and sampling the hair for different colours. Now go to the blunt end of the hair and add some curve to the bottom by swinging your brush strokes upward.

39 **A sparkle in the eye** The eyes are of the utmost importance to every portrait, and one of the most engaging details is a bright spark of light in the eye. Never put it smack in the middle of the pupil, but to the right or left depending on the light direction.

40 **Surface texture** Go to the top Menu bar, and in the window's drop-down menu choose the Library palettes and select the Papers. When you have the Paper dialog box open, choose the Italian Watercolor paper. Now go to Effects>Surface Control and reduce the amount to only 17% to give your portrait just a touch of texture for more interest. (If the texture is still too much, go to Edit>Fade to soften it more.)

The last layers | Are layers necessary?

41 **Lighten the hat details** Go back to the Impasto Thick Bristle brush, and this time pick a medium-grey colour. Now go back over the net that is on the hair to make it stand out where it is difficult to see. This lifts it over the colour of the hair.

42 **More fur fluff!** Now go back to the F-X brush category and choose the Hairspray brush. We are going to add a bit more fluff to the fur on the hat. This is a little tricky, but if you have a stylus pen rotate it so that the spray goes in the direction you want. This will make the fur a bit fluffier-looking, as you can see! Use a very light grey (almost white) colour for this.

You don't have to work with a lot of layers – you may find them unnecessary, especially if you're a traditional artist. However, making a layer for every element in your portrait can be a lifesaver! Layers give you the ability to make changes on every part of your portrait that you create a layer for. This means you can delete, erase, decrease the opacity, apply a selective effect and have complete control over your portrait with more ease and a lot less mess than traditional art! We tend to think it is best to drop them as you work, as soon as you know you are happy with what you have done so far, and then move on to the next stage. Notice that we dropped all the layers close to the end, and left one more layer open for the final touches to the hair and detail work.

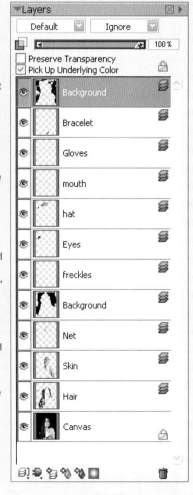

Keep it simple

Sometimes the best background prop for an image is none! In this image all the props are literally on the model. The hat, gloves and beaded bracelet add plenty of interest to the image. If we added even more props to the background then we would create a distraction from this model's pretty face, and have a less attractive portrait. Don't be afraid to keep it simple!

43 **Final highlights** It is always good to take a final look at your portrait to determine what else is needed. We think this portrait is in need of some brightening of the facial highlights. So using the Soft Airbrush tool at a very low opacity, go back and brighten the light on the tip of the nose, nostril edge, bottom lip, forehead and chin. Now flatten the final layers.

A perfect portrait | The elements that add up to the perfect portrait

Let's take a look at some of the elements that are usually present in a successful portrait, that grab the viewer's attention and beckon them in to look...

SUITS YOU
The hat and its netted veil adds a lovely feminine touch. It sort of 'tops off' the image and adds more interest

SET THE MOOD
Expression is of great importance for setting the mood. Here the expression matches the rest of the portrait as it is inviting, yet has an air of sophistication

HAIRSTYLE
The added motion of the hair that was painted in gives this portrait a youthful zest and adds more life to the image

ACCESSORISE
The halter-neck dress, white gloves and beaded bracelets work wonderfully with the black background, and they give the portrait an elegant and timeless quality

IMPORTANT GESTURES
The gesture of the hand enhances the mood in the way the model is poised elegantly and expressively

Working in monochrome

Edith Krueger-Nye reveals how she applies the fine art style of monochrome to her paintings

Tutorial info

Artist
Edith Krueger-Nye

Time needed
Two hours

Skill level
Intermediate

From my days of being a photographer, I have captured many black-and-white images as they are often in demand. There is something about monochrome photos that carries a sense of seriousness – almost like an instant art form.

I came across this photo of a horse that has always been one of my favourites. At university, we learned oil painting by starting off with one-colour paintings. The colour I was given happened to be Payne's grey, and I was off and running!

This painting is a build-up of very thin oil paint. You can perfect the painting according to how realistic you want to paint. Very thin paint allows you to let details show through or remove them, any way you want. I have left the eye portion of this painting real, as I have found

that I prefer it that way, but it's up to you which areas, if any, you want to remain intact.

To make my monochrome painting look more like a painting and less like a photograph, I added a border of about 30 pixels. This gives me more area to paint and allows the overlapping strokes to show just like an oil painting, which gets paint all over the edges.

Only your judgement applies in this method. I used a graphic tablet from Wacom; without it this would not work, or be much too erratic for this smooth painting. Plan your painting out first; do not just paint away. I'm just running through the technique I use here, but if it inspires you to try your own horse painting, there are lots of great photos to download for free from MorgueFile (**www.morguefile. com**). I particularly like 171000 or 98356.

Start at a trot
Set up your painting with a border and some texture

01 Original scanned image My original image was a photograph of 8 x 10 dimensions, I like to use the Show Rulers menu (Canvas>Rulers>Show Rulers). This allows me to find out what size I have to work with. Next, it's time to add a white border. This will allow me to extend my painted brushstrokes out of the frame and give a more interesting effect.

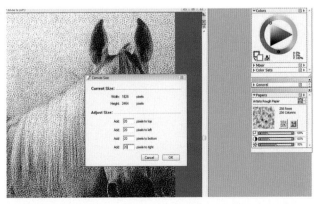

02 The border Start off by following Canvas>Set Paper Color>Eye Dropper and with this selected, click the whitest part of your image. Notice that the main colour box is now white and the additional colour box is white as well. Via Canvas>Canvas Size>Adjust Size, now add 20 pixels per box and then click OK.

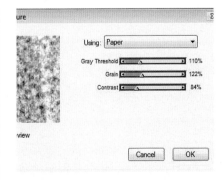

03 A touch of texture Continue now via Effects>Surface>Control. Here you can add texture to your original image to remove it from its photographic origins, as it adds dimension to your original. You can use the numbers shown above but it would be better if you judge your own image's needs for yourself.

Gain pace with a canter

Clone. Paper. Brushes. Done

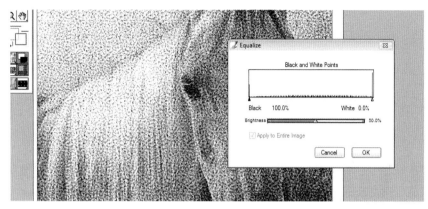

04 **Add effects** If you follow Effects>Tonal Control>Equalize, you'll see that there are two sliders, one on each end. They allow you to control your image's darks and lights. Additionally, there is a Brightness slider. Use both of these and try them out; they will allow you to make your image exactly the way you want it to look. I was taught in school that a black-and-white image had to have bold blacks and brilliant whites; here is the slider that will allow you to achieve this.

05 **Start the clone** You are now ready to clone your image, and doing so by File>Quick Clone should do it. Check that your Brush button is active and the Clone Color stamp is selected in on the Color Wheel.

06 **Your paper**

Minimise your original now, as it is only needed from here on in to check that your strokes are in the correct place. On the clone picture, push the Toggle Tracing Paper button. I used 60%, as I did not want a clear picture of my original. I also chose Artist Rough paper, though you can use very smooth paper as well, as that will add to the smooth look of your painting's surface.

07 **Select brushes** Begin with the Artists' Oils>Wet Oil Blender in two different areas of the background. Your goal should be to check the brushes. Is it the right brush, right size, right opacity, grain, viscosity, blend and wetness? Change them to your needs; one of my favourite things to do is to paint in Dirty mode. It lets the paint stay on the brush and mix with all the other colours. When happy, delete to start properly.

Cloning from monochrome

When you clone from a black-and-white image, you need to make sure you have a good amount of contrast. Simply desaturating the colours won't necessarily work – you risk ending up with a tonally flat image. Use the Correct Colors or Equalize command to boost highlights and shadows and get the perfect cloning base.

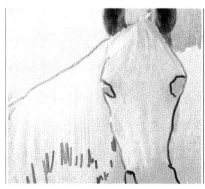

08 **Checking** Now the time has come to start properly. Bring the original photo back up and get a feel for the form. I recommend that you check several times during painting – after all, you want to stick with your original planned image.

09 **Soften the strokes** Here I used the Artists' Oils>Wet Oily Blender to soften the background that comes into contact with the horse, as I wanted the horse to come forward out of its background.

10 **Adding some black** Again using the Wet Oil Blender, at this stage you need to paint in some rich black, right under the head of the horse.

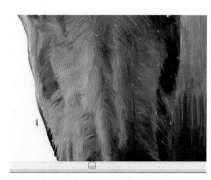

11 Roughly finished The background is roughly finished now. Notice the strokes are bold and lively; each one is expressive and stands alone, yet mixes nicely with its neighbouring stroke.

12 Painting the face Fill in the head section; please be careful about observing in which direction the hair grows. The horse's skull shows through, and your strokes need to acknowledge that. Every stroke counts now, so maybe just change the size of the brush or the pressure used to lay them down.

13 Check the strokes Zoom in on occasion to be aware of your progress. On the face you have many planes of hair growing in all directions. Revert back to the Cloners>Wet Oil Cloner Brush to check the directions of the hair in the face. Be aware of the skull under the facial hair as it needs to be part of the painting.

Follow the form

Even though you are cloning a photo, you still need to follow the shape and form of your source image. A lot of Cloner brushes will obliterate detail if the brushstroke is random and messy. Be sensitive to the basic shape and you'll get a better result. If you want a messier look, feel free to go for a more random approach, but then use more defined strokes on top to get the form back.

Gallop towards the finishing line
Focus on the mane area

14 The mane Now we're finished with the rough draft of the face, it's on to the mane. This is the toughest, most difficult part of the painting. The mane is almost white in places where the sun shines on the horse. I used the Cloners>Smeary Camel Cloner with Size set to 29.7. This was large enough to give me the colour I wanted.

15 Soft blending At this point, go back to the Artists' Oils>Wet Oily Blender with a size of 25.3 to blend the mane hair. Notice the bold, large brushstrokes.

16 Blenders Now use the Blenders>Soft Blender Stump 20 to smooth out the strokes around the highlights of the mane. You need the strokes to be perfect because this is the lightest part of the painting, and you want all eyes to be drawn to the lightest part.

17 Emphasise the mane As the mane needed emphasis, I used the Cloners>Wet Oil Cloner 10 set to 6.4 in Size to pull the mane down. This is done in Dirty mode. Start your brush at the top of the mane and pull down without releasing your stylus, as deep as you want the mane to go. The length comes from pulling the paint down. The facial hair could use a little style, so I used the same brushstroke I used on the mane to pull the facial hair outward.

The final hurdle
Add areas of interest to finish the image off

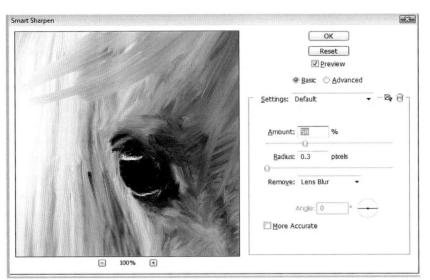

18 The eyes
Now comes one of the hardest parts. The eyes need to be just right, as that is where the soul of this animal lives. I used the Cloners>Straight Cloner sized to 6.4 at 100% – I wanted the eye to look real as if it was looking at me. The highlights in the eye needed to be correctly placed, so I sharpened the eyes in order to bring them out.

19 The border
For the last part, I checked that my brushstrokes had a uniform style showing on the white edge. The overspilling strokes give style to this image, adding interest and showing this off to be a painting.

Horsing about | Groom your horse painting

Hold your horses; before you go galloping ahead with your painting, bear these tips in mind. They may be the difference between a snort and a whinny. You want to get the viewer's focus just right in a monochrome painting so that their eyes are drawn to the right places in the image, and the shadows and highlights placed correctly will achieve this effect.

CREATE MOTION
As I almost finished the painting, it occurred to me to create some motion; the easiest place to do this is over the face, as if the horse just swung its head to look at us. Just follow the hair down to the end

THE RIGHT SURROUNDINGS
Above the horse's mane is the light grey background, which projects the horse out of the paper and makes it the important part of the paper. I used very small strokes and mixed them subtly to call no attention to themselves. The horse is where the viewer is directed to look

DEMAND ATTENTION
The eyes in this face need to look at the viewer. The easiest way for me to do that is to clone them straight from the original image. Make sure you add some white highlights. That way, there is life in your image

FOCAL POINT
Here you need to practise first, as the mane can make or break your painting. The hair needs to look like long flowing horsehair. Start at the top of the mane and do not release the cursor until you have arrived at the point where you want the hair to stop

SORTING THE SHADOWS
The blackest part of the painting should be here, diagonally from the whitest part. Make sure the brushstrokes do not call attention to themselves as their job is to disappear

SAVE UP TO 40%

Subscribe to the **Official Corel Painter Magazine** today and pay only £3.60 per issue if you subscribe by Direct Debit!

Free CD inside iStockphoto images worth £70, plus
40 minutes of video tutorials

COREL®
painter
Official Magazine
™

10-page feature
Clone a masterpiece
Use the Artists' brushes to re-create Sargent, Seurat and Monet's styles

Paint like MC Escher
Draw an optical illusion in the style of this renowned master

Over **50** pages of tutorials

Art skills
Drawing 101
Learn classic art techniques with our real media guide

Improve your portrait
...eed ways of adding impa...

US readers, turn to page 221

Night scenes
Techniques for avoiding dull and lifeless low-light paintings

COREL™ painter X
PC+MAC

For regular digital art inspiration, why not take out a subscription to the **Official Corel Painter** magazine?

Exclusive subscriber benefits

- Subscribe today and save up to 40%
- Never miss an issue
- Each issue is delivered directly to your door
- Free UK delivery
- Money-back guarantee on any unmailed issues

FREE DELIVERY IN THE UK!

About the magazine

The **Official Corel Painter Magazine** is the place to come for artistic inspiration and advice. Each issue will look at a wide range of artistic styles and how to create them. The mag will also cover traditional art techniques – making you a better artist and Corel Painter user!
Jo Cole, Editor in Chief

Subscription prices

➤ **UK:** (by Direct Debit) **£21.60** every six issues **40% DISCOUNT**

➤ **UK:** (by cheque or credit card) **£62.40** every 13 issues **20% DISCOUNT**

➤ **Europe: £70** every 13 issues

➤ **Rest of the world: £80** every 13 issues

This offer can expire without notice

Offer code: KAI CP2

Order securely online at **www.imaginesubs.co.uk**

Order by phone: just call **0844 848 8410** Overseas +44(0)1795 414 611

Take many shots of your still-life scene so you have lots to choose from when it comes to painting

Get creative with brushes

Being loose with custom brushes can render appealing artworks, and a still life is a great theme to play with

D epicting a few everyday objects – either natural or man-made – arranged in artificial scenery has been quite popular among the painters of Western art ever since the 17th Century.

Still-life paintings give the artist far more freedom in the arrangement of the elements within a composition than other types of subjects such as landscape or portraiture. Also, they can be the perfect solution to a bad day of weather or due to the absence of a model to sit for you. Vincent Van Gogh, best known for his landscapes and portraits, discovered in still life a great opportunity to express his art, from *A Pair of Shoes* to a *Vase with Twelve Sunflowers*.

Besides other conveniences, a still life is a great theme for practising a loose style of painting. If you start with a set of a few elements arranged in a composition, you will probably get better chances to play

with brushwork styles than if you were working on a portrait, where the likeness is a crucial matter.

For this tutorial, most of the loose feel will be provided by a category of brushes not included on the original Painter discs. Den brushes are a Denise Laurent creation and this set of brushes is included in Jeremy Sutton's *Painter X Creativity* book (**www.paintercreativity. com**) as well as in Marilyn Sholin's *Painter Tutorial* CDs (**www.msholinprosales. com**). For the sake of simplicity, only three of them will be employed in this tutorial. Don't worry if you haven't got these brushes, though. We've given the Painter X alternatives so you can still enjoy the tutorial.

The source photo is included on the CD, but you can capture your own shot to use. There's also a box on page 33 for some tips on setting the environment for shooting your own composition.

Tutorial info

 Artist
Marcelo Chiarella

 Time needed
3 hours

 Skill level
Intermediate

 On the CD
Original photo and final artwork

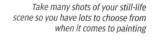

Get started
In the beginning, there was an apple...

Brush settings

Just to make sure you have configured your brush settings accordingly for each step of this tutorial, choose Restore Default Variant from the drop-down menu for the selected brush. Once you've done this you can use the settings we've given and be sure you'll get the same result.

01 **Quick Clone** Start by opening the source image from the CD ('cover before.jpg'). For this tutorial, we will clone the original photo just to establish the main shapes of our work. Choose File>Quick Clone.

02 **Select a brush** Select Dull Conte 15 from Conte brushes and press the Clone Color button in the Colors palette in order to get the colour from the original photo as you paint. Change the Opacity to 10% and Size to around 80. Ensure that Tracing Paper is selected on the Canvas menu.

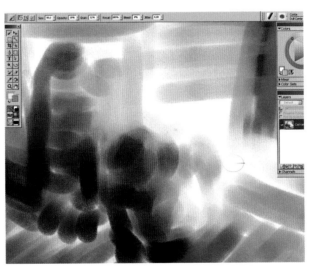

03 **Rough underpainting** Now, let's create a rough muck-up with the main shapes of our composition. For this step you don't have to be worried about being too precise. Use your stylus, varying the pressure and direction to fill in the canvas. Leave some unpainted areas for your image to breathe.

04 **Calibrate colours** Depending on the applied pressure and number of overlaying brushstrokes in some areas, the resulting image tends to be a bit dark. You can compensate for this by choosing Effects>Tonal Control>Equalize and moving the Black slider towards 98%, White to 0 and the Brightness to around 27%. Save.

Respect the values

More important than respecting the colour map from the original photo is constructing a reliable distribution of light and shadows (values). To accomplish this, look at your source photo with your eyes half-closed and compare it with your working image. Try to analyse the values (not the colours) and to change any areas that need correction by using lower and higher values where needed. In the Color Wheel (Window>Color Palette>Show Colors), you select the main colour by using the surrounding circle as well as the value pointing up and down in the inside triangle.

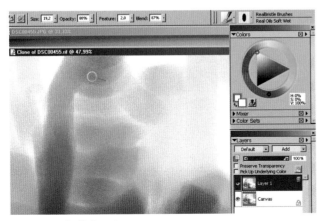

05 **Real Oils brush** Most brushes require stuff in the working layer in order to interact with. Choose Select>All, Edit>Copy, Edit>Paste In Place. Select Real Oils Soft Wet from RealBristle Brushes, set Size to 40,0 and Opacity to 80% and make sure that Layer 1 is selected.

06 **Increasing variety** Start working with this oil brush in order to increase the expressed energy. Be loose in the entire image, but allow some portions of the canvas layer to show up. In the Colors palette, alternate from selecting Clone Color (to get some portions of the original photo) and white (for a blending effect).

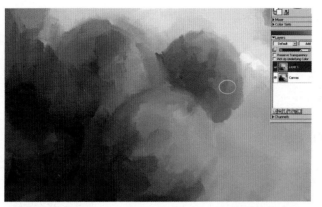

07 **Partially revealing the layer** The purpose of working in a new layer is the flexibility allowed for experimenting with composite method and opacity values. Try to change the opacity to lower values and experiment with other composite methods. This is the result achieved by choosing Gel at 92% Opacity. Select Layers>Drop.

08 **Blend it up** Let's provide a smoother feeling to the image. If you have Den Brushes in your Painter set, choose Oil Brush Blender from this category. Otherwise, use Blenders>Coarse Oil Blender 30 with Jitter set to 1,00. Try to work with sizes around 30. Control the pressure and direction, trying to reproduce the original image movement.

09 **Defining the forms (shapes)** Use Oil Brush Luscious from Den Brushes to establish the shapes' limits (optionally, Gouache>Fine Bristle 30). From now on, avoid cloning. Use the Alt key to select a colour already in the working canvas, and change ever so slightly the hue, saturation or value in order to achieve more appealing results.

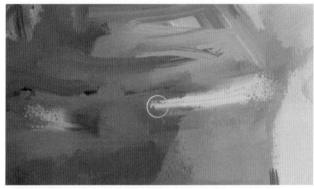

10 **Reinforcing reflections** The bronze pot will recover its shine with some brushstrokes indicating the reflections. Use Den>Oil Brush Luscious, changing Jitter to 1,50, Size 20 (optionally, Gouache>Fine Bristle 30), choosing any ochre colour already on canvas and changing it slightly toward the white corner on the colours triangle and a little in the yellow direction on the surrounding circle.

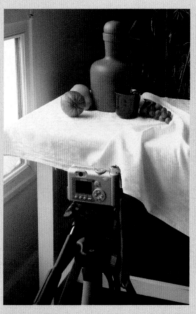

11 **Additional effects** For this step, rotate your canvas using Spacebar+Alt while dragging the image in order get a natural feel. Drawing some arcs for defining the pot shape. Use Den>Oil Brush Luscious with Size 20 and Jitter 0 (optionally, Gouache>Fine Bristle 30) for these lines. Use Den>Oil Spatter Brush, Size 50, for additional effects leaving some splashes here and there (or Pens>Leaky Pen, Size 50, Opacity 20).

Setting up the environment for shooting
Take light and angles into consideration

If you decide to set up your own composition, start with a few elements for experimenting with light and camera controls (although the automatic settings generally can render nice shots, as you can see here).

A good place for the table with the objects is close to a window. This way they will be illuminated by a natural source of diffused light. For the opposite side from the incoming light, you may alleviate the shadows by using a handmade reflector, constructed by gluing a metallic foil to a cardboard.

The tripod is a nice accessory as it helps to maintain steady the camera during the shot. As these indoor scenes generally require low speed because of the weak sources of light, there are far fewer chances to produce blurred images using a tripod than if hanging the camera manually.

Another valuable tip is to use the timer. This way, the instant of the shot will not occur in the instant you depress the Shoot button, but rather a little later, when the camera is not being touched.

Try varying the position of the objects on the scene and always check the camera display in order to get a better feeling of each arrangement.

Use a lamp, experimenting with different positions or even the internal ambient light, so that you can warm up the scene and get interesting effects.

Materials:
Digital camera, tripod (optional), lamp (optional), table, aluminium paper roll, cardboard, towel (optional) and some objects or food to compose the scene.

Create an organic feel

Don't forget your greens!

Be bold with your layers

At some stages of your work in progress, you may be tempted to try a completely different brushwork or style. Creating a new layer is the way for these experiments. The bad point is the fact that some brushes seem not to work with a blank new layer. To compensate this, select the entire work on the canvas layer (Ctrl/Cmd+A), copy it (Ctrl/Cmd+C) and paste it in the same place in a new layer (Ctrl/Cmd+Shift+V). Now you can dare with your brushstrokes without destroying the work already done, and even experiment with the composite methods and transparency in this layer. If you got appealing results, drop the layer. Otherwise, discard it and try another direction.

12 The grapes Using the Den Oil Brush Luscious, Oil Brush Blender and Oil Spatter – or the alternatives we've given – reinforce the grapes' shapes. Always try to create new colours by picking up some green already on the canvas and varying the value, saturation and hue on the Colors Wheel, according to your close observation of the source photo.

13 Remaining vegetables Using the same technique, define the shape of the lemon, tomatoes and apple. This way, you can give more spontaneous brushstrokes and bring back the roundness of the front elements that was lost in the previous steps. Save your work now.

14 Surrounding elements Add some calligraphic signs here and there in order to increase the energy and create an organic feel to your work. For this purpose you can use Oil Brush Luscious, Size 20, picking colours from your work. The Calligraphy brushes also work well. You will realise how diverse the same colour will seem to be, depending on its surrounding!

15 Increasing contrast For reinforcing the overall colour vividness, choose Effects>Tonal Control>Equalize and move the black arrow to around 85% and white to 15%. The image will leave the washed aspect and gain another dimension in respect of its colours.

16 Revealing values Often you must analyse the overall distribution of the values. For this, a great tip is to create a new layer (Ctrl/Cmd+Shift+N), make the current colour white, choose Effects>Fill>Current Color and change its composite method to Color. Click the eye icon of this white layer to alternate the view between colour and black and white.

17 Correcting values Using the tip from the last step, try to reproduce the value map from the original picture by observing both images in respect of the light and shadows. Make the corrections needed by varying the brush and picking up colours from the canvas, changing the value if necessary. Also, observe the details on the bronze pot and only suggest them with some brushstrokes here and there.

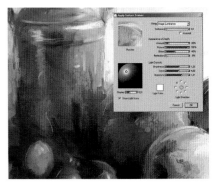

18 Applying some texture Get a convincing impasto oil effect instantly by choosing Effects>Surface Control>Apply Surface Texture, using Image Luminance, Softness set to zero and Amount to around 20%. This will give a discreet rough texture feeling to your work, depending on the luminance.

Put it into perspective

Finalise your painting with the last few adjustments

19 Perspective lines Add some sense of depth, suggesting some horizontal and vertical lines for the background and slanted for the towel, always trying to be loose and to vary in colour, value and expression of the brushstroke.

20 Integrate elements Pick up some blue tones from the towel and using the Den>Oil Spatter Brush at Size 40, create some stains on the background. Repeat this with other colours to integrate the elements on the scene.

21 Final touches For the final touches, use the Pens>Scratchboard Tool on a new layer, setting its Transparency to around 50%. This will create some intermediate tones. Use Impasto>Thick Clear Varnish 20, Depth Lofter and others from the Impasto category in a new layer (with Layer Opacity set to 0) to add some relief details and bring a convincing feel to your work. After the final embellishments, sign your work, preferably in a new layer so you can move it freely and study an appropriate position.

Brushes to get creative with | Experiment with the settings

You can get interesting variants on each selected brush by controlling its Jitter value. This property controls the degree of randomness of your brushstrokes: low values for dabs following directly along the stroke path and higher values for dabs going randomly outside the path. This way, you can produce stunning effects if you explore this property before using each selected brush.

IMPASTO EFFECT

Building up a feeling of thick paint is pretty easy when you use the Surface Control command. It allows for a subtle, yet effective finish and lets you have more control over the look than if you relied on the Impasto brushes.

CUSTOM BRUSH

Although Painter has a vast number of brushes, it's worth investigating some of the ones created by Painter artists. These are tailored to specific tasks and often give phenomenal effects with just a few strokes.

TONAL VALUES

When you are working from a photo, even if you are cloning the colour, it helps to keep an eye on the tonal values. Keep looking at the original and your painting through half-closed eyes. It sounds strange, but it's the best way of seeing the tones!

DEFINE THE ELEMENTS

When you are working with a loose style such as this, it's common for elements to get smudged and obliterated. After laying down the rough strokes, begin the work in the defined shapes.

Before

Create with Palette Knives

Get the knives out, load them up with paint and pile it on your canvas!

Tutorial info

Artist
Cheryl Blanchard

Time needed
40 minutes

Skill level
Beginner

On the CD
Start photo

Have you ever painted with traditional palette knives? Scooping up paint and smearing it on the canvas, sculpting and building into a three-dimensional surface? This is when a painting becomes more than a flat plane; it becomes a form of sculpture. Palette knives, more formally known as painting knives, are springy, shaped spatulas used for painting instead of a brush. They are also used for mixing paints. The building of paint with a palette knife helps to lend spontaneity and bold statement to a piece of artwork. With a little experimenting you can create wonderful effects with the Palette Knives in Painter.

In Painter we have many Palette Knives at our disposal. From the Loaded Palette Knife to the Tiny Smeary Knife, we'll see just

what is possible. The most important thing to discover is how the knives move on the virtual canvas. The width of a knife will also determine the height when it's dragged in a horizontal direction, in its broadest use. Diagonal directions provide the thinnest strokes if the stylus tilt is in the same direction; the left to right tilt of your pen will affect the width of the knife stroke. Think of the tilting of your stylus as turning the knife on its edge and scraping along the canvas. Also, turn your canvas often when using the knives to make the most of them.

Let this tutorial be a stepping-stone for you, a mere introduction. Once you're comfortable using the knives, you'll find many ways to make this tool work in directions that only you can discover with your own experimenting. So, have fun!

Create a bold painting
Turn an average image into a work of art

01 Start with a dynamic image
Let's take this rather average image and change the contrast to add some interest. Load it from the disc. Use Effects>Tonal Control>Brightness/Contrast. Now you can adjust the Contrast slider to add strength to the photograph.

02 Colour it bold
Since we're creating a bold painting, let's take a few moments to ramp up the colour, so the image is as bold as the strokes will be. Use Effects>Tonal Control>Adjust Selected Colors. Select the darkest sky colour in the image. Move Hue and Saturation to the right, and Value to the left. This will add a more interesting colour range to the image.

03 Neutrals to bright
Again, use Adjusting Selected Colors to adjust the neutral tones in the image. Select the main colour of the ground and adjust the Value to the left, to almost full strength. This will give an overall brightness and saturation to the remaining colour in the photo.

04 A simple cloning technique
Go to File>Clone Source and pick your photo. Click Save As. Select all, copy and then Paste In Place. Reduce the Opacity on this copied layer to 50%, and click the eye icon on the Canvas layer. Create a new layer to begin painting on, ensure Pick Up Underlying Color is selected and place it above the copied layer. Painting this way enables you to see where you've painted.

05 Paint the foundation with Artist's Oils
Now we're ready to paint! Select the Clone Color icon in the Colors palette. You can use Palette Knives directly on the image you're cloning if you wish, but this quick painting helps to simplify and provides paint to move around. In Artist's Oils, use the Wet Oily brush with default settings at 80% Opacity. Paint roughly, to block in basic colours and areas.

06 A few painted details
Even though we're roughing in the painting, we need to add some details as reference before using the Palette Knife. On a second layer, paint some smaller shapes in. Here's a handy trick: move this new layer below the one just painted to clone directly from the original image again. When you're finished, move it back to the top of the layer stack.

Tutorial | Palette Knives

Building colour
The beauty of painting with the Palette Knives is in the way the paint builds. The longer you spend in an area applying new paint or pushing around the underlying paint, the heavier and thicker the look becomes. Especially with a bit of Impasto added for effect. The pressure you apply to the stylus will determine how far the original colour will spread before it blends with the underlying colours. Just as the surface of a traditional canvas builds with colour the longer you work at it, so too is the experience here in Painter. You can apply paint in two ways; keep the Resat at 0% to push the underlying paint around, or increase the Resat to sample colours and add fresh paint.

Impasto
All the Palette Knives can be adjusted to use Impasto effects in the Brush Creator. Under Impasto, change the default setting of Color to either Depth, or Color and Depth. Depth will only add the look of volume, while Color and Depth will allow you to build with both. Open the Brush Creator and add Impasto to any of the knives. Experiment with the depth to see what works best in any particular image. The more you work an area, the thicker the paint becomes as you sculpt with the knives. Change the depth of Impasto for a variety of effects as you work through a painting.

COREL painter™ | 37

Impasto and Palette Knives
Use Impasto to bring added spark to your painting

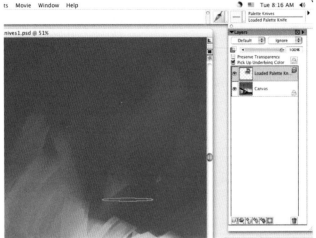

07 Merging layers
Before we begin to use the Palette Knives, merge layers to the canvas by highlighting all layers and selecting Drop in the pull-down menu at the bottom of the Layers palette. This will give you a single foundation to use the knives on.

08 A loaded knife
With the Loaded Palette Knife we can dive right in and push the paint around to shape it, adding interest and volume. You'll notice that the knife makes specific shapes depending on which direction and angle you drag it. Turn the canvas as you paint to make the most of the directional attributes of these knives. The thinnest straight lines are diagonal, and the broadest vertical and horizontal.

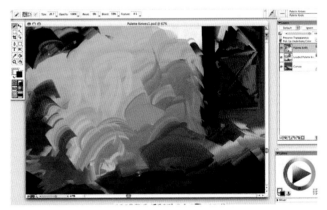

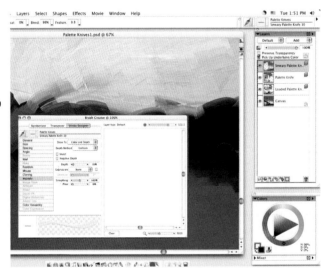

09 Sculpt and build
As with traditional paint, the longer you work in an area, the thicker the paint becomes. The Palette Knife is a good choice for thick colour at this stage of the painting. Set the Resat at 0% to move the paint around, and increase to add colour.

10 Add Impasto
With the Brush Creator, add Impasto effects to the Smeary Palette Knife. For this painting we'll keep the Impasto Depth at 10% in the large areas of the sky and water. You don't need to cover everything with Impasto; leave some areas flat for contrast and interest.

11 New colour
Now open the original colour-corrected photo to use as reference. Add colour sampled from the photo – choose directly from the canvas or from your imagination. Darken the sky a bit to create a twilight scene, adding some detail into the painting. Use the Smeary Palette Knife with Impasto for this as well.

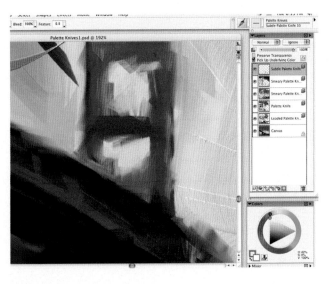

12 Subtle blending Use the Subtle Blending Knives to soften some areas in the painting. You can create depth by varying hard and soft techniques. The softer areas will tend to fade back from the foreground, and give the viewer's eyes a place to rest.

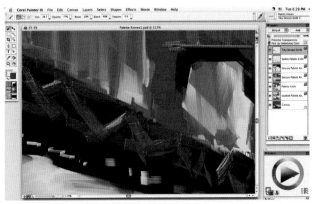

13 More Impasto Use the Tiny Smeary Knife to add some further detail to the painting. With Impasto effects at 25% (Color and Depth) the volume of these strokes will attract the viewer's eye to this detail, and bring added spark and detail to the painting.

The right direction
Different directions for different effects

14 Scrape in some lines Again, an important property of the Palette Knives is the directional quality that's inherent in each. For a fine scrape of paint, set the knife on its edge, make a diagonal sweep from left to right, with Pen Tilt to right. Reverse for a thin line from the opposite direction, with Pen Tilt to the left. To use this knife to its fullest extent, turn the canvas so you can push the paint in any direction.

15 Texture with knives Using any of the knives with a Feature above 0.5 will create a drier knife. Set the Feature to 1.5 with the Palette Knife and add some texture to the foreground. By increasing the Feature even further, you can create some great effects, such as a look of raking dry paint across the canvas.

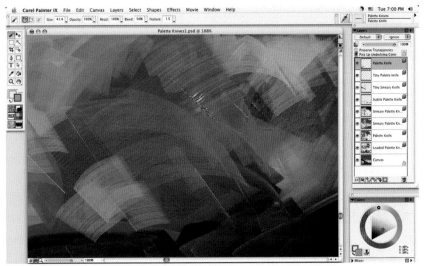

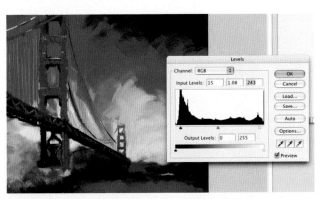

16 Final adjustments Drop all layers to the canvas and bring the painting into Photoshop for the final adjustments. Use Sharpen>Unsharp Mask to define the knife strokes more. Use Levels to add more contrast. Lastly, use Hue and Saturation to adjust colour, to warm and saturate the red just a little for the finishing touch.

Blending with Knives

The Subtle Palette Knives are wonderful blending tools. They can be used with many of the mediums found in Painter. With the right touch and a light hand, this tool can be used to create some very soft and pleasing effects. By varying the opacity and size of the knife, the possibilities are endless. Try them with Acrylics or Gouache, even with the Pastels. The Tiny Subtle Knife is very good for those tight areas that need fine blending. If you keep the Resat at 0% while blending, this will ensure that only the underlying colour will be used in the process.

Playing with knives | Experiment and then create!

The most important thing to do with the Palette Knives is to experiment and play. There's no right or wrong way to use them, and you'll find your own expression if you're willing to forget about perfection and careful edges. Each knife has a multitude of possibilities that you will discover in your own hand.

Palette Knives
Loaded Palette Knife

— Loaded Palette Knife
— Neon Knife 30
— Palette Knife
● Sharp Triple Knife 3
— Smeary Palette Knife 10
— Smeary Palette Knife 20
— Smeary Palette Knife 30
— Smeary Palette Knife 40
— Subtle Palette Knife 10
— Subtle Palette Knife 20
— Subtle Palette Knife 30
— Subtle Palette Knife 40
— Subtle Palette Knife 50
— Tiny Palette Knife 5
— Tiny Smeary Knife 5
— Tiny Subtle Knife 5

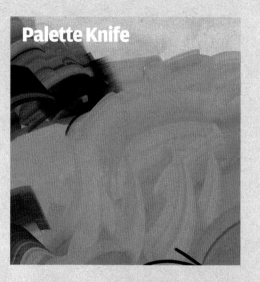

Palette Knife

The Palette Knife is a luscious, wet knife. It streaks and pushes paint in bold swatches of colour. Similar to the Loaded Palette Knife, this one is heavy and wet. Use it for the flattest shaping of colour with the Resat at 0% to push and mould paint across your virtual canvas.

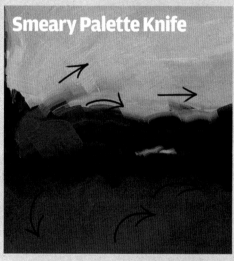

Smeary Palette Knife

Ah, the Smeary Palette Knife. This one is our favourite. One of the smoothest of the knives, it lays down paint in flat, even strokes. With or without Impasto, it is the workhorse of the group, easily moving from pushing and pulling to adding paint, from thin edges to bold surfaces.

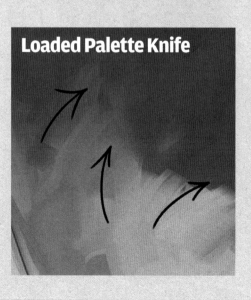

Loaded Palette Knife

The Loaded Palette Knife is a good broad knife to move lots of paint when you begin a knife painting. You'll notice this has some subtle streaking to it, a bit of texture even at a low Resat. This knife also works very well with Impasto features, adding greater texture within each stroke.

Tiny Smeary Knife

This little knife is very versatile. Unlike the larger knives, it has a strong solid stroke at a petite size. The tilt of your pen has just as much impact on the stroke, as does the pressure and direction. For the broadest stroke in any direction, turn the canvas to paint either in a vertical or horizontal direction.

showcase

DAVID DILLON

TITLE	Kiss Me Kate
WEBSITE	www.DDGrafix.com
JOB TITLE	Worship leader / musician

"I have always enjoyed traditional art as a hobby, and this past year moved into digital painting, which I love for the lack of mess and that wonderful "undo" command!" says David. His favourite subject for paintings is people.

eShop
Visit the Official Corel Painter online shop at www.imagineshop.co.uk for back issues and subscriptions

Visit us online at **www.paintermagazine.com**

Create your own art gallery for **FREE** • Meet other artists on the forum • Subscribe and save money!

Original photo

Create family portraits

A combination of drawing, painting and some gentle cloning creates this portrait of Jameslynn and Peanut Butter. Read on, then apply the techniques to your own images

Tutorial info

Artist
Denise Laurent

Time needed
3 hours

Skill level
Intermediate

Ask anybody what makes a good family portrait and they'll probably tell you that capturing a good likeness is the most important thing. People commission family portraits to represent who they are. So a good likeness is surely what we want? Well, not quite. A good portrait should be a lot more than an accurate representation. We want to capture the character and personality of those involved in the painting, and to get a strong sense of them present in the picture.

When planning a portrait you should think about what makes that person tick. Are they lively and outgoing, or quiet and studious? It's important to put all the energy and focus of the painting into expressing your sitter's character. If your subject loves to read, paint them curled up with a book, or if they love the beach, paint them jumping the waves. Digital cameras are great for taking lots of reference photos ready for your informal portrait.

In our painting of Jameslynn seen here, Mum wanted a painting that shows her daughter's wide-eyed, beaming smile – reflecting her lively personality and her love for animals. She didn't want anything formal. We decided on a simple composition that would focus on her smile and include a favourite furry friend. The photo of Jameslynn has a nice pose, but Peanut Butter (the cat) is a little off balance and looks like he's sliding out of her arms. We'll adjust his position when we work on the sketch, as it will give the painting a better balance.

To create a light and casual portrait we'll use a very loose style of painting, keeping the brushwork very simple for most of the painting and allowing some of the sketch to remain. More detailed brushwork will define the focal point – Jameslynn's face and the cat – and some light, gentle cloning will add some of the structure around her eyes, nose and mouth. Once that's done we'll repaint those areas, blending them back into the rest of the painting.

Brush, clone and adjust
Three rules for beautiful art

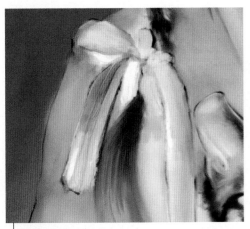

Loose brushwork
Keeping the brushwork very simple for most of the painting creates a more casual, painterly look. Allow some of the sketch to show.

Adjusting the composition
Don't be afraid to change things around to make a better composition. Adjusting Peanut Butter's pose makes for a stronger painting.

Cloning the photo
Cloning is a very useful tool in portraiture, but one that needs to be handled carefully. Use a semi-transparent clone over the top of the existing underpainting, then blend carefully.

Set up your document
Working on the background

Save frequently!

Save frequently using Painter's wonderful interactive save. This really helps if disaster strikes and you need to go back in time to rescue your work – especially if you paint in a more traditional way, with everything created on the canvas layer. It also makes a great visual record of how the piece was created, and has the added advantage of jumping back into the painting process at any point to take the painting off in an entirely new direction, simply by opening one of your saves.

01 Size and resolution Open up your source photo. Start by adjusting the size and resolution of the file. We adjusted the size of our source file to fit the size of the final image we wanted to print.

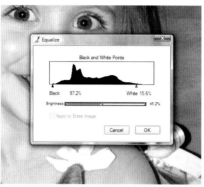

02 Adjust the tonal values Go to Effects>Tonal Control>Equalize and adjust the sliders to give the image a bit more contrast. We also lightened the darks by moving the Black slider to the left a little. This will give a bit more detail in the shadows.

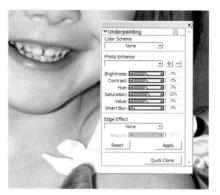

03 Colour We increased the Saturation a little to warm the skin tones. This is best done via the Hue/Saturation command, found in the Tonal Controls option. With some photos you might want to adjust the hue to correct any colour problems too.

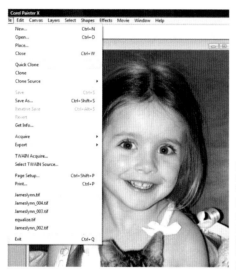

04 Quick clone Now the photo is ready for painting. We made a clone (File>Quick Clone) and turned Tracing Paper off. We are going to make a background for this painting first.

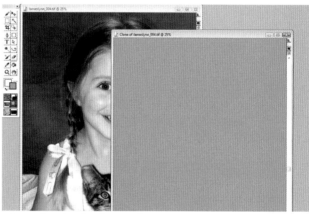

05 Create a background We want a background of pinks and lilacs, as these are Jameslynn's favourite colours. After picking a base colour (pink) we filled the clone. Colours are an easy way of making a portrait fit the person's personality.

The Smeary Wet Sponge

The Smeary Wet Sponge is in the Sponges category. This wonderful brush is a little marvel. You can use it to paint colour on to the canvas, or as a transparent blender. To make a blender to muck up a background set the Opacity to 0, the Pull to 100 and the Jitter to 2. Now mess up that background! If you want to add more colour just turn up the Opacity, or turn down the Pull and the Jitter.

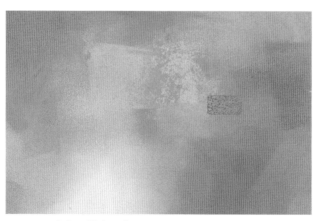

06 Let rip with brushes Using a range of pink, orange and lilac colours (or whichever colours you choose), we painted an abstract background with different brushes. This is a great way to explore Painter's brushes. We used chalks, pastels, oil pastels and sponges.

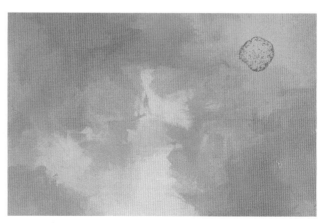

07 Blend the colours together With the colours applied, mess up the background, blending and softening colours together. The Smeary Wet Sponge is a wonderful alternative. Use it to paint, then turn the Opacity to '0' to use it as a lovely soft blender.

Paint over the background
Let the portrait come forth

08 Drawing Jameslynn Turn Tracing Paper back on (Ctrl+T), and start sketching your subject. We used the Thick and Thin pencil – it's responsive to the Wacom pen and great for sketching. Keep the drawing loose.

09 Drawing Peanut Butter Peanut Butter eaesn't quite right, so we adjusted his face slightly to make him look at us instead of looking down. You might find that as you start to paint your image, there will be aspects such as this that need changing.

10 Adjusting the paws One back paw is dropping out of the bottom of the painting, which makes it feel as if he's sliding out of her arms. So we drew both paws facing forwards, which will anchor him in the frame.

Be careful when cloning!
If you include too much cloned material your painting can look quite unbalanced. You can end up with too much detail, or overly complex tonal values in the cloned area. Photographs have a lot of detail that us painters just don't need. For example, look at the teeth in the photo we're using in this tutorial. There are lots of specular highlights on Jameslynn's teeth, and if we keep these in the cloned teeth, they'll look wrong in relation to the rest of the painting. So make sure you paint over all the teeth, and make them much softer and less defined.

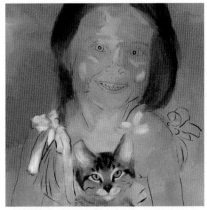

11 Block in the darks and lights Start by painting in the dark and light points of the painting. We used Oil brushes here, especially the Smeary Round, to rough out the dark areas.

12 The under-painting Follow the contours of your subject's face and arms, and gradually paint in the skin. We used Oils, Fine Feathering Oils, Glazing Round and the Variable Chalk to gradually build up her skin tones.

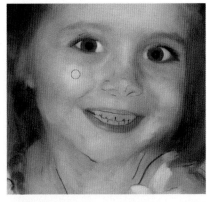

13 Glaze Glazing brushes allow you to build up colour gradually, laying down multiple brushstrokes in several layers. This gives you more control of the colour and texture than trying to lay down a solid colour block in one stroke.

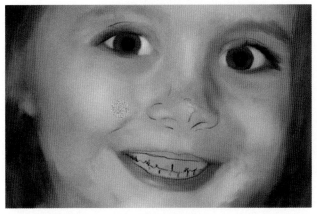

14 Blending Where you need to keep the skin smooth use a very gentle blender to feather one colour into another. Blenders can be hard to control, so turn the opacity on your blender right down and use many more strokes to achieve a subtle effect.

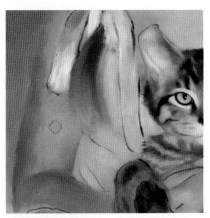

15 Soft edges Keep the legs, arms and clothes very soft, and the brushstrokes simple. You don't want realistic detail here. Leave the sketch showing in places and keep it loose.

Layering the detail
Rushing is not an option!

Make a skin blender

If you do a lot of portraiture you might want to make your own skin blender. Start with the Fine Feathering Oils brush and open the Brush Creator: Ctrl/Cmd+B. In the Stroke Designer under the General tab, change the Dab subcategory from Grainy Hard Cover to Soft Cover. Now choose Well and set Resaturation to 0. Save the new brush, choose Menu>Variant>Save Variant, and give it a name. We called it Soft Blending Oils. Close the Brush Creator.

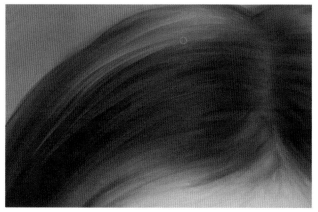

16 Paint the hair The Oils Opaque Bristle Spray is great for hair. Set its Opacity Expression to Pressure. In our painting, we used purple-browns for darker areas, and warm golds for the highlights. Vary the colours you use to give a more natural look.

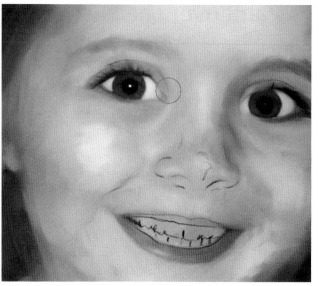

17 Clone the details Use the Soft Cloner at 10% to very lightly clone in eyes, nose and teeth. Keep it light or it won't look natural. It's fine for the painting to show through the cloning.

Make a hair brush

The Oils Opaque Bristle Spray is great for painting hair, but it does need an adjustment to make it respond to the pen, so that each stroke tapers to a finer end. Open the Brush Creator, and in the Stroke Designer under General set the Opacity Expression to Pressure. This works for the Smeary Bristle Spray as well. Now under Color Variability turn up the Hue, Saturation and Value sliders to around 10% each. This will give you some variability in the hair as you paint. Now save the new brush, choose Menu>Variant>Save Variant and give it a name. We called it Hair Spray. Close the Brush Creator.

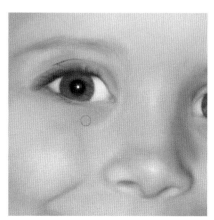

18 Blend in the clone Use a combination of glazed layers of paint and soft blending to merge the cloned areas of the face into the painted areas.

19 The mouth When it comes to teeth, the trick is to be careful. Keep them soft, as hard edges will look too strong. Paint out any bright highlights you might have cloned from the photo. Glaze highlights on the lower lip and make the top lips softer in colour and tone.

20 Define shadows and highlights We added soft lilac shadows to the throat and jaw line with a very light glazing brush. We also applied creamy highlights to her cheeks, nose, chin and throat. A warm pink blush at the edge of her left cheek defined the curve. Don't be afraid of introducing colours like purple into the shadows.

21 Peanut Butter We used green-greys in the cat's fur as well as dark browns, purples and a hint of blue. His eyes are green in the middle and yellow around the edges. We kept his fur loose and fluffy. It's fine if the background shows through a little.

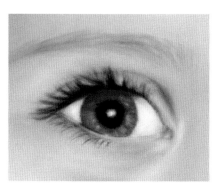

22 Refine the eyes Eyes are important in any portrait. Add tiny details of colour. Use a Fine Detail brush to define the eyebrows and pull out the eyelashes. Add a soft pink glaze to her eye lids, and a soft warm greenish gold to the corners of the lids. Add a grey blue shadow over the eyes.

Final assessment

Don't be afraid of tweaks

23 Making changes We didn't like the way the ribbon on Jameslynn's shoulder plunges into Peanut Butter's ear, so we repainted it in a more comfortable position for them both. We used a Palette Knife for the ribbons.

24 Too tight? When working from photos it's easy to find yourself cropping an image too close to the subject. We thought we needed a bit more background around Jameslynn, so we added some space around the image using Canvas>Canvas Size.

25 Adjusting the background Now we need to paint the background into the new areas of canvas we added. We'll take the opportunity to darken the whole background to bring Jameslynn forward in the painting.

Family art

Painting your loved ones is a rewarding and inspiring project. You get to incorporate a raft of different skills, such as painting skin, eyes and hair, plus you get to think about incorporating extra elements (such as cats!). Here's a summary of our method...

BACKGROUND
The background is simple and soft to bring the focus of the painting forward onto Jameslynn and Peanut Butter

CLONING WITH CARE
Cloning is used very lightly to create subtle form and shape, but no detail

WARM SHADOWS
Careful shading in warm pinks, lilacs and green/golds add form and depth to the face, giving it a warm glow

KEEP IT LOOSE
In the important areas of the painting keep the brushwork loose, and even let the sketch and the background show through the paint

COMPOSITION
Make changes to the pose to create a stronger composition which can tell a better story

Traditional pen and wash

Pen and wash is regarded by many as the prince of drawing media and, as we demonstrate here, it's especially suited to architectural subjects. Sharpen up that quill!

Tutorial info

Artist
Tim Shelbourne

Time needed
1.5 hours

Skill level
Intermediate

On the CD
FInal image

ften, in terms of fine art, less is more. Pen and wash is an ideal example of this, and it's a medium that can really test an artist's mettle. Here you're relying on the power and immediacy of simple, very fine lines, which can both delineate complicated outlines and create areas of subtle shading. It's a technique that dates back almost as long as pictorial art itself, and it's one that can still create very beautiful and sophisticated illustrations. It's also a medium that is very suited to sketching 'on the spot', mainly because of the simple equipment required to do the job. All of these points still ring true within the realms of Corel Painter, and here we're going to take this age-old medium and give it the digital treatment.

One of the most important things about drawing with a pen is the ability to create many different tones, simply by the placement and density of line work, and we've included a boxout on page 52 to illustrate this point. In a pen drawing, the tones are created by placing different thicknesses of lines closer together for dark tones, or further apart for lighter tones. Unlike pencil, we can't rely on varying opacity to create different shades, so you have to rely on an illusion of tone, created by these hatched lines mixing optically. We also need lines and techniques that can describe different surfaces and textures, such as buildings and trees, and you'll learn how to do this here, too.

The wash is used to reinforce some of the main tones in the drawing, and to add interest to areas of less detail. For this we'll use a couple of Painter watercolour variants.

Original photo

A sketchy start
Prepare your painting with a basic outline

01 Choose pen, paper and colour We used a photo from www.sxc. hu as our reference (www.sxc.hu/browse. phtml?f=view&id=209122). Download it and go to File>Quick Clone. Choose the Croquil Pen from the Pens. Go to the Papers Selector and choose Thick Handmade Paper. Set the Grain for the brush to 70% in the Properties bar. Now choose a very dark brown from the colour wheel.

02 Preparatory drawing Reduce the size of the brush to just 4 pixels and add a new layer. Roughly sketch in the main elements in the scene. Don't attempt to include any detail at this stage, as this initial sketch is just so you can get your bearings around the scene and can always be deleted or reduced in opacity.

03 Just outlines Continue to roughly outline the rest of the elements, indicating the trees in the foreground. Don't add any detail to the sky yet, as this will consist mostly of washes in the finished painting.

Tourist attraction
Define your painting and add more detail

Using a ghost image

It's always a good idea to start a project such as this by making a clone of the start image. To do this, simply open the start image and go to File>Quick Clone. This means that if you're not too confident about drawing such a complicated subject, you can always turn on Tracing Paper and use the ghost image as a guide to your drawing. There's nothing wrong with tracing. After all, the object of the exercise is to produce a competent finished drawing. In fact, drawing aids have been used throughout history, even by some of the world's greatest artists!

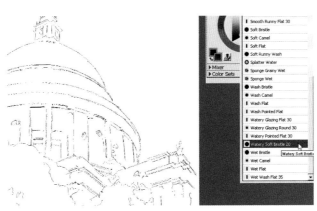

04 Watercolour brush You'd think now that the best thing to do would be to dive straight in with the pen again and start to add more detail. However, it's more useful to define the main areas of the painting with a few light washes, so change to the Watercolor category and choose the Watery Soft Bristle 20 variant.

05 First washes Set Feature to 11 in the Properties bar. Now choose a slightly lighter shade of sepia from the colour wheel and start to lightly brush in the main shadow areas in the building. Make sure not to paint these too dark at the moment – we're still just establishing form and tone at this stage.

06 Adjust the Pen settings Choose a very dark brown from the colour wheel. Add a new layer to the image. Now choose the Pens variants and select the Croquil Pen 5. Reduce the brush Opacity to around 30% so that the ink is slightly translucent. Increase the Grain to around 90% to make the pen lines smoother.

07 Dark details Add detail from the top of the building, using this pen at a very small size. Again, concentrate mainly on the very small, dark details first, using a tight scribble. Try to indicate shapes rather than draw them exactly. By establishing these dark details you'll soon see where areas of lighter shading need to go.

08 Lost and found Where you have long, continuous features, don't be afraid of creating 'lost and found' lines with gaps here and there, or replacing part of a line with some tiny hatching stokes. We're not doing a technical drawing here, and these slightly nervous areas add to the spontaneity of the sketch.

Bright idea

Unlike when you're drawing with pen and ink in the real world, in Painter it's easy to add bright areas of highlight detail within areas of very dark shading – even when you've completed these dark areas. You can do this with one of the Eraser variants. Choose one of the hard Eraser variants and use it at 100% Opacity on the target layer to 'lift out' small areas of ink. This is similar to using touches of white body colour to add highlight details with real pen and ink.

10 Larger dark areas Now you can start to establish the darkest tones in the upper part of the image, increasing the pen size here to around 8 pixels. In bigger dark areas, use quite energetic hatching strokes in varying directions. Refer to the source and finished images as you go.

09 Follow the contours For the moment concentrate mainly on the midtone areas in the image, and use the pen at a very small size of around 3 pixels. Try to make your strokes follow the contours of the area you are shading and remember to leave any highlight areas as blank paper showing through.

11 Judging tones When you're shading flat surfaces in shade, it's a good idea to use horizontal strokes placed closely together and parallel to each other. Remember, the closer your strokes are together, the darker the resulting tone will appear. You need to regularly zoom away from your drawing to judge these tones properly.

12 Indicate, don't draw Start adding the darker tones to the rest of the drawing, but not the trees or the sky, using the same methods as above. Remember the importance of the 'lost and found' broken lines, and also remember that you are indicating shapes rather than drawing them exactly. Often you'll need to zoom in very closely to the image to render very fine, detailed shading.

13 Building tones Again, here you can see how important it is that your shading follows the contours of the building. This adds form and depth to the objects. It's a good idea to first fill the area with midtone shading, preserving any highlight areas, and then go back in with the pen at a larger size to add a few real darks.

Using layers

It's quite an advantage to use lots of layers in this image. The best way to approach this is to use a new layer for each set of objects within the image from distance to foreground. So, you can start with a layer for the initial outline drawing and use another for the main building tone. Use another layer for the details on the building, and another for the trees. This way it's easy to add details to an area behind the trees, for instance, simply by drawing on that specific layer.

14 Finer details Now you can start adding the finer details to the drawing. Use the brush at a very small size (around 2-3 pixels). Don't be tempted to overdo this stage of the drawing, though – it's important to remember that we're suggesting detail here and not carefully drawing every single part of the building. You can see how simply the detail on the dome can be indicated.

15 Less is more Continue to add the details, such as the decorations at the top and bottom of each column and the insets in the tower. Small, nervous lines work well here, roughly following the shape of these details. For the columns themselves, don't actually outline all of them, simply leave white paper showing through.

Fantastic foliage
Brush up on your scribbling technique

16 Scribbled foliage Once you've added all of the details to the building (using the methods described) move on to the foreground trees. To create the trees, refer to the boxout over the page and use the scribble technique with the brush set to around 5 pixels to establish the overall midtone for the trees.

17 Foliage shadows Having established the midtones, increase the size of the pen to between 8-10 pixels and scribble in the darker tones in the foliage. Remember, we are going to add more sepia wash over this area, so don't go too dark – you can always add more later.

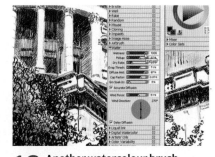

18 Another watercolour brush Choose the Watercolor category of variants and select the Soft Bristle 20 variant. Choose a slightly lighter shade of sepia from the colour wheel and set the brush Opacity to just 15%. In the Water section of the Brush Controls (Window>Brush Controls>Show Water), set the sliders as shown in the screenshot. Set the Minimum Size of the brush to 75%.

Rotating the canvas

There are lots of straight lines and geometric shapes in this drawing, and you may find it easier to draw most of these horizontally rather than vertically. To do this, simply click and hold on the Grabber tool in the toolbar and choose the Rotate tool. Now you can simply drag within your workspace to rotate the entire canvas. Generally, it's easier to draw horizontal lines than vertical ones. When you're done, and you want to return the document to its normal orientation, simply choose the tool again and drag it back into position.

Just add water

Use brushes to give your painting the perfect finish

19 **Loose washes** Start to add the sepia wash to the drawing, using the finished image as a guide. This brush, because of the way we've set it up, stays wet for a long time – so you can paint freely, overlapping strokes as you go. Use the brush at a large size in open areas such as the sky, and smaller on the building.

20 **Smaller dabs** Change to the Watercolor>Soft Bristle variant. Use this brush at a fairly small size to add more washes and dabs of colour in the smaller areas of detail. Also add some more dabs to the outline of the trees, and a few larger dabs in the darker parts of the sky.

21 **Finishing touches** You can now revert to the Croquil Pen and add a few more touches of line here and there, including a few strokes in the sky. Remember, you can easily erase any unwanted penwork by choosing one of the Eraser variants.

Shading techniques | Emulate traditional effects

Individual tones and textures in pen and ink drawings are created purely by the placement of line. There are many shading techniques you can use here, but in this drawing we use mainly the ones shown below. A variety of shading techniques not only helps to establish effective tones, but also adds surface interest to the finished drawing.

FOLIAGE TECHNIQUE

This shading technique consists of using a very loose, random scribble pattern to indicate random foliage. The technique uses the pen at around 7 pixels at first to establish the midtones of the foliage. Try practising this loose scribble before working on the actual trees.

FOLIAGE DARK TONES

Once the overall foliage fill has been established with the aforementioned technique, increase the pen size and then add some more loose, dense scribble over the first layer. This will effectively indicate the darker areas within the trees.

CROQUIL PEN HATCHING

This hatching technique, where short, expressive lines are laid over one another at different angles, is very good for the larger shadow areas in the main building. Place these individual strokes close together to create deep shadow areas.

CROQUIL PEN SHADING

These two techniques are used for midtone areas on the building, and the direction of the individual shading lines should follow the contours of the area that you're shading. The further apart you place these lines to each other, the lighter the tone will then appear in the finished drawing.

DARK VS LIGHT

There are two factors that govern how light or dark shading appears in a pen and ink drawing – namely the thickness of the strokes that make up the shading and how close together they are. The further apart hatching lines are, the more white paper shows through between them, and the lighter the tone appears.

INDICATING DETAIL

Small details are indicated with a very small pen, rather than distinctly drawn. Think of this as a kind of drawing shorthand, which when viewed from a distance gives the impression of intricate details and features. Part of the charm of ink drawings is the contrast between heavy and very light ink lines.

showcase

ANNE POGODA

TITLE | I Died
WEBSITE | www.darktownart.de
JOB TITLE | Digital Painter

Rising star Anne Pogoda is 22 years old and hails from Germany. She's been working as a digital painter for the past three years, producing artwork and tutorials for magazines and books in her high fantasy signature style.

eShop
Visit the *Official Corel Painter* online shop at www.imagineshop.co.uk for back issues and subscriptions

Visit us online at www.paintermagazine.com

Create your own art gallery for FREE • Meet other artists on the forum • Subscribe and save money!

Use brightly coloured pastels

Infuse energy and vibrancy into your portrait with the glorious hues of Painter's pastels!

Tutorial info

Artist
Judy Misquitta

Time needed
2 hours

Skill level
Intermediate

A familiar domestic setting can become a powerful painting of light and form, and pastels can help you achieve dramatic portraits. Over these pages you will learn about choosing a colour palette that may seem unrealistic, but actually follows the rules of colour, value and saturation. You'll discover how to use Corel Painter's pastels in rich, vibrant and brilliant hues.

Although 'pastel' suggests pale, muted colours, the word actually originated from the French 'pastiche' (meaning paste). These chalk-like sticks made from a mixture of powdered pigment and binder are sold in hundreds of colours and tones. Soft and hard pastels are water-based, dissolving into a semi-transparent colour wash, whereas oil pastels can be spread with turpentine or white spirit. The colour brilliance and direct flow from hand to paint surface makes it an interesting medium to work with, and much of its impact comes from the loose texture, flat, block colours and linear strokes used for exciting markings.

The Impressionists loved pastels, with Edgar Degas being the most experimental, combining it with every other medium and surfaces of paper and canvas. Many great contemporary artists use pastels in a combination of bold colours and subtle tones for their creations.

However, real pastels can be rather difficult to use due to their fragile and crumbly nature, and the chalky powder is not easy to control. Real pastels have to be mixed on the work surface itself, by overlaying or blending, unlike other paints which use a palette for such purposes. The abrasive, textured nature of surfaces gives you a limited choice of material, one that has to grip the pigment in its 'tooth', or adherence is poor.

Now we have the wonderful Corel Painter's versatile array of Pastels, enabling us to create the effect of traditional masterpieces with an expressive, contemporary twist. So let's explore the qualities of line and linear shading, and the effects of block-ins, blending and surface texture in an explosion of bold and brilliant colour!

Get started

It's time to put your pastel skills to the test

01 What's your reference? Let's begin by opening our reference image (please use your own for this tutorial), and saving it in RIFF format under a new name. Now the original is safely out of the way. Go to Select All, click Float and your image will be above the white canvas layer. By clicking on the eye icon to the left of the image layer name you can turn the visibility of your reference on or off.

02 Quick trace Click on a new blank layer and using the Artist Pastel Chalk, trace a simple line sketch in black to establish the dimensions and the angles of the pose of your subject, as shown. Change the Composite to Multiply to enable you to use it as a guideline for your painting. Keep the sketch simple, it isn't necessary to crowd it with detail. Turn off the visibility of the reference image for the time being.

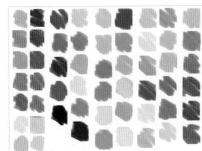

03 Colour mania This is our grand colour palette. The entire tutorial is based on a bright colour scheme of cool and warm colours, to create visual vibration and drama. Blues and purples are chosen to balance the hot-red orange in a lively orchestra of complementary hues. It's a good idea to plan your colours before you start your painting, and then refer to them continuously as you lay down strokes.

Bring out the fun-seeker
Let your inner child run free

Colour techniques

At the preliminary stage, applying broad, grainy blocks of colour with a sweeping motion is the fastest way to cover the canvas. Hard Pastel brushes used with lowered opacity can create endless colours when placed in layers eg: blue and yellow will yield green, red and blue, purple, etc. In addition, blending with Painter's blenders can produce a wonderful effect, similar to those found in oil paintings. Broken colour effects created with short strokes using two or more harmonious colours placed alongside each other gives depth and warmth, and is used in landscape paintings. Cross hatching helps to overlay colours with a mesh like effect. Build up colour effects and achieve balance and consistency by working on all areas simultaneously, beginning with large abstract shapes and moving on to smaller brushes.

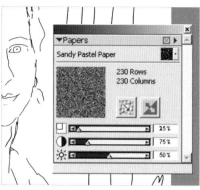

04 Texture and Pastel brush Sandy Pastel Paper is a first choice, since we shall begin with the background first. Alter the Paper Scale to 25%, Contrast to 75% and Brightness to 50%. Get ready to block in colours using the Square Hard Pastel 40 brush.

05 Turn up the heat Select hot colours like yellow, orange, red and red-purple from the background colour palette (shown in step three). Work on a blank layer below the sketch layer. Paint confidently with bold, sweeping strokes, using the Square Hard Pastel. Placement of shapes and patterns is determined by the reference image. Keep the colours clean.

06 Cool off You can use another layer here if you wish. Brush on cool colours of blue, blue-green and purple. Work with the same unhurried, yet decisive brush strokes. Notice how the repetition of colours from one part of the background to another creates visual links. The rule is that warm stands for light and will advance, whereas cool is for shadows and will recede.

07 Best face forward Begin the process of blocking in and loosely modelling facial contours and shadows with the darkest tones. We take our cue from the vivid colour palette and basic colour values of the background, so picking up and applying similar tones for the face is easy now. Shadow areas are either a cool blue or red-purple.

08 Adding mid-tones An impression of mid-tones is now included with the same loose blocky strokes of the Square Hard Pastel. We used a light reddish-orange for the skin, with variations. Links are being established between similar values of hue and tone across the facial structure, and is echoed in the background. Natural flesh tones are now introduced, along with brilliant colours for a vibrant tonal contrast.

09 See the light The best part of this block-in process is working around the image to achieve an impression of solid form. The brightest and lightest tones are applied; the colours of sunlight and shadow understood. The blues depict the reflected light of the sky, and the evening sun lights up with yellow. The local skin colour is red and orange, while the shadows are purple.

10 Dress sense The dress is primarily sketched in with shading, linear strokes and criss-cross hatching in order to paint the colour and pattern. We have chosen a different approach to add textural interest to the painting. Variation in colour, again, determines areas of light and shadow. Refer to your reference image to get a sense of the texture and pattern of the clothes.

11 Curtain call Pastels are ideal for broken colour, shown in the way the curtains are painted. Loose strokes, rough blends and colour mixes create an interesting visual impression of the curtains behind the seated lady. The curtains are identifiable, yet they blend with the background without being overpowering. Remember that our seated subject is the main focus.

Work in the detail

Keep applying colours for recognisable forms

12 Window treatment Soft light coming in from the windows behind the subject are painted in colours of blue-green and purple, and the reflected blue of the sky bounces off the windowpane and strikes the contours of her profile. This window is partially in shadow. The window to the front is bathed with radiant sunlight, creating a dramatic high-key quality and vivid illumination. Notice how the side of her face toward this window is suffused with glowing yellow light.

13 Dress details Sketch and paint in all the tiny pattern shapes that you can see in the reference photo. The Square Hard Pastel and Artist Pastel Chalk will fill in all the details of this delightful dress. Follow the reference image for the pattern.

14 Eyes and nose Brushwork on the facial features is much more detailed. Painting the iris in the right place sets the gaze, so start to draw with a pastel pencil first, before filling in with colour. Use various shades of green, grey and brown. Add catchlights into the darkest part of the iris. The nose is delightful to mould with highlights of blue that reflects the sky colour.

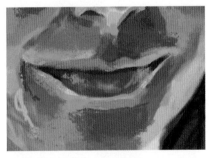

Painter's pastels | A glance at the tools

You get a good choice of pastel brushes in Painter, but when you are starting out it pays to limit yourself to just a few. That way you are forced to experiment with their controls to get the different effects you want. Here are our favourites...

15 Sweet lips A mouth is the most expressive part of any human anatomy. Lip colour is easy to choose, especially if it isn't painted with lipstick. Natural lip colour is more or less the same as skin colour. A moist and full mouth is achieved by subtle highlights. Form and shape is given by shadows placed strategically around the lip area, such as between the chin and the lower lip, and in the little dip above the lips.

16 Hair today Follow the natural flow of the hair. After blocking in colour shades, ranging from very dark to mid-tone, strands of hair can be painted in with a very small Artist Chalk brush. Choose highlights from the colour of the light that falls on the hair. Refer to the colour chart.

Artist Pastel Chalk

This small, hard brush is somewhat like a thin stick of charcoal. It has been used for sketching, linear strokes, colour accents and for cross-hatching. Play about with the opacity and size for various layering effects.

Square Soft Pastel

This is great for producing flat blocks of colour and has a wonderful softness to it. It has been used with lowered opacity to create translucent and radiant skin, and as it has little grain it's excellent for colour washes.

Square Hard Pastel

Beautiful variations in grain and texture can be achieved with this brush. Use it for broad colour block-ins, especially in backgrounds and over wide spaces. Experiment with paper and grain. At a larger size, with 50% Opacity, it's great for layered effects of colour.

Round Soft Pastel

This brush works best for building up colour. It was used to create various textures on the skin and parts of the dress. It has a very organic feel to it and produces soft, subtle strokes. Soft scumbling or squiggly overlapping strokes are best made with this brush.

17 Colour accents These are little abstract touches of colour used to give life and soul to a painting. Colour accents can add zest and vivacity to an ordinary image, and work almost like highlights. Accents work effectively in relation to surrounding colour areas, for example: a mark of bright yellow on a natural lip colour to suggest sunlight, or a streak of bright pink on the hair.

18 Bring it all together Sometimes even our best efforts are 'not quite right'. This is especially so with our choice of hues, our tonal effects and colour values. Corel Painter has the perfect solution with this wonderful feature: Effects>Tonal Control>Correct Colors. Play about with these magical buttons until you're satisfied.

Original photo

Turn photos into sketches

In this tutorial we will show you how to create a 'sketchy style' pencil drawing, using a photo and just four brushes in Painter

Tutorial info

Artist
Jill Garl

Time needed
1.5 hours

Skill level
Beginner

On the CD
Start and final photos

Painter is an awesome program to use for creating this 'sketchy style' pencil drawing. Whether you start out with a photograph or draw your image freehand, the steps outlined in this tutorial will help you to successfully achieve this look.

This style is perfect for drawing people. With its simplistic beauty, you will be able to create a portrait that has emotion and personality. By drawing just a few strokes for the background, the focus will be concentrated on the subject. Using much more detail and shading in the face, compared to the fluid lines in the hair and clothes, is another way to have the focus be on the mood, the expression and the uniqueness of the subject.

There is very little blending or smudging involved here, the contour lines are the basis for this style of art. Your initial pencil lines will become an intricate part of your drawing. It's a beautiful thing to look at your drawing and realise you're looking at a part of yourself in the expression of those lines.

You will learn how to use the Conte brush, along with the Chalk brush and pencils. The Soft Cloner, Eraser, Quick Clone and Equalizer are just a few features you will learn in this tutorial. It is so exciting to watch your subject come to life in front of you, using these brushes, features and techniques. You may find yourself looking through the photographs you already have in a new way – to choose one to use for an expressive new pencil drawing!

Preparation
Start by preparing your chosen photograph

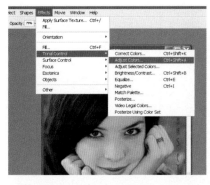

01 Prepare photograph for drawing
Before you begin creating your drawing, you will want to prepare the photograph. We start with desaturating the image. To do this, go to Effects>Tonal Control>Adjust Color. Slide the Saturation bar all the way to the left. Click OK. This will desaturate your photograph.

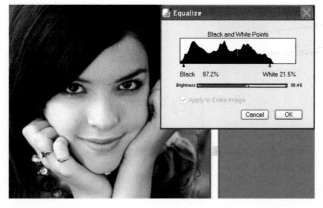

02 Brighten up In order to really see the highlight and shadow areas when you are shading, bumping up the Contrast after you desaturate is an important step. A good way to do this is to use the Equalizer. Go to Effects>Tonal Control>Equalize. Slide the Brightness control from left to right to adjust. Now click OK.

03 Set colour for the background
In this step we will set the Background Paper colour. First choose the colour you want to use from the Color Wheel. For our example we have used an ivory colour. Next, go to Canvas>Set Paper Color. You will not see anything happen to your image at this point, but your paper colour will show up in the next step.

Clone and sketch
Get ready to trace, draw and blend

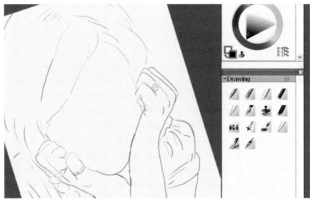

04 **Quick Clone image** Now clone the image and get ready to draw! Go to File>Quick Clone. A duplicate of your image will open up, with tracing paper covering it in the colour you chose from step three. This will happen all in one step! You can toggle the tracing paper on and off by clicking the Tracing Paper icon.

05 **Sketch outline** Trace over the image using the tracing paper and the Cover Pencil variant. Keep in mind that a lot of these lines will become part of your final drawing. Keep your lines nice and fluid. You can always use the Eraser tool, or Ctrl/Cmd+A, to clean up or repeat any lines you want to redo. Angling your paper may help while you are drawing.

06 **Draw features on the face** Zoom in very close to the face. Trace over the features with a lighter touch. Using the Cover Pencil, or Number 2 Pencil, outline the eyebrow area, pupils, irises, eyelashes, etc. Make sure your lines are accurate, as this will be the step that identifies the subject's likeness.

Iterative save

Save your photograph with a new name after you make changes, such as desaturating and Equalizing. Once you have saved, you can click off the original photograph. Your original will remain untouched. The new saved version will be the one you are working on with the tracing paper. It is also a good idea to use iterative saves as you go, saving each step.

07 **Zoom out and check sketch** Check your sketch with the tracing paper off. Make any adjustments you feel are necessary, and will benefit your sketch. Erase any areas that need cleaning up. Redraw any areas you feel could be better at this time.

08 **Adding shadows** Begin to add in some shadows. With the tracing paper on, and using the Conte brush, brush over the shadow areas that you see. The creases around the nose, under the eyes and under the bottom lip are common areas. Take advantage of the pressure sensitivity in your stylus, create heavy and light opacities of colour.

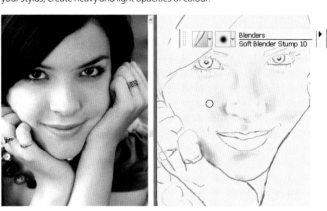

09 **Swatch of colour** Turn your tracing paper on and off to check your progress. Make a swatch of the colour you are using, just in case your colour becomes altered. Even though you are only using a grey tone to draw with, there are many different grey tones available!

10 **Blending in your shadows** At this point we will begin to blend in the shadows. Using the Soft Blender Stump brush, blend the shadow areas. Go in the natural direction of the areas you are working in – for example, round out your shadows around the nose and under the bottom lip. Think of this step as moulding your subject's face.

Face the details

Eyes and ears, and mouth and nose...

11 **Working on the eyes** For this stage we have the original and the drawing open side by side on screen; we can see the detail in the eyes much better this way. Darken the pupil and fill in the irises with the Conte brush. Now blend with the Stump blender, using a tiny brush size. Go over the eyes with the Eraser tool to bring out the catch lights, and watch your subject come alive!

12 **Hands and arms** Next, we will work on the hands and arms. Using the same technique as in the face, brush on your shadow colour and blend with the Stump blender. Shadow and blend around the knuckles, edges of the hands and arms, and into the darkened areas of the photograph.

13 **Clothes detail** For this step we used the Square Chalk brush. With a loose, free motion, stroke on colour inside the lines. Don't worry if you go outside the lines, as long as your strokes have a nice fluid feel then this will just add to your drawing. Avoid the urge to 'fill up' all the outlined space. Let the lines that you created in step five become part of the drawing.

15 **Working on the hair** The hair is another step that will really bring the subject to life. Sketch in the hair with a long, sweeping motion using the Conte brush. Varying the opacity of colour helps the hair to look natural and adds depth. Again, your original lines will show through, giving the hair a nice sketchy, loose style. Leave some areas untouched to create the highlights.

14 **Jewellery detail** Details, like the rings in this example, are drawn freestyle. They are drawn using the Cover Pencil, or Number 2 Pencil, using a very small size brush. The necklace is drawn using the Conte and Chalk brush to fill in colour. The highlights are brought back with the Eraser tool, similar to the eyes.

16 **Preparing to work on the background** We are now ready to add some background strokes. Create a duplicate of the drawing on the screen; go to File>Clone. You can now click off the original. You should have two windows open, the 'Clone of' and the 'Clone of clone'. Check your Clone Source to make sure a check mark is next to the 'Clone of', as this will be your new Clone Source.

Rotate Page

The Rotate Page tool is extremely useful in positioning your page on an angle that works best for you. The page may be rotated in a complete circle in either direction. You may move the paper on its side or upside down to check your composition. The Rotate Page tool is located in the toolbox as a flyout, next to the Move tool (it looks like a rounded arrow). You just grab onto your page and turn it in any direction. Remember to return back to the Brush icon to continue using the brushes. When you want to bring your page upright, choose the Rotate Page tool again and click on your drawing. It will straighten right up.

Tutorial | Turn photos into sketches

Fade tool

The Fade tool is a great option for when you feel you overdid a step with too much saturation, and want to bring the colour or contrast down some. Also, it's a good way to judge how far you may want to go with colour. First, deliberately over-saturate the colour in an area. Then go to your Fade tool and fade to the desired amount. To use the Fade tool, after you have performed your step and want to fade it, go to Edit>Fade. A window will open with a slide bar, where you can fade the last action performed by a percentage. Click OK.

Finish it in style
Complete your masterpiece!

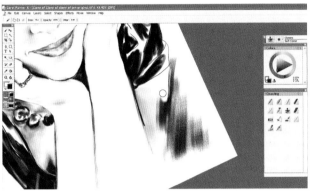

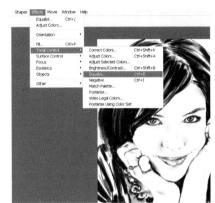

17 **Background strokes** Using the Square Chalk brush, brush over some background areas near your subject, in an angled motion. We sampled a colour from the hair in this example, for the background strokes. If you want to come back into the strokes from the outside edges, just sample the background colour, which is ivory in this example, and brush the new strokes.

18 **Soft Clone image back** Zoom into the area where you sketched the background strokes. With your Soft Cloner brush set at 100%, brush over the areas you want to bring back (in this example it's the arm). The Soft Cloner brush is a tool that tends to spread out a little bit, so be careful not to use too large a brush. Remember, you can always Ctrl/Cmd+Z and try again, it doesn't have to perfect first time.

19 **Finishing up your drawing** That's it, your drawing is complete! For the final step you can play with the Equalizer to get more, or less, contrast. Also, consider warming up your drawing in Photoshop for an alternative look.

Sketchy summary | How to create a 'sketchy style' pencil drawing

Although we have left the Clone command for the shading of this image, the use of a source photo means the technique is accessible to even very nervous artists. The loose style allows you to get away with unconfident lines!

HIGHLIGHT AREAS
If you keep some areas of your sketch without colour it will indicate highlights. This allows your chosen background colour to become the highlights. In this example the effect is most evident in the hair and clothes, helping to bring your drawing to life!

ERASER TOOL
Use the Eraser tool to create the catchlights in the eyes and lips. This tool is also used to create highlights in the rings and the necklace

BACKGROUND
Keep the background simple to bring the focus to your subject. Just a few strokes in the background will help to bring your subject forward and create depth

BLENDING
Do not over-blend in the clothes or hair area. Let the beauty of the line and brushwork show through. Most of your blending will be in the shadows on the face, arms and hands

CONTOUR LINES
Keep your lines free, loose and deliberate when drawing out your initial sketch, as these lines will become an intricate part of your drawing. Have your lines vary from thick and thin for more interest and realism

showcase

HELEN CHIEREGO

TITLE | Poppies and Glass Marbles
WEBSITE | www.paintermagazine.co.uk/user/Helen Chierego
JOB TITLE | Digital Artist

Helen Chierego is from Melbourne, Australia. A traditional painter who started her exploration of digital media a couple of years ago; she now combines the traditional with digital techniques to create impressionistic portraits and still life images.

eShop
Visit the
Official Corel Painter
online shop at
www.imagineshop.co.uk
for back issues
and subscriptions

Visit us online at www.paintermagazine.com

Create your own art gallery for **FREE** • Meet other artists on the forum • Subscribe and save money!

Painting the
seasons

Creating a series of paintings to show the different seasons is a great project. **Cat Bounds** reveals some essential techniques

It's hard not to be affected by the changing seasons. As months pass away, we notice changes in colour, temperature and general feeling. Whether it's blazing sun down at the beach, or frost creeping over a windowpane, each season offers the artist an abundance of potential subjects.

We thought we'd have a bit of fun by taking one scene and translating it into the four seasons. First and foremost, this was an exercise in technique – what needs to be done to capture the look of a season. But it also threw up other questions. What emotions does this season evoke in us? What

memories do we associate with motley-coloured leaves drifting lazily earthward? What is that certain, unnamed moment on a blisteringly cold day when you breathe in a whisper of springtime? And how do we translate it onto the canvas?

All of these questions are valuable in creating your own seasonal image. So as you browse the following pages, have a notebook and pen at hand so you can jot down insights as they occur for creating your own seasonal paintings. Then, once you've taken on board the tips we have here, go ahead and have a go yourself.

Spring

Go for a walk with a spring in your step, and get some inspiration to create a fresh, dynamic painting like the one here

Robert Frost said it best in his beautiful poem, *Nothing Gold Can Stay*. "Nature's first green is gold, her hardest hue to hold. Her early leaf's a flower; but only so an hour. Then leaf subsides to leaf. So Eden sank to grief, so dawn goes down to day. Nothing gold can stay."

Springtime is the awakening, that fleeting, crystalline instant when slumbering earth stirs and all things are new and all things are possible. The golden hues of spring are a lifetime removed from autumn's gold. Close your eyes and think of spring. What are the colours you see there? Colours so delicate, they defy our paintbrushes and shift before our eyes. Gold that is gold for a heartbeat; look again and it's green. Shall we paint a spring morning, midday or afternoon? Early spring or late spring? Springtime in town or in the country? We have so many beautiful choices before us! Here's a look at some of the cardinal rules of painting spring.

Spring swatches

Somewhere between realism and abstraction

Let your true colours shine through

Using local colour throughout your seasonal paintings isn't a necessity, and bringing in at least a few unrealistic colours adds to the excitement. Spring is one season where you can really go to town, as strange, bright colours help give the impression of everything springing to life. So what if you throw a few purple and turquoise leaves into your spring oak tree? The jar in colours will excite the eye and capture the essence of spring perfectly. Here are some good energy colours for spring.

01 **Red rush** Red hues impart life, energy and movement and can lead the viewer's eye through the painting. Like every colour on the colour wheel, reds fall into either warm or cool hues. Warm autumn reds are lush and deep, while cool spring hues of red lean toward pastel. Red complements green, so in landscapes it gives that pop you're trying for.

02 **Painting the blues** Blue is calming. While we want colour schemes that pop, we want rest stops as well. When planning the blues of your sky, consider the time of day, the temperature, whether it's stormy or calm. Will there be clouds? Even if you're painting a cloudless day, remember to break up the expanse with varied hues of blue.

03 **Feeling green** Greens are the most difficult colour pigments to mix and the most challenging to create in digital paint as well. Finding just the right shade of green takes some experimenting. Layer your brush strokes in order to break up the green expanses and describe patches of sunlight and shadow. Warm green goes toward yellow, cool green toward blue.

A map would be useful

Light and dark contrasts map

A map of the light and dark areas of your image will serve you well throughout any painting. Create your map by desaturating and softening the image you plan to paint. Particularly in landscape trees, we need to know where to paint deep colours and where to brush on light colours in order to create shape and dimension. As seasons progress from spring through autumn, those shadows deepen.

Beware!

DON'T PAINT IT BLACK

Our paintings need intense darks in them, whether cool or warm, but beware of true black because black is lifeless. Deep charcoals and intensely dark blues, greens and browns will read as black while retaining the life of your painting.

Soft and bright

Get the correct feeling of light

The light in springtime is a bit of a challenge to capture. It has the crispness of autumn, but the sun's position still gives a softness to the world. We tried to translate this in the image by using a mixture of soft, blended tones in the water, mixed with crisp, defined parts of colour in the bank of flowers. The almost lime green colour of the grass also helps add to the sense of freshness that a springtime scene evokes.

Visual clues of spring

Essential tricks for capturing a season

We've included some classic springtime identifiers here. The first is the fact that the large tree has gaps in it, suggesting there are more leaves to come. The baby ducks are an iconic symbol of spring, as are flowers such as tulips and daffodils. Finally, the dabbed effect on the distant trees and the fact they are such a bright green help give the impression of buds and new growth.

Quick tips

RESEARCH YOUR SEASON

Even if you plan to paint all or part of your seasonal paintings from scratch, photo sites like Stock.XCHNG are invaluable sources of inspiration because their thousands of photos are arranged into categories. Just do a search for 'spring' and then browse through the photos that are returned. Look for the colour, feel and objects that occur most often.

GATHERING BRUSHES

Each seasonal painting may call for its own brush effects, but gathering them all into one palette will result in greater continuity, as you will use at least some of the same brushes throughout the series. We want them to look as if they belong together – which at least here, they do.

PAINT IT TWICE

You need to have a great deal of patience when it comes to painting. It may help to do a preliminary painting to get the feel of things, find the right colours, and plan highlights and shadows.

Summer

Cast your mind back to any summer – or at least those days when the sun was shining! Remember them? Now transfer that feeling of warmth onto canvas

Summertime, and the living is easy... Even more than the words to that beautiful George Gershwin song, the music and the tempo relate the state of mind that is summer. The primary colours of summer are decidedly warm, and earth is fragrant and abuzz with the affairs of creation and becoming, but without the urgency of spring or the bittersweet poignancy of autumn. Can you think of summer without hearing children on holiday from school laughing? What colour is laughter? For that matter, what colour is summer grass? Summer's embrace feels as if it will abide with us always, but summer may take more thought to paint than the others, simply because our wealth of mental images borders on sensory overload. Be patient though; it will sort itself out as you work. The best paintings begin with an idea, not a resolution.

Summer swatches

The lights and colours of summer

The state of mind that we know as summer

Most of us share a collective consciousness of seasonal life on earth. When you were a child, you probably laid on your back in tall grass in summer and watched white, fluffy clouds glide lazily overhead. You may know that crunching sound your boots make in snow, and many of you will have warmed half-frozen noses over cups of hot chocolate with tiny marshmallows floating on top. These are shared experiences that make us all one and which allow us to communicate through our art. By picking the correct colours, you can instantly suggest a mood and get that seasonal feeling.

Sunlight playing on the leaves gives a glow and defines dimension

01 Boat Though summer has its dreary days, our idea of summer embraces its warm sunlight and clear, bright colours. We painted this boat in warm tones to help give the impression of the season, and the act of fishing in itself gives the feeling of summer days. No pure whites were used – yellow tones carry the impression of warmth.

02 Blue sky The typical impression of a summer sky is a lovely warm blue, with little or no cloud. To make this sky different from spring, we simply coloured over the clouds with blue, but still left a touch of highlight to give the impression that something is in the sky. The blue was also warmed a bit to help give a hazy feel to the season.

03 Distant trees We also altered the distant trees. In spring, they were quite acidic, with tones of yellow, bright green and darker tones. Here the whole effect is much softer, with more blended brush strokes to give the impression of lots of leaves on the trees. This softness helps make the light seem hazy and the yellow highlights hint at a sun beaming down.

Creating our neutral colours
Neutrals are the supporting cast in our story

Even when we are focusing on colours that are representative of the four seasons, we ought not to forget to include some neutrals to make our brighter colours more important in the composition. One of the best ways to accomplish this is to combine complementary colours – for example, summer greens and reds.

Summer landscapes
An altogether smoother scenario

In mid-summer, the landscape is often quieter than vibrant spring or robust autumn. Growth reaches its peak, and wild grasses ripen in preparation to drop seeds. The edges of meadows are softened, foregrounds are rich with mature colour and definition, while backgrounds recede into blue haze. Stiffness gives way to curves, and we incorporate these graceful lines into our paintings.

01 Symbols In a softened realistic painting like ours, we can introduce symbols that will read as a tree trunk, parts of a fence, leaves, flowers and so on. It's better not to be too compulsive about these symbolic strokes, as they'll be far more painterly than if we zoomed in and painted painstakingly with a tiny brush.

02 Essence We're after the essence of flowers rather than perfect specimens. The best brushes for painting the essence of things are ones that aren't completely controllable, leaving some of the process to what Bob Ross called "happy little accidents". Colours are the hot reds, yellows and oranges to give the impression of heat.

03 Lots of leaves Summer is when all of nature is in its prime, so it was important in our scene to make sure the trees were packed with leaves. The dark shadows suggest really thick growth and this shadow colour was carried on into the flower bank to show how many flowers were growing there.

04 Smooth and quiet We used the water in the painting to help give the impression of quiet summer days. By painting lots of still reflections, the effect is of a flat surface. The water also allows us to diffuse the light and use it as another way of suggesting hazy days. The deep shadows cast by the trees help suggest how thick with foliage they are.

Beware!

DON'T GO TOO BRIGHT!
It's tempting to paint everything in very strong colours in summer, but often the light is very soft and hazy. Look at free stock photo sites and get a feel for the season. Look at different scenes (country, city, etc) and note any differences.

Quick tips

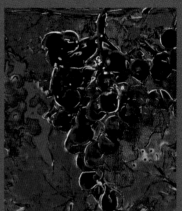

GO MORE ABSTRACT

We've painted literal interpretations of seasons in these pages, but you can still conjure up a feeling of the time of year without relying on landscapes. In the image above, the colours are very reminiscent of hot climates and give the feeling of summer. Try experimenting with different objects and see if you can suggest seasons just through colours.

BEGINNER'S MIND

"In the beginner's mind, there are many possibilities, but in the expert's [mind] there are few," Shunryu Suzuki once said. Approach each painting as if it were your first and open yourself to all the possibilities that exist there on that blank canvas, waiting to become a piece of art worth framing.

THERE ARE NO RULES!

As with everything, the best route to take when painting the seasons is to study photos and paintings, maybe find out if any instructional books have been written, and then decide what you want to follow and what feels right. Don't feel as though you have to do everything we say here - pick a few tips that will work with your style and then make up the rest! Unless you are going for photo-realism, try experimenting!

Autumn

Arguably the most colourful season of the four, do your painting justice by breaking out a whole new colour palette

This scene evokes the work of another of the great poets, this time John Keats. The following is from the opening extract of his beautiful poem *To Autumn*. "Season of mists and mellow fruitfulness, close bosom-friend of the maturing sun; conspiring with him how to load and bless, with fruit the vines that round the thatch-eves run; to bend with apples the moss'd cottage-trees, and fill all fruit with ripeness to the core; to swell the gourd, and plump the hazel shells, with a sweet kernel; to set budding more."

Autumn is the dénouement, those lovely, languid days when we reap what we have sown; a time to reflect, a time brimming with rich, luscious colours pulsating with life and mouth-watering flavours. Is your autumn about tumbling in piles of amber, scarlet and brown crunchy leaves, or maybe about holidays and the smell of pie baking in the oven? Think about how you will strive to paint that aroma and capture those sounds and sights in a few brushstrokes.

Autumn swatches

Capturing the feel of autumn

Autumn – a season in limbo

Take some time to wander back through the autumnal days that reside in your memories. As you read and follow this tutorial, it may even be autumn outside your window with winter beginning to creep in. Scan your neighbourhood for splashes of autumn colour. Can you hear wind chimes through an open window or door? Does your inner child come out and make you go out of your way to step on that slightly crunchy-looking leaf? These are all evocative memories of autumn.

01 Favourite sounds One of the most distinctive autumn sounds is geese flying overhead. There's something immensely comforting about that honking, squawking cacophony, getting louder as they approach and then trailing off again. By incorporating these into the painting, we have set the scene firmly in the autumn months.

02 A gust of wind and a swirl of leaves Falling leaves is a very powerful symbol of autumn, and one we had to include in our painting. They are easy to do, as well. Pick out your autumnal foliage colours and make simple dabs. Try to go for a delicate scattering to suggest a gentle breeze – anything too dramatic and you're in tornado territory!

03 A magical mystery tour Travelling around in the autumn gives you access to many breathtaking examples of fiery and intense autumnal foliage. You'll find it especially in the countryside, but sometimes, when set against a busy concrete city backdrop, that one special scene can be more evocative than you ever believed possible.

Autumn portrait

Apply an autumnal effect

Portraits may also be seasonal. This photo by PBase artist Dave Finley could have been painted as autumn, winter or early spring, but we chose muted autumn colours and softened the background. An interesting painting series would be to paint the same person in season colours.

Beware!

YOU NEED NOT WANDER FAR AFIELD
The world is filled with fabulous photo opportunities to be used as image sources, but your most meaningful and successful seasonal image may be right in your own back yard, just down the road or around the corner.

Autumn online

Some sites to inspire you

These are some sites which, though not restriction-free, can awaken your own seasonal memories.

www.icelandiscool.com/photo

http://news.bbc.co.uk/2/hi/in_pictures/7073411.stm

www.msnbc.msn.com/id/20962060

www.pbase.com/k_amj/image/56777159

The signs of autumn

How we helped show autumn in our image

Autumn is a glorious season to paint, and there are loads of visual tricks you can use to leave viewers in no doubt as to the season. The most obvious is the leaves. Use plenty of reds, golds and bright yellows. We started to thin out our trees to show how nature is slowing down and even had some exposed branches in the right-hand one. Fallings leaves is another obvious trick, and be sure to have some scattered on the ground. Colours are more intense in autumn, so give plenty of punch to the sky and whatever other colours you use.

Quick tips

SOFT FOCUS

Utilise your camera's depth of field settings, or create that soft and dreamy look with your digital software programs, and you've got the beginnings of a painting that is filmy, ethereal and speaks of autumnal timelessness. Further enhance the image with brushstrokes or a combination of filter effects and colour brightening, and you've got art!

SOFT EDGES

Throughout your painting, you will want what are known as 'lost-and-found edges', meaning edges that are soft and blend into the background along with hard edges. Soft edges are most easily achieved with blenders such as the Just Add Water blender in Painter.

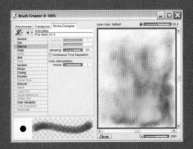

SOFT COLOUR

This is a handy tip to add colour without disturbing brushstrokes. Choose an Airbrush variant set to a low opacity and create a transparent layer above your canvas set to Soft Light, Gel or Overlay. Now as you paint, your brushstrokes will remain safe.

Winter

As you paint this scenario, you'll be excused for imagining yourself walking in a Winter Wonderland…

Yes, we know this one was too easy, but that old song by Richard Smith and Felix Bernard seems nearly perfect for setting the mood for our winter painting. It's so familiar, you're playing it in your mind as you read! If autumn was the time of harvest, then winter is surely a season of fewer responsibilities, of holiday gatherings and finally, of chilly evenings, reading, contemplating and nodding by the fire in woollen socks. We can hardly recall our last deep, drifting snow, but snow remains a part of our winter psyche. Do you celebrate Christmas or Kwanzaa or Hanukkah or other winter holidays? Their colours will likely appear in your winter palette, along with restful greys and whites, blues and browns. Winter colours are cool, recessive, and provide respite and healing for our minds, our bodies and our senses.

Winter swatches

The truth about snow
There's no business like snow business

Pablo Picasso famously once said, "Art is a lie that makes us realise truth." Surely, if you scooped up a handful of snow, you would only describe it as fluffy and white, but if you want to describe it on canvas or paper, then you'll have to look closer and discover ways in which to translate subtle shadows, contrasts and values. Cool purples and blues are wonderful for indicating dimension and a soft gradation among the many shades of these colours, and the white highlights will immediately read as painterly snow. Check out the image on the right.

Footprints in the snow described with shades of blue and purple add beauty to the composition

01 Greys that describe In this little abstract of crocuses pushing up through the snow, there's hardly any white at all, but the cool greys read as snow because of the context and because we expect cool greys to be there. If we had chosen soft tans and browns, then it probably would have read as yellow flowers growing in beach sand.

02 Snow as highlights If the majority of the painting is filled with vibrant colour, then we can get away with painting all or mostly white snow, and it just becomes a beautiful highlight, with traces of snow on the tops of branches, doorsteps and buildings. Our eyes are drawn first to the white, and then we explore the rest of the painting.

03 Journey of discovery Sometimes we choose to let the viewer discover his or her own truth about our painting. In this one, there could be patches of snow in the valley and on the mountains, but those might be glints of sunlight. And so, our painting can be like a poem that means something different to everyone who reads it.

The sky's the limit
Choosing a style for your landscapes

We chose a soft, rather realistic style for our 'four seasons' paintings, but you may want to do yours in a more abstract, collaged fashion – simply because it would be great fun. Will you choose to do them in perfect realism, transparent and splashy watercolour, scrumptious impasto oils or acrylics, coloured pencil, oil pastels or even a mosaic?

Painting winter
There's no chance of mistaking this season!

Like autumn, winter is packed with iconic symbols that leave the viewer in no doubt as to what season they are looking at. We've gone for the most obvious in the painting, namely snow and twigs and even a Christmas tree! However, even if you went for a more subtle approach, just by using crisp blues, greys and purples you would be able to give the feeling of winter.

01 Bare branches Trees with no foliage are a clear indication of winter, and work even if you have no snow in the painting. Using grey tones of brown also helps make the tree look cold and wintry. For background trees, paint some in white and have some in a muddy grey colour. Again, this gives the feeling of winter and crisp, clean temperatures.

02 Under pastel skies The blue sky of the previous seasons is now transformed into a pastel mottling of blues, purples and lavenders. It feels very wrong using these colours, but they perfectly suggest a sky filled with the possibility of more snowfall.

03 Pastel snow Snow is never pure white, and although you can get away with white highlights here and there, your image will look strange with big blocks of white area. You need to think in the same colours as the sky, and have purple and blue shadows to define the snowfall. Bring in touches of yellows to suggest a low wintry sun.

04 Iced water Once again, we have still water but this time there is the suggestion of ice. By reflecting the sky and snow colours in the water, and keeping dark shadows, it feels as though the water has iced over. You could further enhance this by having small flurries of snow on the surface.

Beware!

CHANGING OF THE TIDE
Doing four paintings of the same landscape, it would be tempting to make them nearly identical except for the changing colours. Just as life is never static, true landscapes are constantly changing. Celebrate the changing details in your series.

Quick tips

THINK LIKE SNOW
One way to quickly ruin the effect of snowfall is to get carried away and put it all over the image. In areas such as the trees, you need to consider how snow would land. Just as if you were painting in where light would hit an object, think about what parts the falling snow would land on.

INSPIRATION IN ABSTRACTS
However you may feel about abstract paintings, they are a great way to get the juices flowing. Open up Painter and begin making random strokes and shapes across the canvas. Pick the colours you associate with the seasons, and before long you can have a good mood piece.

KEEP INSPIRATIONS FOLDERS
When you come across an artist's website whose art strikes a chord, bookmark a link to it in your Inspirations folder. Or when you find a single painting that speaks to you, save it in a folder on your hard drive. Then when inspiration runs low, browse your Favourites folders and find that spark that gets you thirsting to create.

TAKE A STEP OUTSIDE OF YOUR COMFORT ZONE
Sometimes we lose the spark if we stop challenging ourselves. If you're comfortable with painting watercolours, step outside your comfort zone and today paint only with coloured pencils. Move your tablet to the left of the keyboard - just change something!

Create painted borders

In this tutorial we'll take you through a step-by-step process to show how a painted border can really add to the overall effect of a portrait painting

Tutorial info

Artist
Daniel Cox

Time needed
30 minutes

Skill level
Beginner

Great modern masters all think carefully not just about the subject, but also how the subject sits in the canvas. Not claiming to be modern masters, we do still try, however, to think about using painted borders effectively in our work.

These borders can add general interest to the painting because they can be bold, strong brushstrokes or even soft, lost edges. Either way, because they don't contain detail, they can help accentuate the focal points of your painting, such as the face and the eyes of the subject. Or the effect can be subtle, where the artist leaves only a few stray brush marks sweeping away from the subject. In a landscape painting, fields, cottages or harbour-side, the effect can be much bolder, using an uneven border as a major part of the composition.

In terms of approaches, an artist could either start with a rough border and then render the subject tighter, purposely leaving the border uneven and rough. Or you can go back and purposely paint the border. This can be tricky though, as the effect needs to look chaotic and unplanned. We've found that it takes some time to get that effect, otherwise the painted border can detract from the painting because it feels staged. It needs to look like you didn't plan it! We'll take you through how we would approach adding a border in these steps. It's just a quick demonstration but should be useful.

Crossing the border

Where neutral colours and negative space are a positive thing!

01 **Just the border** We start this tutorial after the hard part – the actual painting of the image – has been completed. As you can see, at this stage the canvas is actually larger than the final image (for more about this, see the side tip). You don't have to have it larger, but in this case it was really an accident because we were initially planning to paint more background. You'll also notice that we've painted her jacket all the way to the canvas, and this is the main area that needs work.

02 **Conté is king!** Start by using the Conté Brush. Cmd+Alt-click to select a neutral colour that is already present in the painting. Work bold and fast, and don't be afraid to work back into the image. We weren't very happy with the jacket anyway, so we're quite comfortable covering it up.

03 **Negative space is your friend** As you work, always have the negative space in mind. This is important, because the shape is going to affect the impact of the painting. If we paint too much negative space, her head will look like it's on a stick. The idea is to create interest and blend these areas. Here we're working from the border inwards towards the subject.

04 **Creating contrast between border and subject** Don't be afraid to work back into the subject either. Here we want to lead the viewer's eye to her face, and down into the rest of the painting. To do this, paint thick brushstrokes using the Acrylic brush (Size 45, Opacity 22%).

05 **Moving on** As you can see, this part of the image is already very loose. However, it's lacking a feeling of shape, so we worked some of the darker tones that we've used to paint the background trees into the border, and then pulled some of the neutral border colour in the subject. Essentially, we're creating a stronger frame for the subject by doing this. If it's too loose, the viewer's eye gets lost.

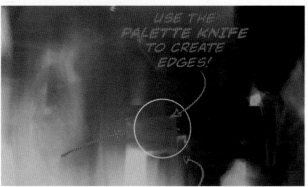

06 **Let's have a Palette Knife fight!** When you are happy with the overall shape, it's time to work on the edges. The Palette Knife is a great art tool in Corel Painter, as it is in traditional media. What's great about it is that it allows you to very easily blend the Conté we laid in earlier, but also by first pushing the paint in one direction and then pulling it in the other, edges are created.

Tutorial | Create painted borders

Use a bigger canvas, and crop later!

As you can see, the canvas is oversized compared to the final image. We do this because it allows us to paint the border wider than planned, and this then gives us the control to crop the image so that it doesn't feel staged. You don't need it to be larger, but for this one we weren't sure how much of the winter scene we were going to paint and how much background would be required. As it turned out, only the hint of some winter trees and a frozen pond were needed, as the snow and colour temperature gave it the required mood and any more detail would just have been distracting.

Selecting border colour/value

Don't guess what colours your border will be, and don't use white. You really only need two to three colours anyway, and these should be a similar value or neutral colour that is already in your image. Anything else, and the effect will call attention to itself. Don't use the stronger blues or warms in the skin tones as they help focus the painting on the subject, and using these colours would give the opposite effect of what you are trying to achieve. Either Cmd+Alt-click a colour in the painting, or select from your palette. Either way, it should be a tone and colour already present in your painting.

Borders and boundaries

Crop your image once it's ready to lose unnecessary space

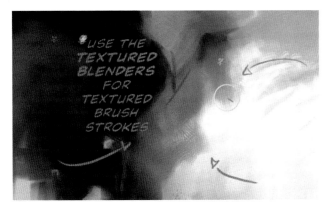

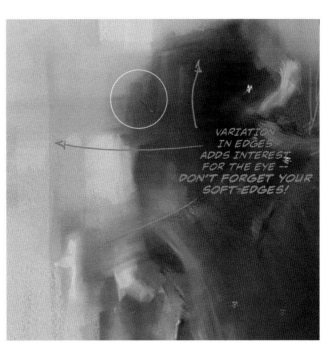

08 Soft edges are good too As the focus of our painting is the subject's eyes and smile, it's fine to soften her beanie hat into the border. This is really the last place we want the eye to go, so the Dry Palette Knife (Size: 62, Opacity: 30%) is great for this area. Work fast, and pull the paint in one direction, then immediately move the Knife at 30 degrees to it.

07 Textured blenders and brushstrokes Another good tool to apply here is the Blender. We want to blend the darker value of her collar into the border, but we don't want it to be a lost edge. Use the Coarse Oily Blender (Size: 41.0, Opacity: 7%) to pull the darker value into the light value, in doing so adding texture and therefore interest for the eye.

09 Everything is lost After looking at it full-frame, we decided we want to just totally lose a few edges. Maintain contrast between the subject and the snowy area, but totally blend the snowy area into the border colour. Use the Loaded Palette Knife (Size 52, Opacity 22%) to drag snow into the border. Then use the Dry Palette Knife again to just blend some of the area completely.

10 Cropping This is where cropping comes in handy, because you can choose the areas that have the most impact and lose areas that don't. So to enhance the composition, crop tight on the top and back and leave more room on the right, which allows the viewer to follow the subject's gaze.

Simplify the shapes first

This is all about enhancing the painting, so remember your basic principles of composition. Simplify the shapes in your head, so that the border basically becomes white space. What areas need to be painted into, and what areas need to be painted out from? If you're a beginner, then you could paint a thumbnail first to see what works. In the end though, the painting should have more impact with the border and enhance the composition. If it doesn't, start again!

11 Creating the look of traditional canvas Now that we are happy with the border, there's still a final step that we can do to create a convincing canvas effect. First, create a new layer and then set the Opacity to 0. This is the most important step.

12 Select the Impasto Oil Choose the Artists' Oil>Impasto Oil (Size: 90, Opacity: 100%) and begin painting. In the thumbnail, you will notice that you are using paint, but it won't show up on your canvas. However, the impasto-like effect will show through, without affecting colour. The trick is to follow the paint strokes you've already placed down for an authentic effect.

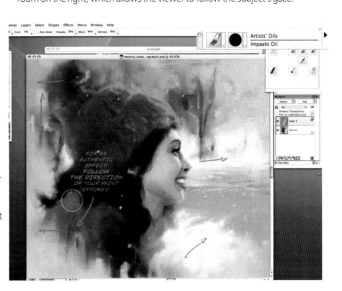

Brush selection | The best brushes in the borders business

These are the brushes we mostly used while creating the painted border, mainly because we thought they'd give us a good mix of texture and pigment that we required (the Conté and Acrylic brushes), blending ability while retaining this texture (Coarse Oily Blender and Loaded Palette Knife) and very importantly, being able to easily create edges (Dry Palette Knife and the F-X Squeegee Brush). However, these are just our personal preferences and we're sure you could get a similar effect by trying out some of the natural Bristle brushes and the Artists' Oils. Let us now explain our choices in more detail.

Conté (high and low opacity)
This brush is great for laying in colour quickly. At low opacity, the texture is more evident and by laying a stroke next to another one, it creates small edges. Also the grain is very evident. Use it at a higher opacity for large blocks of colour when you want more opaque colour. Alternatives would be the Sponge for a similar grain, and of course any of the Bristle brushes.

Coarse Oily Blender
This is great not only for blending, but also creating textured effects as you do so. With a soft Blender, the area can quickly look like it was blurred. With a textured Blender like this one, the effect looks more like a brush was used to blend the area, similar to dry-brushing in traditional painting.

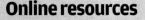

Dry Palette Knife
Once again great for blending, but this tool is also nifty when it comes to creating edges. A handy technique is to lay in colour with the Conté, and then work in a zigzag motion with the Dry Palette Knife. Try it and we're sure you'll be very pleased with the edges you create.

Loaded Palette Knife
You may find that the Loaded Palette Knife is similar to a dry brush technique. If you use it on a lower opacity, paint and colour is applied but texture and grain is retained.

F-X Brush>Squeegee
This brush wasn't used in the tutorial, but it deserves a mention because we could easily have used it. Basically, the Squeegee brush creates some really hard edges; if you just lay in a few blobs of paint, this brush will quickly blend them and create some dynamic hard edges at the same time.

Online resources
Know more about your subject

Richard Schmid
Painted borders can accentuate the focal points of your portrait, such as the face and the eyes, as in Richard Schmid's portrait above (www.greewhichworkshop.com).

Morgan Weistling
Morgan Weistling's portrait shows that the effect can also be produced subtly, where the artist leaves a few brush marks sweeping away from the subject (www.morganweistling.com).

Jeremy Lipking
In a landscape painting, something like a house, cottage or waterfall, the effect can be much bolder. Here, in this Jeremy Lipking landscape, he uses the uneven border as a major part of the composition (www.lipking.com).

Create realistic rays of sunlight

Painting a sunlit woodland scene can be a real challenge in lifelike lighting, but here we shed a ray of light on the mystery and majesty of sunlight

Tutorial info

Artist
Tim Shelbourne

Time needed
2-3 hours

Skill level
Intermediate

On the CD
Tonal start sketch

Whether you're painting landscapes, still life or portraits, one of the most important factors to achieve a convincing result is that of light. Light itself is the single thing that quite literally allows the scene to exist at all, so it needs careful consideration and handling. One of the most fundamental hurdles you'll face when it comes to painting a highly lit scene is first deciding where the light comes from and exactly what quality it is.

A good strategy for working this out is to start with a tonal sketch. This is a monochrome sketch, which simply shows the light and dark parts of your painting. To get you started, we've supplied a tonal sketch that helps describes the light.

We'll show you how to paint the scene using a variety of brushes, complete with typical rays of light filtered through the leaves of the trees. One of the brushes is customised to paint the leaves too.

You'll notice that there is quite a limited colour palette with this one. There's not a great deal beyond brown, orange, green and yellow, but of course we need shades of each of these to bring the depth and realism to the whole piece.

Tree time

Use the sketch on the CD as the base for your sunlit scene

01 Blocking in the main trees Open the 'tonal' sketch in Painter. Choose Linen Canvas from the Papers, and then add a new layer to the image. Within the Layers palette, check the option for Pick Up Underlying Color. Next, choose Thick Wet Oils from the Oils variant category. Now use this brush to start roughly blocking in the main trees using a very dark brown.

Fill with colour
Bring warmth into the painting

02 Adding midtones Use a slightly warmer, lighter brown for the lighter parts of the trees. Continue to add in the trees and the fence posts. Adjust the size of the brush as needed. When you have blocked all of these areas in, using the screenshot as a guide, lock this layer by clicking the padlock in the Layers palette.

03 The dark distance Add a new layer. Use the same brush but increase the Bleed to 85%. Choose a dark green from the Colors palette and start to block in the distant, darker area of the woodland. Choose other green/brown dark tones from the Colors palette or the Mixer Pad now and then, and use short, dabbing strokes here.

04 Into the light Reduce the Bleed to 25%. Choose a lighter green/yellow and start to fill the tree areas towards the left with this colour, again, choosing a slightly different colour of approximately the same shade here and there. Use short strokes at different angles. Refer to the tonal sketch for placement of these tonal areas.

Light plan | Use this as a guide to see the effects of light

As you'll see from the illustration below, it's very important that before you start to paint, you know both where the light comes from and also where it goes. In the light plan below, we've highlighted the main source of the light and also the points in the finished composition where it features at its strongest.

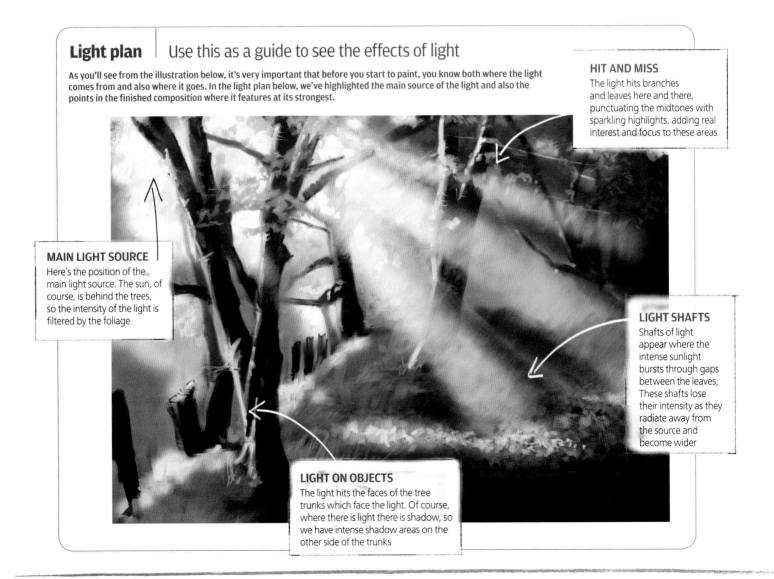

HIT AND MISS
The light hits branches and leaves here and there, punctuating the midtones with sparkling highlights, adding real interest and focus to these areas

MAIN LIGHT SOURCE
Here's the position of the main light source. The sun, of course, is behind the trees, so the intensity of the light is filtered by the foliage

LIGHT SHAFTS
Shafts of light appear where the intense sunlight bursts through gaps between the leaves, These shafts lose their intensity as they radiate away from the source and become wider

LIGHT ON OBJECTS
The light hits the faces of the tree trunks which face the light. Of course, where there is light there is shadow, so we have intense shadow areas on the other side of the trunks

05 Light and loose For the bright areas, choose a light yellow and reduce the size of the brush. We'll add the brightest highlights in these areas later. These areas can be fairly abstract with lots of energetic brushwork. Continue to add these various tones of light greens and yellows to all of the areas between the trees.

06 Ground level For the woodland floor in the bottom-right of the painting, choose dark browns and tan colours, filling this area with small strokes and using the brush at a fairly large size. Return to a selection of light greens for the lighter ground areas near the fence.

07 Branching out Unlock the upper tree layer. Reduce the Bleed of the brush to 10%, and at around 10-15 pixels, use a very dark brown to add some branches to the trees. Brush the branches in the directions shown in the screenshot with short, flicking movements.

Creating the leaf brush

Creating the leaf brush is easier than you might think, as it's simply a modified version of the Artists' Oils' Soft Grainy brush. Choose this variant and then go to Window>Brush Controls>Show Artists' Oils. Set the sliders as follows: Amount 50%, Viscosity 68%, Blend 65%. For the lower sliders, set these values: Bristling 67%, Clumpiness 65%, Trail-Off 80%. Set the Wetness slider to a medium value. Remember to set the Angle Control to Random as detailed in Step 8 of the walkthrough. Remember, one of the joys of Painter is that making small changes to brush settings can yield great results, so feel free to adjust these settings.

Let there be light!
Let the sun brighten up your image

08 Magic leaf brush! Return to the layer below and add a new layer, checking the Pick Up option. Select Artists' Oils>Soft Grainy Brush and customise it using the settings in the side panel on this page. Go to Window>Brush Controls>Show Angle, and set Expression to Random. Now use this brush at 30 pixels to add all of the lightest leaves behind the trees on the left.

09 From dark to light Again, use very light greens and yellows here, adding the odd touch of white in the brightest areas. Vary the size of the brush as you go and use the finished image for reference. It's best to build up these areas in layers of colour, starting with darker areas and then gradually adding more leaves in lighter and lighter shades.

10 The dark side You need to carry on adding this leaf detail in the darker, distant foliage areas, again starting with dark tones and building up to the lighter ones. Vary your brush size and use darker shades of greens and browns here. You may find it useful to soften these areas slightly with the Round Blender brush.

11 Ground cover For the large area of leaf mould on the ground, revert to the Soft Grainy Brush and first use a very dark brown to paint in the shadows. Gradually change your colour through lighter and lighter tan colours, using the brush in quite a random fashion, slowly adding lighter details. It's important to use the finished image as a reference here for the placement of the various tones.

12 Foreground leaves Click on the Tree layer and add a new layer. Still using the custom leaf brush, add the leaves on the trees in the foreground in quite a random fashion, using various greens and varying the brush size as you go. Add a few bright green and yellow ones here and there, giving the impression of them being caught by the sunlight.

Miracles of the Mixer

We're using a lot of shades of similar colours in this project, so the Mixer palette can be a real life-saver here. After choosing a colour from the Color Wheel, you can use the Apply Color tool below the palette to apply each of these to the Mixer Palette itself. By doing this with a number of different greens, yellows and blues, you can mix these together with the Mix Color tool below the pad. This will give you a variety of colour that you can pick up with the small Eyedropper tool. You can always add some white to the mix to extend your range of colours even further.

Rays of light
Give it an autumnal glow

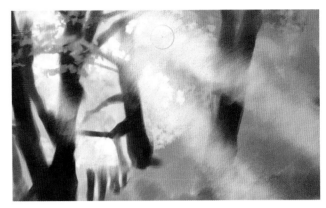

13 **Shafts of light** Add another new layer. From the Oils brushes, choose the Thick Oil Bristle 30 variant. In the Properties bar, use the following settings: Resat – 70%, Bleed – 82%, Feature – 4.6. Now use this brush at around 60 pixels and use a very light yellow to paint in the rays of light, using short, diagonal strokes as shown in the screenshot.

14 **Light intensity** Make sure you keep to the shapes shown in the final image for these shafts. The upper part of the shafts need to be lighter than the lower parts as the light is stronger here, so choose an even lighter yellow and gently apply more paint here. Remember that these shafts are wider at the bottom than at the top.

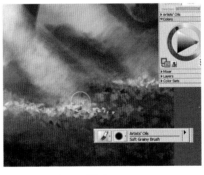

Dodging and burning

Painter features Dodge and Burn tools, and these can be useful when you're working on a painting that uses light. The Dodge tool lightens the tone of brush marks and the Burn tool darkens them. You can immediately see the usefulness of these tools. After choosing one of the tools from the Toolbox, set a low opacity. Now you can accurately lighten or darken small areas simply by brushing over them. If you haven't got Painter X, you can use the Dodge and Burn variants in the Photo brushes.

15 **Filtered light** Using this brush with a very light yellow over the upper branches of the foreground trees will give the impression of diaphanous, filtered light in this region, giving a diffused effect.

16 **Patches of light** The light rays illuminate the patches of ground they hit. To add these bright patches, use the Soft Grainy Brush with Opacity at 50%. Now add some bright orange and yellow patches of leaf directly below the rays of light. Start with the darker shades and overlay them with brighter ones.

17 **Light on the trees** From the Palette Knife category, choose the Loaded Palette Knife variant. Add a new layer. Now use this brush at around 20 pixels to add some subtle highlights to the sunny side of the trees. Use long, flowing strokes with light tan colours and yellows. Add a few sharp strokes of near-white here and there.

18 **Grass in the sunlight** Still using the Palette Knife, start adding the bright grassy area. Use a variety of greens and yellows, and use short, upward flicking strokes, varying the size of the brush and the angle of your strokes. Use the brush at a very small size and with bright colour to add the odd flick here and there to indicate sharp, sunlit blades of grass.

19 **Sparkling highlights** Now reduce the size of the brush and using very light colours and white, add some really sharp highlight accents to the trees, grass and various fence posts, etc. By using the brush with horizontal strokes, you can easily create the impression of sharply highlighted branches springing from the tree trunks.

Woodland wonderland
Add punch to the rays

20 Clarify the light Add a final new layer at the top of the stack. Choose the Thick Wet Oils brush from the Oils brushes. In the Properties bar, set the Bleed to 10%. Zoom into the top-left of the image a little and using very light yellows and whites, add some defining highlight areas to the lightest parts of the image. Simple, random strokes will add interest and light here.

21 Bright leaves Revert to the Soft Grainy brush and use it at 50-60 pixels to add some bright leaves across the upper area of the painting. Painting these leaves large and in bright colours suggests them being both in the foreground and being lit by the shafts of sunlight.

Soft and hard light

Sometimes, especially when painting distant areas, some of the brush marks you make can be a little too sharp, especially when you're painting leaves. Here, you need to use one of the Blender variants. The Round Blender brush is ideal for this. This will also help in the areas of light in the top-left of the painting. Here, we need to combine sharp accents of light with soft, unfocused areas. When you've completed painting this area, use the Blender brush to blur a few areas a little to heighten the effect of diffused light.

22 Linking branches It's worth adding a few of these touches to the bright grassy bank by the trees. You can use the Palette Knife again to add a few linking branches between these leaves. Paint these with a light, bright orange colour, using short calligraphic strokes.

23 Define the trees From the Artists' Oils variants, choose the Oily Bristle Brush. Now add a few real dark colours to the trees, and a few lighter details within the tree trunks themselves to add a bit of detail and interest. A few very fine lines around the outlines can help to define the form.

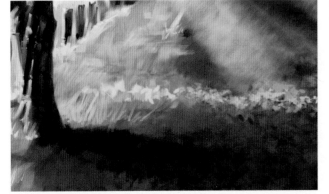

24 Final touches Using the brushes and techniques above, you can add as much additional detail to the image as you want. Here we've intensified the shadows cast by the foreground tree a little and added a few more foreground leaves here and there. We resolved the tones in the image with a little Dodge and Burn (see boxout on adjacent page).

Light changes everything!

When it comes to light and how it affects a scene, essentially three things can change it dramatically. The first variable is where the light actually comes from, for instance, is the sun directly above or lower down in the sky? Both produce different results. Next, the colour or temperature of the light can alter the look of the scene completely. Compare a sunset to a moonlight scene. Finally, how intense is the light source? In the image here, the light is very intense indeed, but had this been a rather overcast day, then the scene would be very different and much more subtle in regard to the lighting. With a few tweaks, we've turned our sunlit scene into a moonlit dream. What a difference light makes!

Before

Working with patterns

From backgrounds to costumes, including patterns in your painting can create a stunning amount of detail. Save yourself some time by using Painter's Pattern function

Tutorial info

Artist
Anne Pogoda

Time needed
3 hours

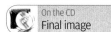
Skill level
Beginner

On the CD
Final image

t's easy to find a reference to Painter's Patterns palette when you search books and websites for one, but it's not so easy for beginners to find the palette itself. Sometimes we wonder if all those great tool tips out there really are meant to help people who have never worked with a specific feature before? Well luckily you won't have the same problem as we had when we first wanted to work with this feature, since we're here to explain everything about creating patterns in Painter, and to make it as easy as possible for beginners and advanced painters alike. With this tutorial you'll learn how to apply patterns to your paintings, how to add more detail to surfaces and backgrounds quickly and easily, and how to work with stock photos to create patterns (in case you're not comfortable with painting).

Patterns are useful things, because a lot of detail provides a lot of space for a story to be told by your painting. Using patterns

gives you a lot of freedom to add things that could explain what kind of person you see in the painting, why this person is in this location and how this person feels. The painting we made for this workshop was about temptation. At first, the girl was supposed to summon the viewer to

receive her apple, but then it turned into a girl lost in the woods and all that she had left was one last apple. Her rich clothes contrast with the cold forest; the detailed, jewelled patterns mark her as running away and out of place. Now it's time to give it a go yourself!

Lost and found
Find your missing patterns

This is a very important point, since it really confused us when we were new to the Patterns function. We'd just created a new pattern, but it wouldn't show up in the Patterns window. So we sat there for a moment, wondering where our new pattern had gone, and then decided to capture it again until it would finally show up. After endless tries we finally got the idea to click the little symbol next to Lotus Petals (which is the first default pattern in the list), and then we found our capture had been added to the Patterns list four times! We deleted three of them and proceeded with our painting. We don't know why it always jumps back to Lotus Petals once you re-title your captured pattern, but it helps to know where it has gone.

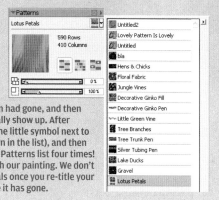

After

Start simple

Begin with some easy branch patterns

The direction of strokes

The direction of brush strokes can affect the way the pattern is turned. This might happen with the Oily Cloners for instance, or if you've used a very painterly brush to create your pattern. It can also be affected by whether you use a mouse or a tablet, and by the Dab Type. Go to Brush Controls>General to experiment with different Dab Types.

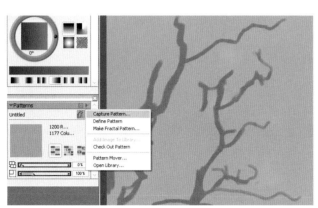

01 Capture a pattern Go to Window>Library Patterns>Show Patterns. Your Patterns palette will pop up. Let's start with something simple. Open a new canvas and make it 1000x1000 pixels in size at 300 dpi. Use your favourite brush to paint some branches in the background. Now hit the arrow next to the Patterns menu and choose Capture Pattern.

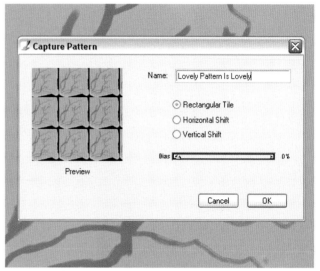

02 Name and save A new window will now appear. Here you can choose settings for your pattern, but we'd suggest you work with the default settings until you're comfortable with creating patterns before you start experimenting. Name your newly created pattern and click OK.

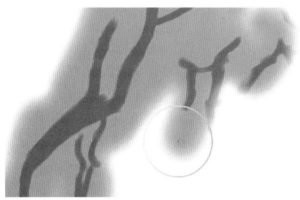

03 Check it works Now open another canvas the same size as before to see if the pattern works. Go to File>Clone Source>Current Pattern. Select the Soft Cloner brush because it will adapt to exactly what you have painted. You might want to try out some other Cloners as well, but remember that you're looking for a precise effect.

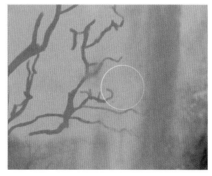

04 Apply to your painting Now that you know your new pattern is working, select the 'WO Patterns' image from the disc and create a new layer. We've painted in the branches pattern using the Soft Cloner. Don't be afraid that some of the detail might be taken away by this, you can work it back with the Eraser later.

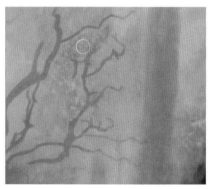

05 Blend it! Now that the branches have been applied, pick the Eraser tool. Set this to Airbrush, as you want the edges of what you're going to erase to blend in with the background. This will work best when the Opacity is set no higher than 50%.

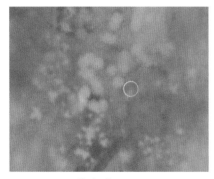

06 Many little dots You can create a more painterly effect for your pattern. Go back to your patterns canvas and make a new layer. On this layer, paint in many random dots to suggest the shape of leaves when seen from far away. We used a combination of the Acrylics Bristle brush and the Fine Tip Soft Airbrush.

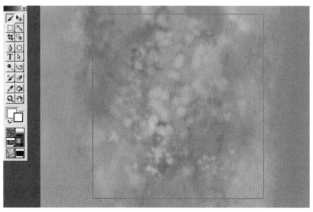

07 Make your selection Now pick the Rectangular Selection tool from your toolbox and make a selection of the area where you painted the most dots. This will be your leaves pattern. Choose Capture Pattern again, now name and save it.

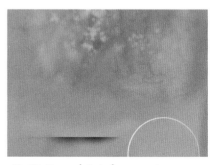

08 From dots to leaves Select your painting again, make a new layer and paint the leaves in wherever you see fit. Since our created patterns usually end up with some black borders on their lower parts, we had to erase these to make the patterns fit into the painting. We suggest you do the same and just proceed with another leaves structure on a new layer.

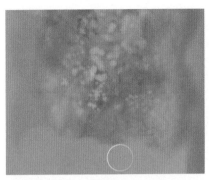

09 Avoid repetition When you have a pattern that you want to use repeatedly, try to avoid too many obvious repeating elements, as this would give the painting a rather artificial look. You can erase parts, flip and transform them or change the Blend mode of your layers to add some variation.

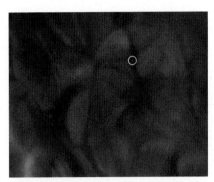

10 Flowers for the dress Let's advance a bit further now. Colour the background in the same colour as the clothes and give it some shading if you already know exactly where you want the pattern to be. Now paint some flowers on your pattern canvas. We used the Acrylics Bristle once again for doing this.

11 Build up the pattern This is what our canvas looked like after we rampaged with the flowers. You are free to paint more detailed flowers than we did of course, or to choose a different design. We usually paint the final details in when we know that we're not going to change anything about the final concept of the painting, and so we prefer to have it more loose at first.

Paint textures

The best thing about patterns is that you can apply a texture to your painting that you have a massive amount of control over. You can give the texture a hand painted look using the Oily Cloners, or just control how much it covers by choosing different brush sizes. Remember, patterns can be absolutely anything you want!

Dress up your patterns

Clothing patterns need variation and movement to look realistic

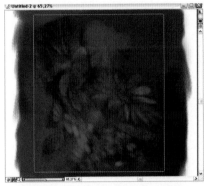

12 Select and repeat Next, we made a selection of the flowers we painted in the middle. You don't have to cover the whole canvas when capturing a pattern – it will still create a repeated element once you apply it to your painting, so try standalone images, like flowers.

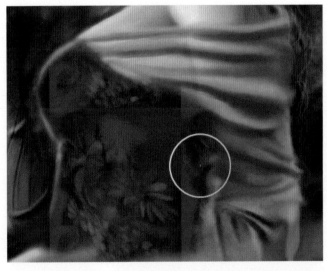

13 Look at the sizing Create a new layer now, but don't forget to collapse your pattern layers every now and then, since your computer will be very thankful for every extra memory you can provide it with! We randomly painted a flowers pattern on this layer – but unfortunately it doesn't fit!

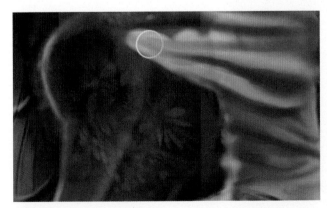

14 Move pattern elements Luckily the parts that don't fit aren't a problem. Just hit V and then move the pattern block to a better position. Choose the Eraser and erase everything that covers the wrong parts of your image. This includes the cloth – scrunch up a piece of patterned fabric and you'll notice that the pattern seems to disappear into the folds.

15 Add more definition After we fixed the position of the flowers we chose the Acrylics Bristle brush again and painted some extras for the flowers wherever it seemed necessary. At this stage we also brought our attention to this area again to paint in some more highlights and details for the flowers to make them stand out more.

Experiment on the same layer

Some brushes will look strange when you apply them on a new layer. For instance, the Acrylics brushes need previously applied colour to work well. That's why it works best to duplicate the layer of the pattern that you have just applied to your painting to avoid it being ruined by any mistake you might make while adding detail to it.

Capture ready-made patterns
Use stock photos or scanned elements

The texture shines through

Now, you might wonder why it should make sense to have a texture shining through in a way that makes it hardly visible later on? It's because of the suggestion of detail. The more detail you see, the more you will have your eyes fooled by the shape and movement of your patterns, suggesting that you are looking at a real person.

16 Use a photo If you don't feel comfortable with painting at all, don't worry! You can also just apply some colour that generally fits well for your painting (we chose green because of the very greenish palette) and then take a photo or use a stock image of something that could fit as a pattern, like fabric or lace. Cut the part from your photo that you want to use and paste it on the patterns canvas.

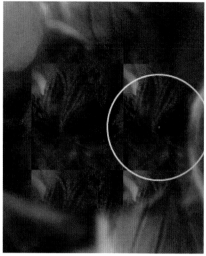

17 Pretty texture We used this flowery photographic texture to create the sleeves. After we tweaked the photo, we took the Acrylics brush again to work it over a bit. Then, using a new layer, we applied it to our painting again.

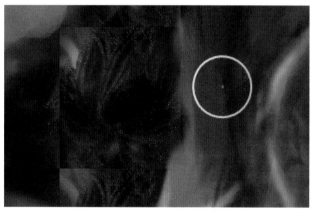

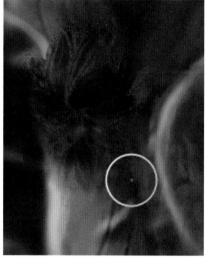

18 Soft and tiny We had to be very careful not to destroy this tiny pattern as we worked it over with the Eraser. The Eraser had to be quite small to avoid damage, and we had this layer visible at 40% Opacity to see the exact shape of the arm while we were working.

19 Work with the body Finally, here is the little sleeves pattern! We suggest that you always create a new layer once you have applied your pattern, since it's simply impossible to paint them beforehand in a way that will make them perfectly blend in with the shape of the body or lighting situation. That is why we worked each body pattern on a new layer after we had applied it to the painting.

Painterly patterns
Make precise patterns

On the right you can see what the dress looked like after we applied our pattern to it. It took a lot of time, but didn't necessarily mean that the dress would be finished. Adding a pattern can help to give the subject further definition and push it forward. After that, there is a lot of room to make a copy of the patterns layer and work it over with some brushes. This will give it a more painted look if you have worked with a photo or scanned element, and it will add much more life to your pattern and make it stand out. We'd suggest that you work the shape of the body in, like the areas that should be dark or lit, to avoid the body looking flat. Create a new layer for this and work your way through with an Airbrush for the darker areas, and an F-X Glow brush for the highlights.

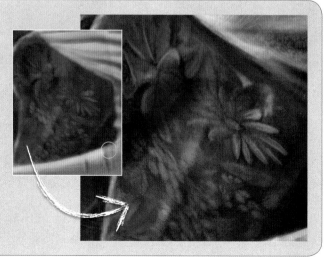

20 The pattern shines through Here we have another example of a photo used as pattern. It is essential that the patterns layer is used with around 20% Opacity, and that the background of the photo fits the colour of the image area that it is applied to. Use the Eraser carefully to work around darker areas and have the pattern structure shine through the lighter parts.

showcase

LARRY DOUGLAS COBLER

TITLE | Orange Reflections
WEBSITE | www.paintermagazine.co.uk/user/Cobler
JOB TITLE | Retired packaging designer

"I have spent thirty-five years involved with photography, art and design. I now have a bit of time to experiment with some of the art that has been in my head for most of my life."

eShop
Visit the
Official Corel Painter
online shop at
www.imagineshop.co.uk
for back issues
and subscriptions

Visit us online at www.paintermagazine.com

Create your own art gallery for FREE • Meet other artists on the forum • Subscribe and save money!

Create a sports painting

Work with Pastels and the Airbrush to capture the action, anticipation and the roar of the crowd in a sport painting

Tutorial info

Artist
Jim Scullion

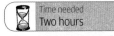
Time needed
Two hours

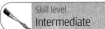
Skill level
Intermediate

On the CD
Start sketch and final image

For centuries, sport has been captured by artists and sculptors in all of its glory. They have striven to capture the atmosphere, the colour, the action, the elation, the joy and the bitter disappointment that sport can bring to its participants and followers. Sport offers a wide and varied range of subject matter to the artist that can combine portraiture, figurative work, movement, landscape and even still life.

In this tutorial, we will create a painting that will convey the power and anticipation in one particular sport – baseball. We shall not be working from photographic references, but will use a sketch created in Painter as the basis for painting. You can also make this a bit of a fantasy work if you choose to; who hasn't dreamed of hitting a home run for the Yankees or scoring a goal in the World Cup or skating with either Torvill or Dean? Whatever your fantasy may be, this may inspire you to capture it in a painting.

We will create a fairly realistic moment from a game frozen that split second before the bat hits the ball. We will use standard brushes from Painter and will use a method of adding colour lightly to the painting and blending it. This will be repeated throughout the painting process to build up a realistic portrayal of the ball player. We'll try to dispel the myth that you need to add lots of detail to make it look realistic and we will add a simple background using the Airbrush, which will add depth and give the impression of a crowd on game day. So now it is time to boot up the computer, crank up Bruce Springsteen and sing "take me out to the ball game!"

Home plate

Step up to the pitching mound and let's begin

01 Sketch Load the Baseball JPEG from the disc. This sketch was drawn in Painter using the Thick n Thin Pencil, and will be used as the basis for our painting. Note that we will not paint on the sketch layer as it needs to remain intact for reference throughout. A Wacom tablet with a drawing surface larger than A4 was used in our painting process. Set up Brush Tracking in the Preferences section before you begin.

02 Getting started To create the baseball player, we will use only four brushes: the Artists' Pastel Chalk and Pastel Pencil 3 from the Pastel variants, and from the Blender brush selection, the Round Blender and the Just Add Water brushes. We dragged these into a custom palette for easy access. Add a new layer above the canvas layer and highlight it. We will paint our character on this layer, leaving the sketch intact on the layer below. Select the Artist' Pastel brush, Size 11.3, Opacity at 10%, Grain 17. Use this to add a light blue grounding to the helmet, shirt collar, cuffs and the socks. Paint strokes should be lightly applied and follow the contours of the surfaces.

03 Blending Using the Soft Blender Stump (Size 30, Opacity 30%), blend the pastel into the surface of the paper, being careful to follow the contours of the surfaces. Here we are laying a basic undercoating, which we will continue to gradually develop during the course of the painting. Save your file as a RIFF file at this stage.

First base

Flesh out the painting with more colour and tone

04 Step back

It is very beneficial to step back from the painting from time to time to view it in its entirety from a distance. Painter allows us to do this by zooming in to close detail and zooming out to view the whole image. Do this regularly in order to ensure that the painting is progressing as a whole. It is easy to get caught up in working on fine details, which can detract from the overall feel.

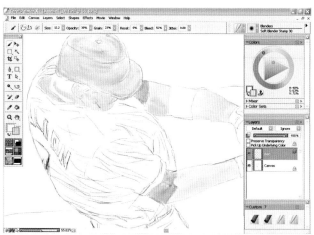

05 Flesh

Using the Artists' Pastel brush, add a mid-tone flesh colour to the face and the arms, again at an Opacity of 10%. A low opacity setting such as this allows us to gently apply light layers that are easily blended, and helps us to resist the urge to add masses of colour that will quickly become unmanageable in the way we are working. Continue with the Blender brush to blend the pastel into the paper. Don't get overly concerned about the actual colour that is used for flesh, as this is not a portrait.

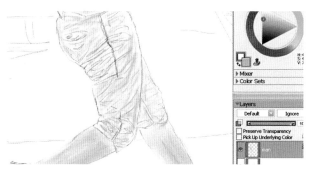

06 Clothing

In any figurative work where the figure is clothed, the clothing plays an integral part in setting the image context. In sport art, this is vitally important. The treatment of the uniform will help us to convey the movement and power of the ballplayer. In the initial stages we continue to lay a foundation of colour, a light grey, onto the clothing using the same process as the previous steps, laying pastel colour followed by blending. Follow the contours of the clothing folds indicated in the sketch.

07 Adding dimension

The aim of this painting is to produce an almost three-dimensional figure on a two-dimensional surface. The gradual building up of colour and blending process helps us to create that illusion. Add colour to the helmet by progressing through three or four layers of added colour and subsequent blending. Add slightly darker shades of colour, and overlay lighter shades for highlights.

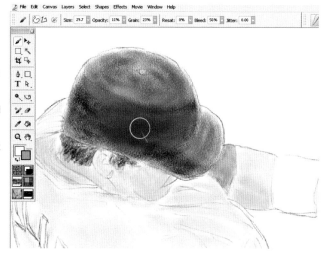

Saving as a RIFF file

RIFF is Painter's native format. If using any features unique to Painter, saving as RIFF will preserve these features. This is important when using layers. Preserving layers, watercolour layers, shapes or many other functions allow you to continue from the point of saving. However, RIFF layers can be very large, so ensure that you have lots of free hard disk space.

08 Shadow and tone

Add darker tones to the flesh areas to define muscle tone and contours. Continue to work with a brush at 10% Opacity for gradual build-up and ease of blending. Detail in the face is fairly minimal; the outline of the ear, hair and the indications of the mouth and chin are added with the Pastel Pencil brush at Opacity of 35%. Don't overwork these features as it would only detract from the final overall image.

09 Use your loaf

Highlights on the face and the helmet are detailed by using the Eraser at 4% Opacity to gently remove colour. This gives a more realistic highlight than adding a white pastel. In traditional pastel work, artists roll a piece of bread until soft and doughy, and use this as an eraser to remove the pastel from the paper, as normal soft erasers damage the surface. Here we have used the Painter equivalent of a bit of bread.

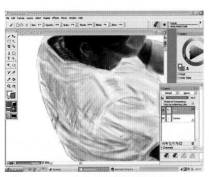

10 Clothing development Back to the clothing. Use the same methods as before to continue adding colour followed by blending. The helmet aside, we are not working on a smooth surface. Attention needs to be paid to the shadows and highlights of the material; accuracy here will add to the dynamic posture.

11 Clothing detail Add some areas of light pastel and leave unblended to give a degree of texture. The impression of a sewn line across the shoulder and the dark pastel shades in the deeper material folds are added with the Pastel Pencil. Add your own name to the back of the uniform as it personalises the piece.

12 You don't need hands We added gloves because many professionals wear them, and also as it helps to simplify the painting process. We don't have to worry about painting accurate hands and detailed fingers. The gloves have been built up using the same pastel and blend method and don't need any real detail.

Iterative function

When working on a detailed painting, we find it useful to save frequently, gaining new versions of the file during the process. Saving the various stages of a painting allows you to not only continue from the last saved stage, but also to go back to earlier stages and change things if you so wish. The Iterative Save function is a time-saving function that quickly saves sequentially numbered versions of the painting. If you are working in the RIFF format, the saved files will also save your layers, etc.

Second base
Add to your ballplayer with a few final details

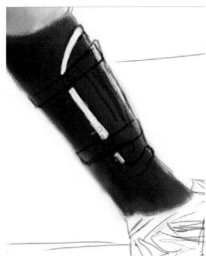

13 Leg detail After the success of the gloves, we decided to add a shinguard to the player's left leg. Using the Pastel Pencil, a very basic sketch is created. The white outline was painted by using the top of the Wacom stylus as an eraser.

14 Footwear The shinguard is completed using the Artists' Pastel brush, with highlights added using the Pastel Pencil. The baseball boots are blue and black, and again have been created using the gradual pastel-and-blend method. Detail is added to the boots with the Pastel Pencil. When working on commissions relating to a sportsperson, the detail of footwear is often important as many are sponsored by sports manufacturers, and it is necessary for them to be portrayed wearing their sponsor's brands.

Get up and dance

While painting, artists often listen to music or audio books. If we concentrate too hard on a painting, we may clam up our creativity. By allowing our thinking part of the brain to listen to the audio book or music, we free our creative side to create without too much worrying about colour and composition and all the boring stuff that stifles expression. It is also important to get up and wander away from the screen from time to time. Too long in front of the screen starts to physically take its toll on you and affects your work. Grab a cup of tea or coffee and have a wander around the room. When you return after even just a few minutes, you return refreshed and with new energy. Also, if you are listening to upbeat music and are feeling good, this will reflect in your work.

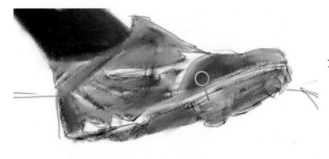

15 Additional detail Although we have omitted fine detail from the painting as it can detract from the overall image, it is sometimes useful to add subtle detail to complement the image. Using the Artists' Pastel, add a light reddish brown tint to the rear of the trousers and carefully blend into the folds. This gives the impression that the ballplayer has been involved earlier in the game and has slid in the red blaze while attempting to steal a base.

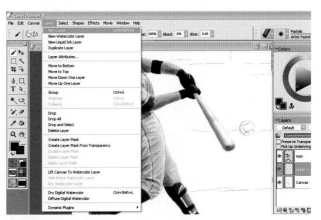

16 Background The main figure is virtually complete. We now add a new layer that sits between the canvas layer and the layer we have been painting on. Highlight this new layer and we shall now proceed to create the background.

Third base

Add a bit of background and a crowd to cheer you on as you paint

17 Ground Using the Artists' Pastel (Size 78, Opacity 23%), add a light reddish brown base to the lower part of the background layer. Gradually build this up to cover the area indicted in the painting. Do not blend this pastel work.

18 Background development A light coating of green paste is added to the background layer, as well as an umpire. Highlight the canvas layer and using a light grey colour and the Pastel Pencil, sketch a very basic outline of a figure in the background. Return to the background layer and select the Soft Airbrush 40 (Size 66, Opacity at 10%). Now start to build up the background.

Use your painting

When you finish a painting and save it, don't forget about it. Post it on an online gallery and let other people enjoy it. Also revisit it from time to time. Take the painting in this tutorial, for example; when completed and saved, reopen it in Painter as a clone source. Use it in a new painting as the source to help you create something perhaps more free-flowing in watercolour. You may create a less-detailed painting but one more vibrant and impressionistic using the Bristle Oil brushes with your original painting as the cloning source. Painter is basically an art shop full of all sorts of materials, so you use your own work as the basis to experiment.

19 Airbrush detail Continue to use the Airbrush to add form and colour to the background figure and the wall. It is important that the background is very light in overall colour in comparison with the main figure. Just as we would lighten faraway mountains in a landscape to convey distance and depth, this is also relevant in sports painting. It helps to bring the subject to the fore and draws the viewer's attention to the intended point of focus.

20 Crowd The challenge of creating a crowd is very daunting to newcomers of sporting art. However, if we remember that detail is not always of importance and that we only want to create the impression of a crowd, the task becomes so much simpler. Using the Airbrush, overlay light pastel-coloured shades in a random pattern. Initially, it looks like a lot of little snakes that a child would paint, but as you continue to overlay these at random, the impression of an out-of-focus crowd appears.

21 Further background detail The crowd is gradually and softly built up. It is important not to get this too dark as it can detract from the main subject. As we have painted the background on a separate layer, if we do paint it too dark, then the transparency of the layer can be reduced to compensate. Finally, a light green grass is airbrushed into the background.

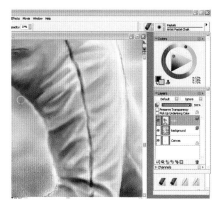

22 Excess paint Return to the layer containing the ballplayer and erase any excess pastel that has strayed across the layer while blending. When erased, it will reveal the background layer below.

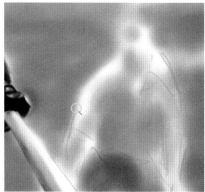

22 Remove sketch Highlight the canvas layer containing the original sketch and then erase sketch lines from background. Also remove any sketch lines that can be seen around the ballplayer.

Tips and techniques | Batter's box

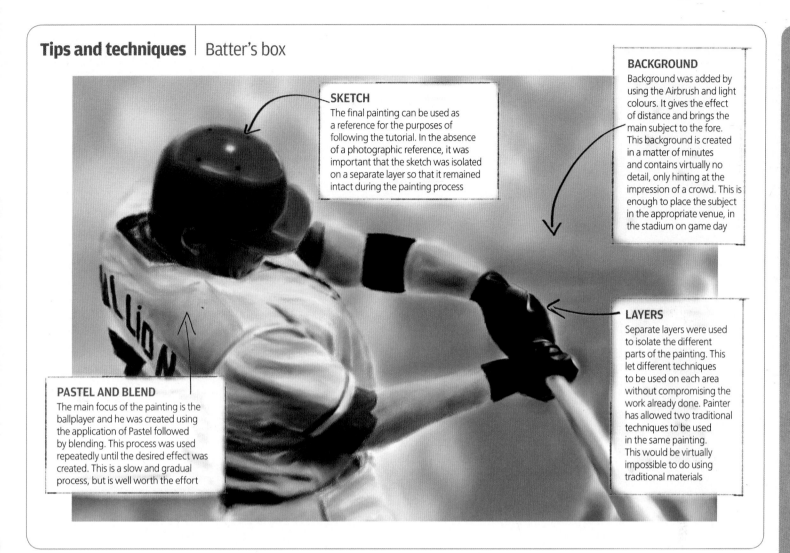

SKETCH
The final painting can be used as a reference for the purposes of following the tutorial. In the absence of a photographic reference, it was important that the sketch was isolated on a separate layer so that it remained intact during the painting process

BACKGROUND
Background was added by using the Airbrush and light colours. It gives the effect of distance and brings the main subject to the fore. This background is created in a matter of minutes and contains virtually no detail, only hinting at the impression of a crowd. This is enough to place the subject in the appropriate venue, in the stadium on game day

LAYERS
Separate layers were used to isolate the different parts of the painting. This let different techniques to be used on each area without compromising the work already done. Painter has allowed two traditional techniques to be used in the same painting. This would be virtually impossible to do using traditional materials

PASTEL AND BLEND
The main focus of the painting is the ballplayer and he was created using the application of Pastel followed by blending. This process was used repeatedly until the desired effect was created. This is a slow and gradual process, but is well worth the effort

Home run!

Enhance the foreground with a bit of texture, then go on a lap of honour for finishing!

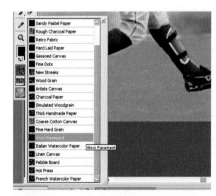

24 Ground material We will now add some detail to the foreground. Open the background layer and create a selection box around the area from the bottom of the picture to just above the dark grass area. Open the Paper Textures and select Worn Pavement.

25 Detail foreground Using the Artists' Pastel brush (Size 206, Opacity 48% and Grain lowered to nine per cent), paint a reddish brown over the selected area. This adds a texture to the ground area. Using darker browns gradually builds up the texture of the red blaze area. Using darker greens, build up the grass area textures.

26 Finishing touches Add some white chalk markings to the red area and using the Eraser (Size 12, Opacity 23%), carve your signature into the red ash. Save your image as a RIFF file, then flatten the layers. Save in whatever format you choose. Make yourself a cup of tea and come back and admire your finished work.

Andreas Rocha shows you...
The principles of speed painting

Capturing the essence of an image in a quick painting session

Tutorial info

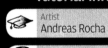
Artist
Andreas Rocha

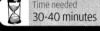
Time needed
30-40 minutes

Skill level
Intermediate

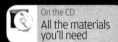
On the CD
All the materials
you'll need

When I first started painting digitally, I always wanted everything to look very smooth and finished, hiding the brushwork as much as possible. Throughout the years, I began to understand that a painting looked much richer if the actual painting process was made apparent in the final version. This could be obtained with faster execution and less care in avoiding mistakes. It was also a great way to practise painting with confidence and concentrate on the soul of the image, rather than its final presentation.

I came to this conclusion when I found out about the works of such artists as Craig Mullins and John Wallin Liberto. It was amazing how much energy they could transmit through their paintings. It seemed that all the brushwork was laid out in front of you without hiding behind smooth, clean textures. I believe that speed painting is very closely related to these kinds of paintings. At first I thought that it would be just a quickly executed image. But speed painting is so much more than that. As soon as I grasped the

idea behind it, I understood its value as practice for putting down the essential ingredients of a painting in the least amount of time, like line, value, colour, composition, light, theme and mood. Concentrating on the essentials infuses the painting with character. Digital speed-painting benefits from some really helpful tools software has to offer these days, like custom brush creation, painting at different magnifications, ease in picking colours, layers and their associated blending modes and keyboard shortcuts for almost every command. Everything converges to a creation process where the mind goes beyond the tools and focuses only on content.

Regarding the image of the tutorial, it was inspired by one of several giant World War II bunkers that I saw in Vienna, Austria. These giant structures are truly amazing and their concrete mass is something to behold. Taking this form as a starting point, I aimed for a dark, post-apocalyptic scenario. Even if these subjects are synonyms of war, they can produce some interesting environments, full of fantasy and mystery.

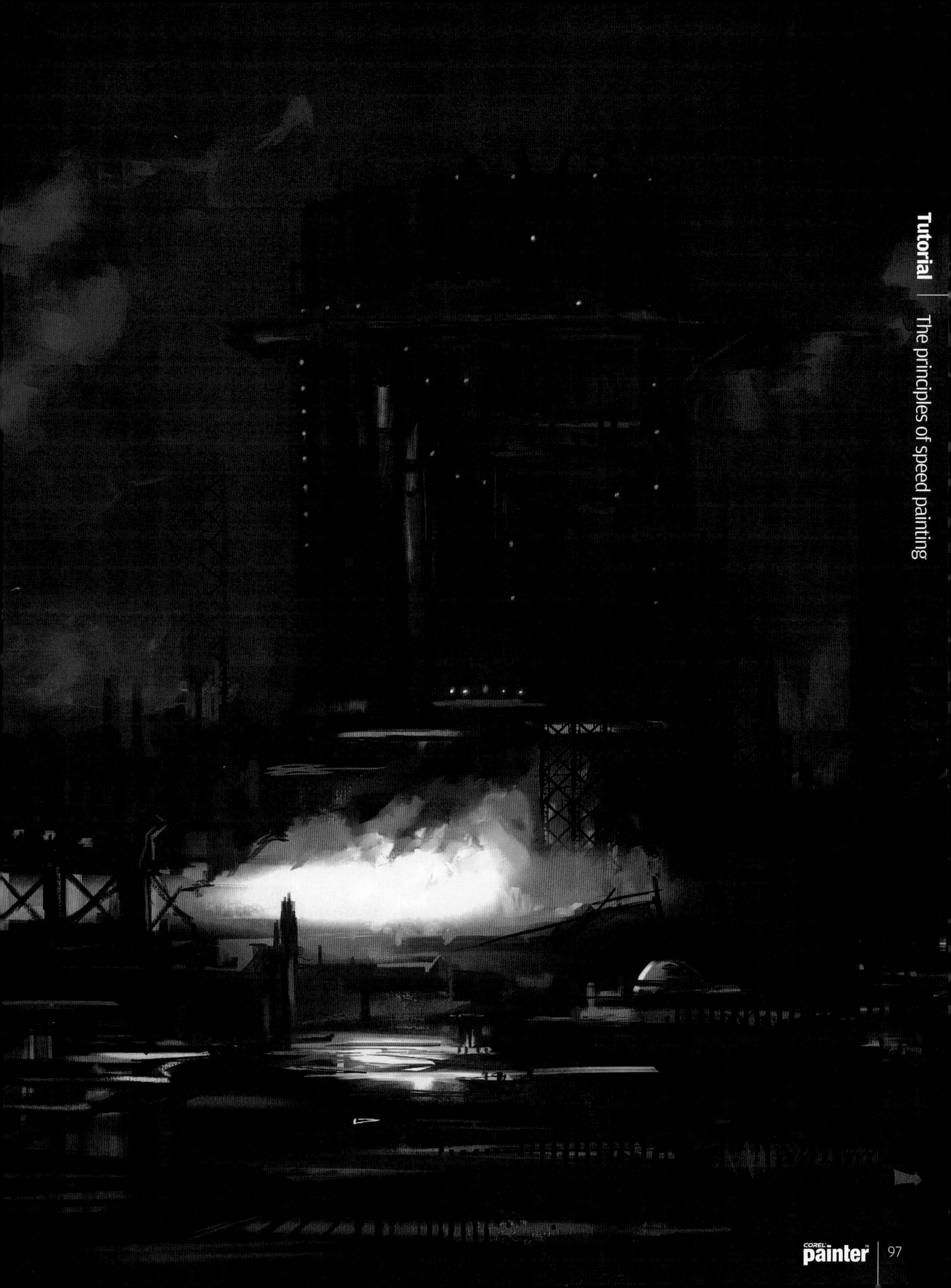

Be prepared

Preparation is the key to creating a well-thought-out painting

Zoom keyboard shortcuts

It is very useful to assign shortcut keys to the Zoom In/Out, Zoom to Fit and Zoom to Actual Pixels commands. Go to Edit>Preferences>Customize Keys. The Zoom In/Out and Zoom to Fit are in the Shortcut>Application Menu>Window, and the Zoom to Actual Pixels can be found in the Shortcut>Application>Other. If you assign these to the F1, F2, F3 and F4 keys, this enables you to do all your Zoom commands with one hand. After a while, these actions will become intuitive and really speed up the painting process.

Speed painters to admire

As already stated, you can find some truly wonderful speed paintings at Craig Mullins' (www.goodbrush.com) and John Wallin Liberto's (www.johnwallin.net) home pages. Other fantastic digital artists are Ryan Church (who has some great tutorial DVDs at Gnomon) and Erik Tiemens. To really contemplate the work of these two artists, check out the artbook *The Art of Star Wars – Episode III* to be really impressed. Last but not least, check out the astonishing artwork of Matthias Verhasselt (http://mv.cgcommunity.com), who also has work up on YouTube.

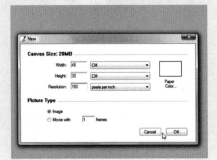

01 New document Create a new document, 48cm wide and 30cm high, with a resolution of 150ppi. This will be half the resolution of the final image, which guarantees speed and sufficient texture to look good when upsampling the image. Later on, when you start detailing the image, you can resample the image to double its size.

02 Creation of custom watercolour paper Make the Papers palette visible by going to Window>Library Palettes>Show Papers. Then open 'paper_watercolour.jpg' from the disc. This will quickly lay down texture and pattern. Select>All, go the Papers palette, open the side menu, click on Capture Paper then name it 'Watercolour'. Close this document without saving.

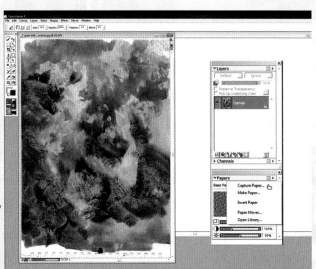

03 Reference images and laying out the documents It's helpful to collate some images in a document for quick reference during the painting process. These images can feed you with visual information during the actual painting. Open 'medley.jpg' from the disc and put it side by side with your document. Also, zoom out the main document to about 25 per cent. Depending on your hardware, this could be more or less.

04 Initial value pass Click the Chalk brush category, select one of the Square Chalk variants and drag it out to a new custom palette. In the Papers palette, select the recently created Watercolour paper. During painting, tweak the paper's parameters to obtain more or less texture, depending on the desired effect. For initial brushstrokes, use a 150-pixel brush while for finer ones, use a 15-pixel brush. Lay down marks to compose something that looks more or less balanced in terms of value.

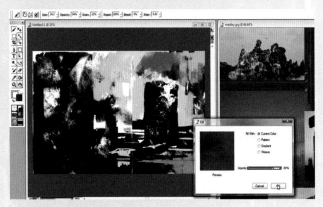

05 Colourise pass Go to Effects>Fill, and reduce the Opacity to 80%. Select a dark grey/blue from the Colors palette and press OK. The introduction of colour in this initial phase helps to establish an overall mood early on. Also, all subsequent colours will always relate to this dominating one, which helps in keeping colour harmony throughout.

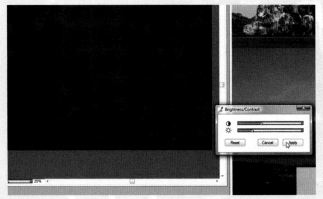

06 Brightness/Contrast pass Go to Effects>Tonal Control>Brightness/Contrast. Reduce the Brightness and Contrast as seen in the screenshot. The image needed a contrast boost after the previous step. Since this was envisioned as a cloud-filled moody sky, the overall scenario ought to be quite dark.

07 The wonderful Palette Knives

Go to Brush Selector>Palette Knives, and drag both the Palette Knife and Loaded Palette Knife to your custom-created palette. Go to Window>Show Brush Creator to tweak these brushes. In both variants, go to the Angle Property and change the Expression to Bearing, and change the value to 1% in the Color Variability Property of the Loaded Palette Knife.

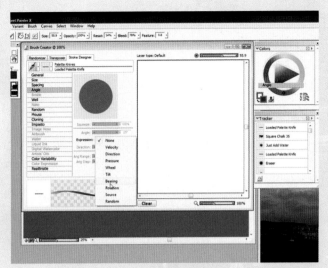

08 The wonderful Blenders

Go to the Blenders bar and drag the Just Add Water variant to your custom-created palette. Again, open the Brush Creator and select the Just Add Water variant. Then go to Variant>New Variant and name it 'Just Add Water Hard'. Select this new variant and change the profile icon in the Size Property to 1-Pixel Edge.

Palette Knives

If you harness the power of the Palette Knives, you can have some truly amazing tools at your disposal. First change the Angle property in the Brush Creator palette to Bearing. The only other thing that you need to do magic is own a tablet with tilt sensitivity. Depending on the bearing, pressure and tilt of the stylus, you now have an endless possibility of brushstrokes to apply. This possibility makes this brush category both expressive and impressive.

Just you and your tools
Check out the brush selection box for our favourites

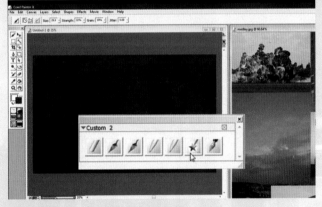

09 The last three tools

Go to Brush Selector and the F-X category, then drag the Glow variant to your custom-created palette. Do the same for the Eraser in the Eraser category and the Croquil Pen 5 in the Pens category. Now you are ready to rock!

10 The magic of the Glow brush

Select the Glow brush from your custom palette, pick a dark saturated brownish colour, start painting in light with a large brush and watch the magic happen. It's like illuminating the scene! Try to paint in light where you know it will probably hit, and keep resizing the brush with Opt/Alt+Ctrl/Cmd to add both large and small areas of light.

11 Let the details begin

With the Loaded Palette Knife, start defining the structures. This is where the reference images come in handy. Also, try to stick to the colours already on the canvas to keep the present colour harmony by using the Opt/Alt modifier while painting. This will pick up underlying colours.

12 Lighten the sky

Going back to the initial Square Chalk brush with the Watercolour paper selected, paint in a dark-blue sky. If you paint and no colour appears on the canvas, try to reduce the scale or brightness in the Papers palette.

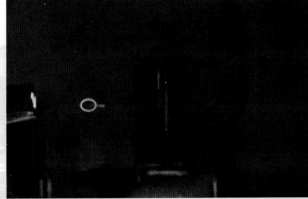

Important details
Increase the depth and texture

13 **Blending the sky** Using a mixture of the Palette Knife, the Loaded Palette Knife and the Just Add Water Hard brushes, paint and smooth the brushstrokes in the sky. However, try not to overdo it in order to retain some brushwork. These brushstrokes are mostly applied in vertical and horizontal movements.

14 **Going on with detailing** With the Loaded Palette Knife, more details are added to the structure, the sky and the fire. Zoom in to 50 per cent in some areas to apply more precise brushstrokes. You will probably have to rearrange the open documents, making the main document occupy as much as possible on your desktop. This is important so you don't lose notion of the overall picture. Use Tab to hide the palettes.

Resolution

Each painting phase should have its appropriate resolution. Start paintings with low resolutions for two reasons: first, the brushstrokes are applied in real-time, and second, the image will always be seen at 100 per cent magnification and no resampling has to be applied to the image, which sometimes can result in some ugly textures when viewed at 66.6 per cent magnification for example. As soon as you established the overall look of the painting, resize the image to the final resolution and start detailing. Many times it is also beneficial to oversize the image to add even more details. However, reserve this for the final steps, as sometimes this can make your computer somewhat slow.

15 **Detailing the main tower** With the Loaded Palette Knife and the Croquil Pen, details are added to the main tower. A good way to make details appear is to paint in the reflected light from the fire.

17 **Adding metallic structures** In the Layer palette, click the Create New Layer button and name it 'Structures'. With the Square Chalk and the new Structure paper selected, paint in these new elements, taking care to pick colours depending on distance. When you are satisfied with the results and don't need to paint behind this layer, you can drop it on the canvas.

16 **New papers to add details** To hint at detail in the structures, create two new papers. Open a new document about 500px by 450px, paint some stripes with the Square Chalk brush, Select>All, in the Paper Palette>Capture Paper and name it 'Stripes'. Do the same with a narrower document but this time paint in a metallic structure and name it 'Structure'. You can also use the ones provided on the disc.

18 **Adding depth** There are several ways to add depth to the image. A great effect is to add dark silhouettes in front of bright areas, like the bridge-like structure in the centre. Also, paint in lines of bright orange to simulate puddles of water or metallic structures reflecting light. Try to do this in perspective with larger lines in front and narrower ones further away. You can also blend some of the structures with the sky using the Palette Knife or the Just Add Water brushes.

19 **Liven up the sky** Using the Loaded Palette Knife and the Just Add Water Hard, apply and blend some blue hues to the upper part, and some dull green hues closer to the horizon. The first is to show patches of blue sky seen through the smoke and the second for green light reflected from chemical fires in the ground.

20 Detailing the fire

Now zoom to 100 per cent and with the Loaded Palette Knife and the Just Add Water Hard brushes, detail the fire, referring to the photo of the burning car. Also, use the Digital Airbrush variant from the Airbrush category in the Brushes palette to soften the fire and add a slight glow.

21 Check Brightness/Contrast
Again, go to Effects>Tonal Control>Brightness/Contrast, and adjust these settings to make the image even darker and moodier. However, be careful not to exaggerate this step. It is sometimes better to do it several times in small increments along the painting process.

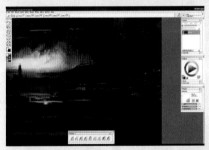

22 Overall detailing
Following the techniques described above, using the several custom-created papers, go ahead and add detail to the overall image. Remember to hide the palettes, leaving only your custom-created palette visible and working as close as possible to 100 per cent magnification. Keep panning with Spacebar, and don't forget to zoom out to keep track of the overall image.

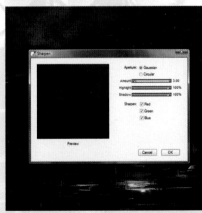

23 Final sharpening
In the end, go to Effects>Focus>Sharpen, with an amount of three to enhance the overall brushwork. And that's all, folks!

Brush selection
The brushes used in this tutorial

With so many brushes and tools at your disposal in Painter, you will often find yourself wondering which ones achieve the best results. We have supplied you with a selection of the brushes that we used, however, art is very much a subjective medium, so you may find that with a blend of knowledge and experimentation, you end up using different brushes to those suggested and create something very personal to you.

Square Chalk
This brush is great for filling large areas quickly, at the same time adding interesting textures. This was mainly used for the initial value-establishing phase.

Glow
A great tool to add light to a painting, it works best on darker scenes and with dark, saturated colours. This brush was used to add the fire and its reflected light.

Loaded Palette Knife
This tool has great versatility and expression. This is best employed when used with tilt-sensitive tablets. After tweaking it, this was the most-used tool in the painting.

Croquil Pen 5
Other variants in the Pen category could probably have achieved the same effect, but it's good to use what you have at your disposal. This was used to add precise opaque details.

Just Add Water
This is a wonderful tool for blending. Together with its hard-edged variant, both these tools are perfect for all kinds of blending. They were used in the sky and the fire.

Digital Airbrush
The Airbrush is fantastic for adding atmospheric effects, whether they are glows, clouds, halos, dust... Preferably used at low Opacity for best results.

Create mixed media textures

Pat Brennan explains how to turn a photograph into a colourful, textured digital collage

Tutorial info

Artist
Pat Brennan

Time needed
4 hours

Skill level
Intermediate

On the CD
Texture files

I have always loved the glamour, elegance and sophistication of the stars of the Forties; the last great decade of Hollywood's golden age. A great many studio shots from that time are done in partial shadow to highlight the facial structure of the actress or actor, and the skin is always flawless. In this tutorial I shall be re-creating that look, but with a contemporary twist, using a range of photographed and scanned textures to add a fantasy art feeling. I'm hoping to encourage those of you who have never made or used textures in your work to give it a try.

Corel Painter is the perfect program for making textures because it can digitally re-create any traditional medium you can think of. In this tutorial I'll show you how easy it can be to make a texture with traditional mediums, then merge them with Painter to create an amazing collage effect.

I used one sheet of watercolour paper and two coloured inks to make one of the textures used in this piece. I didn't use any brushes. These textures are scanned, but you could just as easily photograph them. And you don't need expensive materials either. Cheap, and even free, materials, can provide wonderful effects, including: scraps of cloth, paper, leaves, flowers, fur, bird feathers and even wood. By using image-editing software like Paint Shop Pro Photo X2, you can turn them into transparent layers while still retaining the textured surface, which means that you can create truly individual images.

After using them myself I share my textures online at **www.lunartex.deviantart.com.** Some of my textures are also included on this issue's disc, so you can get started straight away.

Create textures
Scanning tips

Here's a few tips I found useful when creating textures. If you're scanning lace or other open fabrics, place a sheet of coloured paper (I find soft brown very good) on top of it before you close the scanner lid. Don't forget, most scanner lids are removable to enable you to put larger objects on; just drape a piece of cloth over it to keep the light out. When using paper and paint, experiment with anything that makes a mark, like sponges, crumpled tissue, flicking the paint with a toothbrush, or even dropping it from a great height!

Lace is a fantastic texture to apply to your images and makes a great background

Use traditional ink to make your own patterns and then scan in for your textures

Watercolour paper is an excellent surface for your ink backgrounds

Set up your photo

Perform some edits and then get in position

Shortcuts

Don't forget to use the keyboard shortcuts when you are working on details in a large image. Having to switch tools to move your image around the canvas is time consuming and interrupts your workflow. A quick and easy solution is to press the Spacebar to temporarily activate the Hand tool. Release the Spacebar and the Hand tool will revert back to the tool that you were working with. This is the shortcut that I use the most, especially when I'm nearing the end of a project and I've increased the file size significantly.

01 The photograph

We haven't supplied the start photo for you, so please feel free to use your own. I placed my subject against a plain background and set up a sidelight. But if you prefer, there are many free to use stock images available on the web. Try www.deviantart.com. Read the artist's terms of use carefully. When you're working from photographs in Painter, you should always work on a duplicate. Choose File>Clone to make a duplicate of your original.

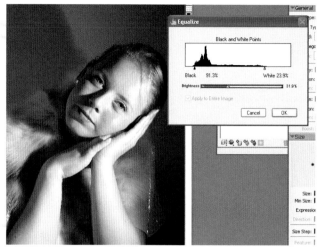

02 Lighten the image
Open the photograph in Corel Painter. Go to Effects>Equalize and move the black and white sliders around until the level of brightness is to your satisfaction. Be careful at this point not to destroy the all-important shadows on the face. Lower the saturation slightly with Adjust Colors>Saturation. All that's necessary at this stage is to have a clear, fairly bright image to work with.

03 Remove the background

To separate the subject from the background, draw a fairly rough line around it with the Lasso tool, invert the selection, then fill with your chosen colour. Proceed to paint fairly accurately around the head with a Digital Airbrush at 100% Opacity, reducing the brush size as you get closer to the figure. Select the background colour with the Magic Wand, invert and cut. Open a new document the right size, colour and resolution. Now paste.

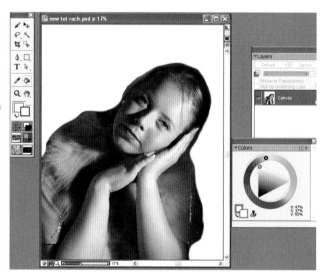

04 Float the image
To make the area around the image transparent, choose the Magic Wand tool, select the background, and invert the selection. Go to Select>Float, and you now have two layers. The shape you cut out with Float is now visible on the bottom layer. Select this layer and use the Paint Bucket tool to fill it in with the background colour.

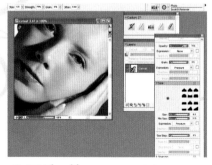

05 The skin
To get a wonderful smooth skin finish, select the Photo Scratch Remover at 79% Strength and 6% Grain. Set it to Pressure and carefully go over the skin in small circular movements. This gives that flawless airbrushed look. Another good tool to use is Blenders>Just Add Water. These tools only work well though if the skin is not too blemished.

06 Eyebrows and lashes
The stars in the Forties always had their eyebrows set high up in a thin arch, and the obligatory long eyelashes. To get a similar look, create a new layer and airbrush the original brows out by colour picking the original. I used Airbrush>Soft Airbrush 50 at 9% Opacity. Using Fine Detail>Soft Air 3 at 17% Opacity, paint in new eyebrows with light small strokes in the direction of growth, and lengthen the lashes. Now drop the layer.

07 Add first texture
Drop in the ink texture provided on the CD behind the figure. On the figure layer, start erasing part of the head and most of the original clothing to integrate the figure with the background texture. I used Erasers>Gentle Bleach 7. Leave a faint suggestion of the outline of the clothing at this stage. Notice how I've placed the darkest part of the texture just around the top of the head. Experiment with the placing of the texture to suit your chosen image. Try flipping it horizontally or vertically.

08 A second texture
Using the ink texture for a second time, apply it over the top. This applies it to the whole image, so set it to Multiply. With the Eraser>Gentle Bleach 7 at 20% Opacity, erase parts of the image where it's not required, notably the face. I like the suggestion of fingerless gloves, so I'm going to leave it on the arms. You can experiment with lightening and darkening this layer, and scrolling through Blend modes.

09 Third texture
Apply the same texture for a third time. With Preserve Transparency unchecked, set layers to Gel Cover at 58% and apply the section to the bottom half of the image, below the second texture. Erase any parts not required. The placement may leave a hard line across the image, so zoom in and remove all traces with the Eraser.

Mix and match
It is possible to create entire visual images within Painter, without needing another application. It's an artist's studio without the mess. Having said that, if you have acquired a lot of expensive art equipment it makes sense to use it all. Traditional paints and paper, scanners and photo editing programs are all part of the optional toolkit for this tutorial.

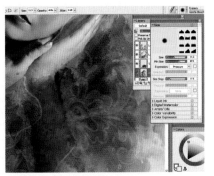

10 Add a collar
With an Airbrushes>Fine Detail 3, airbrush on a new layer. Draw in a ruffled collar to replace the clothing that was erased. It doesn't need to be too painterly. Select Choose Distortion>Pinch. Now run this brush along a drawn line to narrow it. Parts of it can be erased slightly when you are happy with it.

11 Fourth texture overlay
Open the antique lace texture from the CD, and place it at the top of the layers stack. I chose Magic Combine at 19% Opacity, but other layer styles (such as Gel Cover or Multiply) give interesting effects too. I erased all the lace outside the collar area with Erasers>Gentle Bleach at 40% Opacity.

12 The lips
On the figure layer, use a soft brush set to Multiply at a low opacity, and gently stroke more colour onto the lips. I'm brightening and darkening them without losing the original highlights. I've colour-picked red from the texture visible behind the head. I think it's important when creating artwork with multiple colours and textures to try and unify the image wherever possible.

Splatter brushes
The paint splatters I have used in this piece came from the generous www.corelila.deviantart.com. These brushes are free to use. You can, however, use a saved scan of your own home-made splatters instead. Put your paper on the floor and protect surrounding areas. An eyedropper is a great tool for this, and you can vary the height for different effects. I prefer using ink, as the dye concentration is higher. Flicking with an old toothbrush is a tried and tested method that's very useful (and cheap) for fine splatter spray.

Extra make up
Final flourishes to the face

13 Eye colour
On the figure layer choose Lasso and carefully draw around each pupil. Go to Tonal Control>Adjust Color> Uniform Color and move the Saturation slider to the right slightly. This has the effect of enhancing the original eye colour without it looking too artificial. If you prefer the look of brown eyes and your subject's are blue, this can be easily achieved with Tonal Control>Adjust Color>Correct Color.

14 Eye make up
To add make up to the eye area, open a new layer above the figure and set it to Multiply at 52% Opacity. Choose Airbrushes>Soft Airbrush 50, colour-pick the eyes and stroke in as much or as little required. I've kept this make up quite subtle. You could try something completely different; there is great scope in this step for experimenting with all the different styles and colours of eye make up.

Colour tweaks
Enhance hues and then apply painted strokes

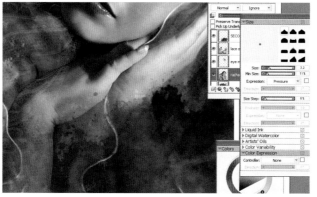

15 Blue forehead Add some colour to the forehead. On a new layer, set Multiply to 52% and choose Airbrushes>Soft Airbrush 50 at 12% Opacity. Now stroke in the colour you have chosen. By doing this, the gentle highlight above the eye that helps give the face its form has disappeared. With Erasers> Gentle Bleach 7 set to about 7% Opacity, I carefully removed some of the colour to reinstate this highlight.

16 Redefine edges With all the textured overlays, some of the edges of the collar have become indistinct. On the first texture layer choose Erasers>Pointed Bleach 15 at 30% Opacity and stroke the edges you wish to redefine. If you have used blue colours throughout your piece you could make a feature of the edges by using the Pattern Pen>Decorative Ginkgo Pen.

17 Random brush shapes Apply some random brush shapes and blobs of colour all over what remains of the hair. If the colours are applied with different opacities and colour modes, this heightens the effect of overlapping,

19 Add to the brushes
Keep adding to the decoration of the headpiece with the brushes. With each one on a different layer you can change the order of the layers and put one behind or in front of another for different effects. Try different blend modes until you are happy with the look and placement of the individual elements.

18 Add a brush decoration The two add-on brushes I'm going to use in this piece are free to use from the handy www.gvalkyrie. deviantart.com. In the photo-editing application of your choice, start applying the different brushes available in the sets. Place each brush stroke on its own layer where you can skew it, rotate it, erase parts and change the opacity – whatever looks right! Or pick your favourite Painter brush and do the same!

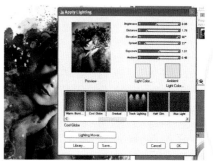

20 Add some spatter texture On a new layer, add some textured splatters and blobs. Use colours that are already present in the image, and remember each brushstroke can have a different blend mode. To achieve this look you can use a texture you made yourself by flicking ink or paint, set this to Multiply or Magic Combine, and erase where you don't want it to show.

21 Save and drop When you are satisfied with what you have achieved so far, save your layered file and duplicate it. To do this, open the file in Painter and choose File>Clone. Now, on the cloned file in the Layers palette, choose Drop All. It's important to save your layered file and to do the final steps on the copy.

22 Lighting effects Now to make the lighting more dramatic. Luckily, Painter has many lighting effects that are easy to customise. Here I have chosen Apply Lighting>Cool Globe, but I changed the lighting colour to a deep cream. I moved the light source pointer down and to the right to make sense of my shadows. Then Edit>Fade to your satisfaction.

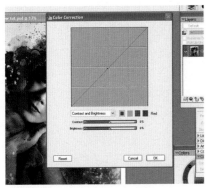

24 Dodge and burn

I feel that some of the darker parts of the image would benefit from some selective darkening. Choose Photo>Burn at 9% Opacity. Where the shadows would be deepest (like under the chin and where the hands overlap) I carefully darkened the areas. The same with the Photo>Dodge tool – I lightened areas very slightly that lost their sparkle with the successive layering, such as the eye's catch-light.

23 Final colour correction

In Painter choose Effects>Correct Colors. With this selected you can adjust the gamma curves for individual colours, or all of them by using the black master curve. Here I have concentrated on saturating the reds.

25 Final check

I check every square inch at full resolution for elements I feel could be changed or removed. I then look at it full screen from a few feet away. If I was working on a traditional painting I would look at it through a mirror to see obvious flaws. In Painter, choose Canvas>Rotate Canvas>Flip Horizontal. This new perspective gives a completely different view.

Mixing media | Merge traditional with digital

Mixed media images are great fun and definitely worth experimenting with. It's incredibly easy to create your own background patterns with ink, watercolour or other paints and then scan in to be used on your Painter canvas. Once applied to a photo and treated to some Painter magic, you can end up with a very pleasing piece of art.

BRUSH MARKS
A Painter creation wouldn't be right without some brush marks. We have applied lively strokes but you might prefer a more subtle approach

SKIN SMOOTHER
Painter has some nifty controls when it comes to working with skin, and the Photo Scratch Remover is excellent for smoothing skin and making it look like it's been airbrushed

TEXTURE FILES
Have a look around you – chances are you are surrounded by textured objects that would work as background elements. Photograph curtains, tables, cushions – anything that might work in a composition

HAPPY ACCIDENTS
When placing your texture files, you might inadvertently create something you hadn't planned. In this case it was the feel of lacy gloves over the arms, and was a look we decided to keep!

ENHANCE PATTERNS
As you lay down the background elements, don't be afraid to paint in detail to help the eye decide what's going on. In this example, we gave a subtle outline of clothes ruffles

Create with perspective

Use the rules of linear and aerial perspective to help your landscape paintings

Tutorial info

Artist
Celia Yost

Time needed
4 hours

Skill level
Intermediate

On the CD
Layered files

Linear and aerial perspective are very useful tools for an artist to have in their arsenal. Linear perspective is a system used for creating a sense of depth in a painting or drawing, with the desired effect being that of looking through a window, instead of at a wall. The idea that's the basis for linear perspective is that as objects approach the horizon line, parallel lines appear to converge at the same point. There are three basic types: one point, two point and three point, which refer to the number of vanishing points used in the image, and the angle at which you are drawing determines which one you'll use. If you're looking at an object straight on, you'd use one point, if you're viewing the object on edge you'd use two point and if you're looking either up or down on it, you'd use three point (three point is the only one that has a special vanishing point

that's not on the horizon, and is used for showing either extreme height or extreme depth. You'll see it used a lot on comic books.) Most of the time when drawing, you will find yourself using two point, however, in reality you can have as many vanishing points as there are objects in an image, as unless it's a city, things are rarely situated on a perfect grid. Conveniently then, we're going to draw a city in order to demonstrate two-point perspective and then show how aerial perspective can give the feeling of distance. This is achieved by altering the colours in the background and also cutting down on the amount of visible detail used.

Scenic skyline

Import a sketch into Painter or do it in the program

It's all boxes

Linear perspective is all about boxes. What we mean by that is we're sure you've noticed that while it's pretty easy to draw a box in perspective, things suddenly get a lot more difficult when you try to draw just about anything else. The trick is to turn everything into a box. You figure out how whatever you're trying to draw would fit into box straight on, draw that box in perspective and then align the object to its box. This is also easier said than done, but it still works as a good place to start with more complicated geometric or organic objects.

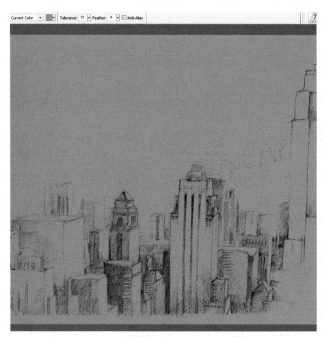

01 Getting started We started out with a rough sketch that we scanned in. You could also do this step in Painter, but it all comes down to whether you feel more comfortable doing the initial drawing traditionally. Set the layer to Multiply and added a fill colour to the canvas using the Bucket tool to help you visually as you work. Either create your own or use the sketch on the layered file on the disc.

02 Initial colour Add a layer between the canvas and the sketch, and start rendering some basic lighting and colour. We're using the Fine Feathering Oils brush and an Artists' Oils brush that has been modified so that it lacks a trail-off point, but still blends very smoothly.

If nothing else, remember where your horizon is

Another important thing to remember when using perspective is that no matter how many vanishing points you have, there will be only one horizon line. Now, we say that and immediately think of some exceptions (like free-falling objects), but the main point is that the horizon line is actually the viewer's eye level, and regardless of what kind of crazy things are going on with space and the ten billion things that aren't parallel with each other, you only have one set of eyes to look at it with.

03 Initial lighting Using mostly the Wet Acrylic brushes, we threw some colour in the sky to help remind us of what we'll be doing with lighting later on. As an aside, working back to front when using the blending brushes on different layers is a good idea, though it's not the end of the world by any means if you move around the canvas as you work.

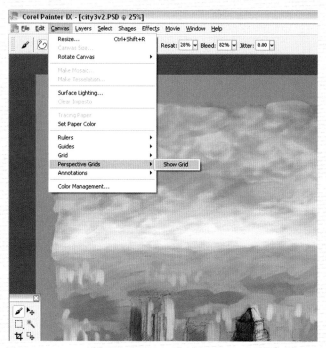

04 Introducing the grid Now it's time to start working with linear perspective. Our sketch is really rough and we didn't bother calculating out where the vanishing point where, and while it looks all right now, we need to adjust things. One of the main tools we'll be using in this tutorial is the Perspective grid. Go to Canvas>Perspective Grid>Show Grid.

Building work
Utilise grids to make your life easier

05 Using the grid To make use of the grid, we need to align it to our drawing. We only want the vertical grid at the moment, so uncheck the horizontal box and move the horizon line so that it's on the same level as the horizon in the drawing. Then adjust the grid, moving the vanishing point and the far edge so that it more or less is at the same angle as the buildings.

06 Altering the grid The perspective grid can be manipulated in a few different ways. Grabbing the horizon line will move the grid back and forth, while grabbing the far edge will move it from side to side. The vanishing point is a bit difficult to see. It's just a small notch on the horizon line and will shift the entire grid if it's moved.

07 Colour and adjustment
Add another layer above all the others and start working on the buildings, using the Perspective grid as a guide. Throughout the entire process, you will be making constant small adjustments to the original orientation and position of the buildings this way.

08 Save the grid Since this is two point, we need a second grid. Use the exact same process to place it as you did with the first one. So you're not having to constantly redo this, it's helpful to save them. Just click on the + grid next to the pull-down menu and name it something descriptive.

09 Tweaking the settings We worked using the Wet Acrylics, Detail Oils, Conte, but use whatever you feel like using as the brushes in Painter are very much a personal choice. Slowly work in and adjust what you have drawn to the grid.

10 Rotate canvas Another useful function is Rotate Canvas. This allows you to turn the image to an angle that's more comfortable to draw, like you would your paper in real life. It's located under the Grabber tool, or a hot key of E.

Perspective and realism

Despite initial appearances, linear perspective generally doesn't create a completely realistic portrayal of reality. This is easy enough to test for yourself. Look at a 3D model of a street that's computer rendered, and thus by definition has mathematically perfect perspective. Look at the edges, and notice how distorted things look. That's where linear perspective starts to break down. This happens for a couple of reasons. First of all, in reality the apparent vanishing points are miles away, and this is rarely practical to measure out. Also, we see in 3D and the picture plane is 2D, so because we have two eyes we're always seeing two slightly different perspectives. We're constantly glancing around, and rarely will you be looking fixedly at one spot, whereas an image forces just that, so it can never be completely realistic.

COREL painter | 111

Staying on the straight and narrow
Custom gridding and more tricks of the trade

How to evenly space receding objects
Windows made easy

This is most practical for things that are box-like, such as windows. First, determine where you want the top and bottom of the nearest object to the viewer to be. Draw two lines to the relevant vanishing point, and divide off the front and back so that you have a rectangle in perspective. Now draw lines connecting the opposite corners. The centre of the resulting cross is the midline. Draw a vertical line through this and you will now have two boxes. Continue dividing boxes until you have your desired number. If you want three windows, follow the same steps, but instead of subdividing at the centre of the crosses, your dividing lines will be where the secondary crosses intersect with the original one.

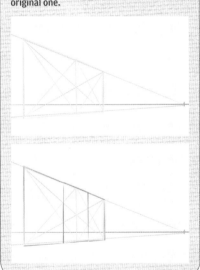

11 Straight lines The Straight Line tool is handy when you're drawing something like buildings. It's hot key 'V', or can be accessed on the left side of the Property bar. Use it to define edges, lines of windows, etc, and then go back in with a regular brush so that it looks more organic.

12 Custom grids Now we have a bit of a problem. You need to work on the far right of your image, but as your vanishing point is just off the edge, there's an area where the grid doesn't cover. So to compensate, add a new layer above the others, title it 'grid' and, using the Straight Line tool and an obvious colour, build your own.

13 Other grids It's helpful to have a grid layer to make other notations as well. Here, we added some guidelines for the windows on the Empire State Building. We also turned on the regular grid (Canvas>Grid>Show Grid). Being able to adjust the transparency of your notes is handy and using the Layer palette is easier than having billions of perspective grids for one image.

14 The longest step Now that we've made the first pass, it's time to go back in, add details and generally tighten up the image. This is a lot of slog work, and there's really no short cut for it.

15 Spacing There is a trick for evenly spacing objects in perspective. This works best if the number is something like two, four or eight; three and six are possible, it's just more complicated. After a certain point, you're better off eyeballing it. See the side tip for more information on this.

16 Progress so far This is our progress so far on the foreground. Sometimes it helps to jump around a bit when painting, so even though this section clearly isn't finished, we're now going to work on another part of the image.

17 Rendering the background Here, we start to go into the far background and try to make it look more like buildings and less like an amorphous blobby mist. This has far more to do with atmospheric perspective (see the Atmospheric Perspective side tip) than linear perspective.

18 Atmosphere Atmospheric perspective is very helpful for creating convincing, deep space. In some ways, it's trickier than linear to manage because it's more subjective and variable. In general, as things recede their colours become duller, there's less contrast between the darkest dark and lightest light, and edges become softer.

19 Rendering the sky Start to go back into the sky and make it a bit more interesting now, perhaps using the Wet Acrylic and Fine Feathering Oils brushes. Gentle, circular strokes work especially well for rendering clouds.

20 Detail work We're getting close to the end now, so we're at the point of fiddly detail work. Go through the image and tighten up the buildings, fix little things and add more detail to the background.

Finishing touches
Lighten up a bit with highlights

21 Endless detail work More of the same here, this stage could potentially last indefinitely and there's a danger of overworking the image. Don't overdo it and make the buildings in the background as detailed as those in the foreground, as that will flatten out the apparent space.

22 Final lightening adjustment The last thing to do is add another layer for lighting. Use the Soft Airbrush to just gently soften some of the background a bit more, adding in general highlights and shadows in a couple of places.

Working from reference
We worked with a couple of reference images of New York for this image, but while we tried to stay reasonably accurate, we were not married to the photos. There were several areas where the way buildings lined up with each other that made it unclear as to what was going on, due to unfortunate tangents or lighting. So it's a good idea to be working from more than one photo of the same area, preferably ones that are taken from slightly different angles. Also, having a readable image and composition is more important than being accurate to the photo.

Atmospheric perspective conditions
This tutorial focuses on linear perspective, but keep in mind that when you're dealing with a landscape, atmospheric perspective is almost as important in creating the illusion of depth. We went over this a little in one of the steps, but in general your background should be have colours that are closer to being neutral, have less contrast between highlights and shadows and be softer-edged than your foreground. These are all effects that a lot of air or atmosphere has on things, and encourages the idea that you're looking at a large amount of distance in one shot.

Learn to paint skin tone

Paint realistic and natural-looking skin tone starting from scratch, using traditional techniques and just three brushes

Tutorial info

Artist
Mayrhosby Yeoshen

Time needed
3 hours

Skill level
Intermediate

On the CD
Final image and skin tone swatches

Every digital artist has their own way of painting skin tones for portraits. However, not everyone is able to get a very realistic look, since at first glance it seems hard to avoid a fake-looking human face due to the nature of the media. It is easier, though, to achieve an organic feeling when we do it the traditional way. It's not just a matter of airbrushing and blending colours. It's a matter of adding your own personal touch and paying careful attention to every single detail: from the colour on the lachrymal to the crease in the lip. It looks like hard work, but it's not what it seems to be. At the end, the results matter. Not only can you make beautiful portraits, but your observation skills will improve drastically.

The traditional technique here is no more than crosshatching. But don't be fooled. Unlike the way you did it before with pencils, this technique achieves what it sets out to achieve. The fact that we can work on canvases several thousand pixels in height, and can zoom in for maximum detail, will let you take control of every single part of the painting. No more than three brushes are used for this technique. One is created from the Round Blender, one is freely downloaded from the internet and the other one is the Cover Pencil.

We paint the base tones with the first two brushes, and for the crosshatching we just need the pencil. This way, your understanding of shapes and three-dimensional environment will improve as well. After we choose the colours for shading, we will blend them, get rid of the line art and then start with the fun part, which is adding the extreme details. You'll find a layered file on the disc to paint into, and you'll also find swatches for other skin tones. You can use these with the techniques shown here to create portraits for different nationalities.

Beginning with the base

Base all round! Choose the base image and the base colours

01 The line art First we need to begin with a sketch, be it tracing your favourite photo, tracing from a scanned sketch or using the 'skin tone for tutorial.psd' file from the disc. In this case, we just have the line art for the face and ear. Since everything else is pretty much done, we can concentrate on painting and texturing the skin.

02 Pay attention to the environment and mood Is it day, is it night, is it dusk? Natural light, artificial light? Which mood do you want to transmit? Those things will influence your skin, as they will with the rest of the picture. Here, the atmosphere is warm with natural light, so the skin colours pretty much won't be altered.

03 The colour palette Using your reference, find out which base colours you'll choose for dark, mid and light shades. Also, pick more colours for the cornea, the iris, the lips and subtle shades like eye bags or blush, if any. There are provided swatches for this tutorial, not only Caucasian, but for other skin tones.

Starting with shading

Enhance the base with shading

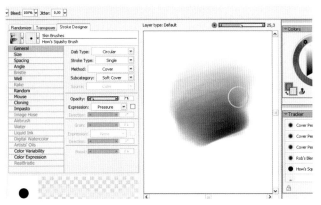

04 The brush
On the CD, you will find instructions on how to create the first brush. Load up the Round Blender brush from the Blenders and then open the Brush Creator. Now click the Stroke Designer tab and enter the settings. Start with a low Opacity of approximately 7% and Size set to around 24-30px.

05 Beginning the shading
Check the Preserve Transparency box on the skin layer. Now let's start shading the mid-dark areas. Choose a light warm brown and use your reference to see where these areas are located. In this case, the skin under the eyebrows, the eyelids, the chin and left side of her face will be shaded.

06 Blend the colours
Don't be afraid of picking more tones from your palette mixer, like pinks and oranges darker than the base skin tone. Maintain the low opacity and blend the colours using the brush's inner features. Don't forget to tackle the rest of the skin, like the neck and upper chest.

07 Keep on with the dark shading
Set the brush to a smaller size (around 10-15px). Now use a darker brown for the shading. Don't be afraid of picking the different colours resulting from this mix using the dropper, so you can make the shading richer. Try to blend the colours using the brush's inner features.

08 Apply light
Now with a lighter version of the initial skin tone, let's start applying the light to the right side of the nose, the forehead and the upper cheekbone. We're still working with big areas, in a way that's not detailed. Always look at your reference and understand the three-dimensional shape, and why the light is hitting areas like the cheeks, centre of the nose, etc. For the brightest light tones, you can use a light cyan with low opacity to make the skin look more organic.

The Rotate Image tool

One of the best tools Corel Painter has to offer is Rotate Image. The fact that it works during real-time is reason enough to overuse it! The shortcut is 'E'. Once you have got the desired angle, press 'B' to use the brush again. To have the image again in its original angle, double-click while the tool is selected. It's just like drawing on real paper or canvas, without waiting for any rendering.

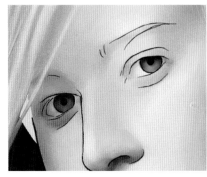

09 The eyes
Add the basic colours to the eyes, bearing in mind that the white of the eye is actually greyish. Start shading the iris and pupil, and remember the spherical shape of the eye by adding shadow underneath the eyelid and close to the tear duct. In the extreme sides the eyes tend to have a reddish tone due to the blood.

10 The mouth
As you did with the eye, start painting the lips, filling them with a red-pinkish colour, and shade with a darker red. You can also draw the line that separates the upper lip from the lower one with a smaller size and higher opacity.

11 Subtle skin colours
There are further picked colours for subtle shades, like the ethmoid sinus, located between the upper part of the nose and the eye. In this case we pick a nice lavender, painting with very low opacity, using the brush's ability to blend with the colours underneath. The area close to the tear duct is often found in a yellowish tone, so with a smaller brush add that touch, rounding it.

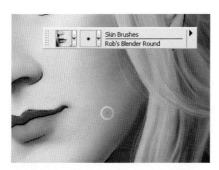

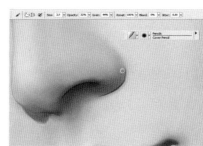

12 **A touch of blush** For the cheeks, use a bright carmine red. With a big brush (around 30px), shade the cheeks, blending with the colour underneath.

13 **Blending the colours** Now that you have the basic colours on the skin, blend them using Rob's Blender Round brush with an Opacity of approximately 25-30% and Size between 35-40px. You can find details of where to download this on the disc. This will give us a smooth feeling, making what we have done look less sketchy.

14 **Time to get rid of the lines** Now you want to leave all the features defined, preparing the skin for texturing. Hiding and showing the line-art layer while defining the contours of the skin, use the Cover Pencil set to around 2 pixels and 30% Opacity. Always using a darker (or lighter) colour, fill in the gaps with this pencil in a bigger size, or the brush created earlier in a small size and high opacity.

Flaky skin?

If you feel that your skin is lacking something, you can always play around with the levels, the contrast or saturation, making your skin tone even richer. Another way of making your skin richer is with crosshatching. Making little bits of crosshatching here and there, almost in a random way, will help give the appearance of small bumps or even pores.

Continuing with crosshatching
Draw and get drawn in by the eyes and mouth

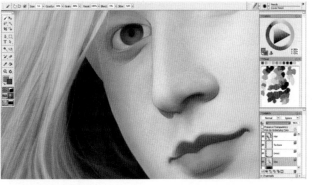

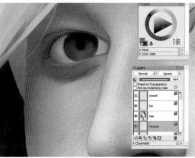

15 **Let the texturing begin** What we've done up until now is prepare the skin for the massive texturing job. We're now going to start working on a macro method. Create another layer called 'Texture'. Uncheck Preserve Transparency and check Pick Up Underlaying Color. With the Cover Pencil, Size set to 1-6 pixels and Opacity at 20%, start to crosshatch. You can practise in the Brush Creator.

16 **Start crossing** You can start crosshatching from whichever point you want. We've gone with the right cheek. With fast movements, start crosshatching with arc lines that go along with the shape of the surface. A common mistake is to get in a very different angle than the one the face is shaped. If you are not happy with what you're doing, erase and do it again, until you get the trick of it. The use of the Rotation tool is a must.

17 **Pay attention** This technique's success resides on the amount of subtleties we can control. Pay close attention to the creases, the folds of the skin and the very different tones on it. You may also want to use the Dropper tool as much as you can. We're now focusing on the used tones on the painted skin and the colour wheel, not in the Mixing palette any more.

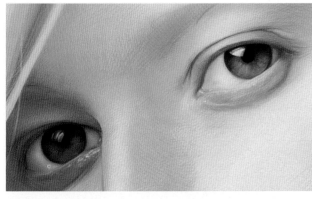

18 **Refining the eyes** The eyes are often the very first thing we see in anyone's face. And that's why we must focus on them more than any other feature of the face. Details like the tear duct, the inner part of the eyelids, the iris lines and the usual shine will make them pop out, making the face richer and giving it more personality. Do not forget the lower eyelid creases.

19 **More of the mouth** Another big feature of the face, it deserves great study and detailing. The most common mistake is to draw lines randomly, without even bothering to study why they are there, and the three-dimensional shape. Take your time to notice all the lips' features, seeing where to add the light and where the shadow.

Finishing the face
Pay attention to the other details

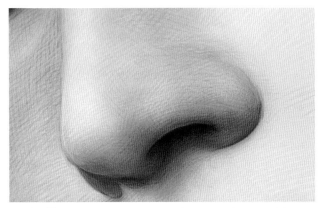

20 The nose The nose can be great fun to draw, due to its subtle colours. It can have the lightest tone on the whole skin, yet the darkest one at the same time (the nostrils). Pay attention to the skin around the nostrils. Usually on Caucasian skin tone, this area is full of bright oranges and carmine reds.

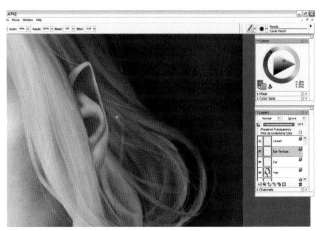

21 The ears If you decide to include ears, bear in mind that like the nose, the ears in Caucasian skin can have a lot of bright red, pink and orange tones. Ears don't require detailed attention like the eyes or mouth.

Adjust skin to perfection

If you feel that one area of the skin needs something, be it a darker tone or lighter, more saturated or not, then take into consideration the following. Add a new layer on top of your skin, make a selection of the area you want to modify, and feather it. The amount of feathering needed depends on how big the area is, but most of the time a number between 20-40% works. Then fill in with a colour you think might make the skin change. Let's say, if you need more shadow then add a darker tone. Set that layer to the Multiply blending mode. If you need more saturation, try Overlay. For a lighter tone, try Screen. To achieve the desired effect, change the opacity to the desired level. Then erase the bits you don't need and flatten it with the original skin layer.

22 The neck and upper chest After working on the face, we can concentrate on the rest of the skin. As they are much bigger areas with much less attention to detail, the result can be a little bit boring. Usually, it's good to switch to other elements of the painting before attempting this part. Notice the very dark shadow below the chin, and don't forget the shadow cast from the hair and dress, for instance.

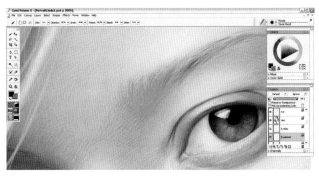

23 Eyebrows Although eyebrows are not skin per se, they still sort of blend with it. In a new layer, start drawing the eyebrow with the same pencil, this time a little bit bigger (2.5 to 3 pixels) and Opacity set to 50%, beginning with the darkest shading and finishing with the lightest one. Pay attention to the flow of it – don't overdo it or else it will look fake. For more blending with the skin, draw some strands the same colour as the skin underneath.

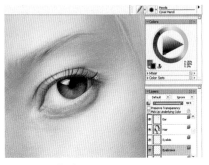

24 Eyelashes For the eyelashes, use the same brush as for the ears and a very dark colour (almost black). To avoid a fake look, draw them more randomly but in an accurate way – don't get messy. Follow the direction of the eyelid they come out from. Whenever you draw an eyelash you think looks wrong, Use Undo and try it again.

25 Finishing up We now have all the skin features done. What's left to do is to make sure everything is all right. Make sure that the shadows from the hair or clothes are cast onto the skin. If you see any part of the texturing too dark, you can always take the Eraser and with a very low opacity (5-10%), erase the tiny bits. Or you can use the Blender with low opacity as well. Or even correct the colours. The world is your oyster!

showcase

eShop
Visit the
Official Corel Painter
online shop at
www.imagineshop.co.uk
for back issues
and subscriptions

MARK HOLLIS

TITLE	Country Pile
WEBSITE	www.markhollis.co.uk
JOB TITLE	Freelance painter, illustrator, video artist and musician

Mark is based in Bristol, UK and says of his art "I make work about what life is like in the 21st century, with a nod to our history. I depict scenes of humour, hope, loss, and social commentary with a sardonic twist."

Visit us online at www.paintermagazine.com

Create your own art gallery for FREE • Meet other artists on the forum • Subscribe and save money!

Turn sketches into retro art

Re-create the spirit of vintage travel posters using your own sketches or holiday photos

Tutorial info

Artist
Brad Sutton

Time needed
5 hours

Skill level
Intermediate

On the CD
Sketch and final artwork

Creating a vintage travel poster can make an illustration look nostalgic and make the image look a bit more classic. Travel posters were used to entice travellers to come to the chosen destination. Railroads and cruise lines used these posters to get people to visit different countries, cities, states, beaches and anything else you can think of. It was used as an early form of marketing. Artists like John O Brubaker, Roger Broders and others created these illustrations and helped to catch the fancy of would-be travellers. Even earlier, railways like Southern Pacific and Santa Fe used photographers, like Edward S. Curtis, in marketing their rail lines and destinations. These illustrations can be found on posters, brochures, stamps, magazines and in travel agencies.

These sorts of posters were at their prime after the Art Nouveau and Art Deco eras, when the artists used limited colour palettes to create their idyllic scenes. Colour combinations were also important for these travel posters as they had to be colourful to grab the attention of the viewer and appeal to them. Even today, companies will use these same colour combinations because they know which products sell with certain colours.

Creating this style of poster can be a challenge. Choosing the right colours and making them work together and look harmonious can be difficult, but it can also be rewarding at the same time. Text can accompany the illustration if you wish. If the viewer cannot tell the location by the recognisable and iconic images, putting the location or name in the image can help. Hopefully you'll enjoy this project and it persuades you to take that trip, and get out to see the world! Or maybe you'll end up seeing your artwork advertising a place or on a stamp!

The Seattle skyline became the inspiration for this project. Notice how we have emphasised the Space Needle landmark and added the sailboats for an idyllic feel

Begin your vintage travel poster
Even the roughest of sketches will do

Changing your Preferences

This is a good area to fool around in as it can make things easier and more user-friendly for you. One of the features is the Undo button. You can change the number of times that the Undo button can be used. In the toolbar, go to Edit>Preferences>Undo and a window will open for this option. Set it at the maximum. It currently goes to 32 levels, but it would be nice in the future if it went to 50 levels, maybe in Painter XI..?

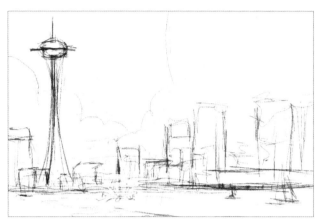

01 Rough sketch First scan your sketch on to the computer. For this illustration we drew directly onto the canvas, using the Opaque Medium that we will also be using later. This is the same technique that we use with traditional mediums. You can find the sketch on our disc.

02 Cleaned up sketch If your sketch is as rough and quick as the one we did you may need to clean up some of the lines. For this we used the Eraser and the medium that we sketched with. Select the white of the canvas to erase any unwanted lines.

03 Making changes Take another look at your composition and decide if things need to be changed. We felt that the two buildings on the far right were too similar. Copy and paste a section of the buildings and move it to the desired height. It's not correct to how they are in real life, but that's the beauty of artistic licence.

04 Block in colour For blocking in colour use the Digital Watercolor. We used the New Simple Water brush. Start at a low opacity around 25%, as this will make it easier to blend colours. We even went to 12% at this stage to get the colours roughed in.

Customise your keys

This is a good way to make things easier for you to use in the program. We like to just push one button to open a file, or to dry the watercolour. In the toolbar, go to Edit>Preferences>Customize Keys. In here you will see all the Application commands. This is where you will want to change the command you are using and pick an easier button for you to use. We changed it to the letter P because we can push it with the end of our stylus quickly and without having to push two keys.

05 Background to foreground Start with the objects in the background first. Using Digital Watercolor enables you to colour outside the lines. Then you can carve the next colour over the one in the background, which is very similar to painting traditionally.

06 Finalise blocking in colour Finalise the main colour schemes in the illustration. This is very quick and rough – additional colours and shadows will be added later. It's just a way to get the colour on the canvas.

07 Dry Digital Watercolor Now to dry our watercolour. Go to Layers in the toolbar and go down to Dry Digital Watercolor. Note: You will want to customise a hot key for this, as it will be a key that you use a lot.

08 Start to blend Start to blend the colour that you laid down. We used the Smudge Blender. This gives a soft look, like pastels, and can also add texture to your poster.

09 Direct and delicate brushstrokes Some of the initial lines that you put down as the sketch will blend when you go over them. So be careful. Some of the lighter lines will just blend into the colour. Good thing you have the Undo key!

10 Use an Opaque brush Now use your opaque medium. We like the Wet Gouache Round 10. Experiment with all the mediums and brushes that are at your disposal. You will eventually find ones that just seem to work better for you.

11 Clean up sketch lines With your opaque medium, start to go over the lines and block in colour like you did with the Digital Watercolor. This step can be avoided by having the lines cleaned up prior to painting. It's a good opportunity to re-draw aspects if needed.

Artistic license
Bending the rules

When you set about re-creating your own vintage travel poster, don't be constrained by what it is you see in front of you. Always remember what these posters were used for – to depict an area as the absolute ideal and as somewhere that people just had to visit.

Your job is to pick out the elements that make the place you are painting special, and then build around that. In our example, the Space Needle is a recognisable sign for Seattle, so we have brought it in as the main focal point. The waterfront view of the city is beautiful in its own right, but by adding sailboats we have turned it into a dreamy place where you can feel relaxed. The soft, warm colours help add to this.

And talking of colours, notice the distinct lack of them. The original artists didn't labour under a ton of different hues, so pick maybe three colours and work around them. You'll be amazed at what can be achieved.

Deepen the colours
Boost colours for maximum impact

Don't worry about layers

We have painted this entire scene pretty much on just one layer. This has allowed our blending process to work, but make sure that you have the maximum amount of Undo's possible!

12 **Change a couple of things** You can see as you go along that there are things that need changing. We noticed that the clouds look too perfect, like ice cream scoops. We made them look more organic by carving into them with the colour of the sky.

13 **Unifying** Now go back to Digital Watercolor, at 12-20%. Use yellow for the highlights and purple or blue for the shadows. You want to choose a colour that is high in value and tint, close to the white.

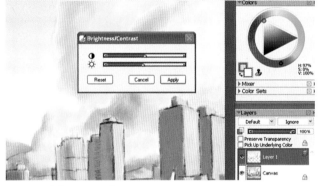

14 **Back and forth** You want to build this up in layers, drying digital water in-between each layer. This will help to set the mood of the illustration.

15 **Build up layers** Working back and forth with lighter and darker values can be helpful and faster. You may also notice that things can start to look too dark in certain areas.

16 **Brightness and contrast** You might want to make the clouds fall back further. Copy the layer and make sure it is directly over the first image. Go to Effects>Tonal Control>Brightness/Contrast and then move both sliders to the right. Now erase the buildings and water, and drop that layer to the canvas.

17 **Darken foreground elements** Now you will want to add more contrast from the buildings in the foreground to those in the background. Use Digital Watercolor again by working back and forth until you get the desired look. Don't forget to Dry Digital Watercolor.

18 **Reflections in water** Using Digital Watercolor, start to add some of the shadows and reflections from the buildings in the water. You may have to use your Opaque to make certain areas lighter.

Finer details

Add the small, important touches

19 **The fun part – making things pop**
Now this step can seem tedious and mind numbing, but this is what adds life to the picture and makes it 'pop'. For a lot of the windows we used Digital Watercolor, because you can draw lines and then erase them to make the windows, by taking the colour to Pure White on the Tint.

20 **Finish up the water** Add details to your water to make more of the little nuisances that appear in real moving water. You will need to be aware of the sky because the water is reflecting it.

21 **Finalising** Finally we used the FX–Glow tool for some of the highlights in the water. We also painted purple clouds behind the building in the middle as it looked like we were painting around the building.

Constructing retro art | Get the elements as they should be

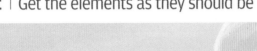

It's very difficult to stop fiddling with an image, especially when you're re-creating a style. Have some time away and then look at things with a fresh eye. In our example here, one thing we might add is some text, maybe saying something like 'Welcome to Seattle!' or, 'Come sail on the Puget Sound!'.

REDUCED YOUR COLOURS
Keep your colour palette nice and simple. In our example here, we have chosen yellow, blue and lilac as our main hues and then built the tones around them. Despite the lack of colour, the art is anything but dull.

SIMPLE DETAIL
Although we have spent some time adding detail such as the windows, the forms are relatively simple. The original posters were more illustrative than photo-realistic pieces of art.

PICK A LANDMARK
We have put the most famous Seattle landmark in a prominent position, letting it absorb the best of the light and shading. The boats help lead the eye towards it as well, which if it was a true travel poster, would help sell the area.

ALTER REALITY
It's highly doubtful you would see a cluster of sailboats merrily bobbing around the city's waterfront. But they are the perfect addition for a calming mood.

Add people to your landscapes

Enhance the illusion of life in your landscape by adding people

Tutorial info

Artist
Brad Sutton

Time needed
1 hour

Skill level
Intermediate

On the CD
Start landscape

o you have a landscape that you like? One that looks really good, but you have a niggling feeling that it could be improved somehow? Well, adding people to your scene can be a nice way to improve it. The viewer can also relate to the painting more by picturing themselves within the landscape. Many famous painters have used people in their landscapes throughout time. L.S. Lowry used a large accumulation of people in his industrial settings and if you look, the people seem to be alive and moving throughout the scene. Fragonard's paintings are intimate and give the viewer the sense of tranquillity. Bouguereau's paintings of people in a landscape are life-like. With his *Shepherdess*, you can feel how hard the ground is on her bare feet and there's a sense of weight to her.

Look at art that has both landscape and people; see what choices the artist is making. Which aspect is more important, the figure or the landscape? Deciding how much of the landscape you want to show will depend on how big or small your figures will be. The landscape can also be a character in your painting. It can have its own narrative characteristics – is it a scary forest or a peaceful meadow? The choices you make will help to determine how you want your people to interact with your landscape. So take your painting and increase its sense of believability by making the subjects live in your landscape.

Lively additions
Take your landscape to new heights

Mix up the colours

For an easy way to figure out the colours of the trees in the background, make a mark in the sky with the colour of the trees in the foreground. Select the colour that is at the end of that mark, then Undo the mark. This is a quick and easy way to mix colours. It is also used with traditional mediums – you mix a little of the tree colour with the sky to make the colour for background elements.

01 Start your painting Start with your established painting (ours is on the disc). Try to use the same medium that you used on your landscape for the people. We used Acrylics for the landscape and kept it quite painterly. Look at your painting and start to visualise what might be going on and who encompasses this area.

02 Select your drawing tool Now start with the Acrylics Dry brush and use a low opacity (like 25%). Make a couple of marks to decide what level of opacity works for you. Using a low opacity will help build up the colour intensity.

03 Add a layer You may or may not like using layers in Painter. If you work traditionally then that's fine, but we'd suggest adding another layer so you can draw out where you desire the people to be. And more layers if you feel safer working that way. Adding a layer can be found in the Layers box at the bottom, or going to the Property bar>Layers>New Layer.

04 Start sketching out figures Now start to sketch out your figures. This should be done on the new layer that you created on the last step. Have fun with this, keeping everything loose. Keep in mind distance, and what the subjects are doing in your landscape.

05 Watch size ratio Watch your size ratio. We like the size of the person under the tree on the right. But the person in the background on the left is a giant! Using the tree level is a good way to determine how tall to make your subjects as they recede into the background. Watch the relation of the figures and the edge of the canvas.

Use a few handy tricks

We decided that a hill would be nice in the far background to add more depth, but we had already painted the sky and trees in. Using Digital Watercolor, paint the hill in over the trees and hills, then move the colour to pure white and erase the colour that is over important elements that you do not want to cover. This is a simple (and useful) trick that can be implemented on other aspects of your paintings.

06 Think about composition Now, take a step back and look at what you've drawn. Does it flow? Do the figures help move your eye? Consider these things when drawing. We added the kite to help in the triangular composition. We also want the landscape to stand out more.

07 Move things Move things around if you do not like where you have drawn them. Use your Rectangle selector, outline what you want moved and then use the Layer Adjuster to move it. We moved the kite down a little and moved the people under the tree to the other side. On this side of the tree the people create a better silhouette.

Building up the scene
Liven things with colour and expression

08 **Clean up and drop** Now that you are satisfied with where the people are, start to clean up the lines that you've drawn. We used the Gentle Bleach at 25%. We like the way this eraser works, it almost has a kneaded eraser feel. Next, drop the sketched layer (Property bar>Layers>Drop). Or you can go to the Layers window on your screen, click on the stack of papers, then drop.

09 **Start painting** Working on the Canvas layer, start to paint the figures in – adding more detail to the figures in the foreground. We used Acrylics Captured Bristle, Dry brush and Digital Watercolor. With the two main figures and the kite we used shades of red to reconfirm the triangular composition.

10 **Add shadows and highlights** In this step you'll want to use the Digital Watercolor New Simple Water. The Digital Watercolor will help to add dimension and unify your shadows. Remember to dry Digital Watercolor. Go back to your acrylics to add highlights (an opaque medium will be needed).

11 **Create more details** Add more details to the figures. You will also want to work back and forth with the figures and the landscape to make it look natural. We thought the kite was too dark, so we used Airbrush Fine Tip Soft Air. Select the colour of the sky next to it, or even a shade a little lighter. Now gently brush over it to make it fall back in space.

The best brushes | Brushes that will help your painting

ACRYLICS – CAPTURED BRISTLE
The acrylic brushes are very useful and add a nice texture to your painting. The Captured Bristle is a great brush to use. Used at a low opacity, the paint is applied and can be built up in layers.

DIGITAL WATERCOLOR – NEW SIMPLE WATER
Possibly the best thing ever invented – Digital Watercolor is a beneficial tool for starting a painting. You can block in the painting and change elements quickly with this brush. This brush will help to change moods and tones, add depth and help to add volume. It works well with all media.

12 **Finish it up** In your final steps add more details that take your fancy, and start to finalise the piece. We added another figure to the lone one in the background, to help distinguish between shrubs or rocks. The figures in the background are left over from step eight (they were a part of the original sketch, and kept really loose with nothing added to them). It really enhances the landscape to wonder about what they might be doing.

BLENDERS – SMEAR
Blender brushes are good for getting rid of hard edges. The Smear brush creates a soft, almost pastel look to the painting. A lot of the other blenders are great for adding texture to a piece too. We use this brush for the sky – it helps to create a more realistic, organic sky instead of the dreaded gradient which makes things look artificial.

ERASERS – GENTLE BLEACH
The Gentle Bleach brush is a nice eraser for allowing the soft touch of a kneaded eraser. It will allow you to pull the desired amount of medium off. We usually use this brush when sketching, as it allows us to erase the exact amount that we want to erase.

Create a Japanese woodprint

Use the principles of an ancient technique to turn your Corel Painter canvas into a tool for making woodprints

Tutorial info

Artist
Charlene Chua

Time needed
Two hours

Skill level
Intermediate

On the CD
ukiyo-sketch.jpg, woodcut.grd

rintmaking enjoys a long history with culture and civilisation. In Japan, the art of printmaking is most apparent in its famous woodblock prints, also know as Ukiyo (or Ukiyo-e). Japanese woodblock prints typically feature expert craftsmanship, apparent from the fine, intricate line work and masterful application of colour. The art form began in the 17th Century, and by the 18th Century it had become a discipline involving highly specialised artists and artisans.

Traditionally, the art form required a team of experts. The artist created a sketch on thin paper, which was glued to a carving block, whereupon the carver meticulously stripped away portions of the cherry wood, creating the black key block. Separate blocks were then carved, one for each additional colour. Colour was applied by the printer and then dampened, handmade paper was laid onto the blocks. Printing was done by hand with a baren (a flat, disc-like burnishing tool), under the supervision of the artist.

The themes found in Ukiyo artwork, although rather broad, are also fairly consistent. Popular themes include Japanese landscapes, animals and plants. Depictions of beautiful women (often courtesans) and kabuki actors were also hugely popular, to the extent that they were subject to censorship approvals for possible violations of good conduct. However, the most controversial were the highly explicit shunga, or erotic prints.

For this tutorial, we will tackle something a lot less controversial, yet no less interesting. The artwork we'll be creating is adapted from a piece by one of the most famous woodblock artists, Utagawa Hiroshige. Hiroshige is remembered for his landscape compositions, where he usually weaves together rural backdrops with buildings and people from everyday life. We will show you what brushes to use to re-create the fine black outlines of the artwork, and explore how to apply some interesting texture effects to make your artwork look closer to a real print.

Brush marks

All the black outlines in a traditional woodblock print reside on the key block. The non-printing areas were carved away. Despite this, master carvers were able to produce hair-thin lines by skilful cutting. In Corel Painter, lines and line effects can be replicated with these brushes:

Calligraphy brush   **Scratchboard tool**   **Leaky Pen**

Scratchboard Rake   **Croquil Pen**   **Soft Pastel Pencil**

Hard Charcoal Pencil   **Sharp Charcoal Pencil**   **Tapered Conte**

Colour swatches

Colour in woodblock prints was applied by preparing a separate carved block for every colour. The arduous process meant most prints usually had no more than two or three colours. Gradients were archived by inking a block, then wiping off some of the paint to produce a toning effect. Originally, most of these colours were bright and vivid. Many old prints appear desaturated due to the fading of their colours over the years. The aging of the paper also gives old prints a yellowish tint.

COLOUR PALETTE
The chart here demonstrates some common colours in Ukiyo prints. The swatches at the bottom suggest how the colour might look in an aged print; the swatches at the top suggest how the colour may have originally looked.

Let's begin
Arm yourself with the files from the CD and get stuck in!

01 Getting started Many Japanese woodcut prints feature traditional scenes from Japanese culture. You can easily create your own composition by referencing popular themes on the internet, like Japanese castles, cherry blossoms and, of course, Mount Fuji. We decided to borrow from a piece by Hiroshige, with the addition of the castle on the left.

02 Importing artwork Create a new file and choose a light tan for the paper colour. Hit File>Place and locate 'ukiyo-sketch.jpg' on the CD. Enter a suitable number in the Scaling boxes to scale the file appropriately. In the Layers palette, change Composite Method to Gel. Select Pastel>Soft Pastel Pencil 3 as your brush of choice.

03 Drawing the border Set the brush size to 21.5 and choose Straight Line strokes. Use the Colors palette to choose a dark brown for your main colour. Create a new layer above your sketch called 'Border'. Next, use the brush to draw a rectangular border around your artwork. Now select Freehand Strokes in top menu, and draw in the rounded corners of the border.

The floating world for sale

Japanese woodblock prints are commonly referred to as Ukiyo-e, literally 'pictures of the floating world'. Many pieces by woodcut masters survive in varying conditions. The best are reserved as museum treasures, but many other reproductions of lower quality can still be found for a reasonable amount at speciality dealers. Some dealerships can be found online:

Ukiyo-e Gallery (www. ukiyoe-gallery.com)

Stuart Jackson Gallery (http://jacksonarts. com)

Degener Japanese Fine prints (www.degener.com)

Japanese Gallery (www. japanesegallery. co.uk)

Japan Print Gallery (www. japaneseprints.net)

(Galleries frequently deal with 'Shunga' erotic woodblock prints, which are meant for adults only.)

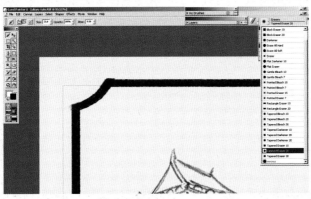

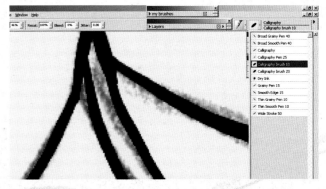

04 Touching up the border Select the Eraser>Tapered Eraser 20 brush. Use this to erase away the unwanted corner edges. Tidy up any protruding strokes. You can lock the border layer by clicking the lock icon in the Layers palette to prevent further changes. Create a new layer and name it 'Outline'. Move this new layer above the sketch but under the border layer.

05 Drawing in the outline Set the Outline layer's composite method to Gel and select your brush via Calligraphy>Calligraphy Brush 10. You can choose another shade of dark brown or grey for some subtle variety. Next, carefully outline the castle and the hills in the background. Use the Size slider in the top Property bar to vary the size of your brushstroke for effect.

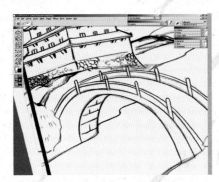

06 Drawing the bridge Reduce the size of your brush to about seven or eight and draw in the curved arches on the bridge. Tilting the canvas may help facilitate the natural curve of your arm – hit E or use the Rotate Page tool. Draw in the pegs in the bridge, and use an Eraser to tidy up flyaway and intersecting lines.

07 Trees To draw the trees on the right, use the same brush but try using more angular strokes to simulate the shape of the tree trunk. Since this picture was intended to be a winter landscape, avoid drawing in an outline for the crowns of the trees. The negative space treatment will help give the trees a softer look.

08 Leaves and grass Master carvers were able to carve out the extremely fine details that are the hallmark of Ukiyo prints. You can simulate some of this artistry by using different brushes to complete the finer details of the outline. Choose the brush Pens>Scratchboard Tool to draw in the grass and leaves in the bushes near the bridge with short, sharp strokes.

09 Stone texture
Switch over to Pens>Leaky Pen. Use this brush to paint in the stone texture on the castle walls and the bridge, varying the pressure with your tablet. You can use the Pens>Croquil Pen to draw in the fine stem on the lower bush, and the Pens>Scratchboard Rake brush to create some additional texture on the tree trunks.

10 Make some snow
Create a new layer named 'White' and move it between the sketch and the Outline layer. Select the brush from Gouache>Broad Cover Brush 40. Use this to paint in patches of snow on the castle, bridge and background. Also, paint in the outlines for the trees and bushes. Lastly, paint in the thin strip of forest in the far background.

Tutorial | Create a Japanese woodprint

Signatures and seals

Traditional Japanese woodcut prints were not signed. Instead, they were embossed with several seals. These were carved letters or logos that indicated various bits of information, including, among other things, the artist, the title, the publisher and on some prints, the censor. At the turn of the 19th Century in Japan, in an effort to control public sentiments, books and prints were subject to approval from authorities before they could be sold. In the later half of the century, publishers were required to include their names and addresses as well, which they usually inscribed on the side of a print.

Bringing it to life
Insert some colour and texture to the image

12 Adding Texture
Hit Effects>Surface Control>Dye Concentration. Select Paper from the Using drop-down. This will apply the Retro Fabric paper texture to the Light Blue layer. You can make the paper texture or less apparent by adjusting the Minimum and Maximum sliders in the Dye Concentration pop-up window. When you are done, hit OK.

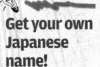

11 Light Blue
Create a new layer, name it 'Light Blue' and move it below the White layer. Select a light, dull blue for your Main colour. With the Gouache brush from before, paint in the bridge, background and small mounds in the foreground. When you're done, use the Paper Selector in your Toolbox to choose the Retro Fabric swatch.

Get your own Japanese name!

Here's how we made our own 'seals' for the artwork. First, we went to this very cool website, www.japanese-name-translation.com, and converted the names 'Charlene Chua' and 'John Smith' into Japanese characters. We then wrote them down with a brush pen (you can get these at art stores, or you can use Painter's Calligraphy or Sumi-e brushes as an alternative), and scanned in the calligraphy. After importing them into Painter, we changed their mode to Gel and created a red rectangle on a new layer below behind the words. We grouped the two together and reduced their Layer opacities slightly.

13 Creating more texture
Right/Ctrl-click on the Light Blue layer and choose Select Layer Transparency. Create a new layer, change its composite method to Gel and position it above the Light Blue layer. Select the Lasso tool and set it to Subtract from Selection. Use this to deselect the blue mounds in the foreground. Set your Additional colour to white.

14 Apply a gradient
Select the Paint Bucket tool and choose Fill: Gradient. In the Gradients palette (Cmd/Ctrl+8), select Two-Point from the drop-down menu, and set the gradient type to Circular. Click within the selection boundaries to apply the fill. Select the Artists' Rough Paper swatch from the Paper Selector, and apply the Dye Concentration effect as before.

15 Colouring the castle
Create a new layer called Light Grey for the castle. Paint the castle a dull blue-grey with the Gouache brush, then apply the Dye Concentration effect (change your paper swatch back to Retro Fabric). Create another layer above this and call it 'Dark Grey', and repeat the process to create the darker portions of the castle's roof and stone walls.

Finishing touches

Gradients are the order of the day for completing your masterpiece

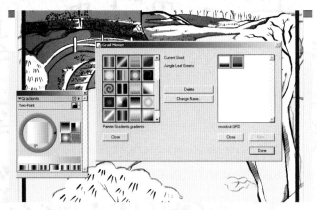

16 **Foreground gradient** Create a new layer and move it below the Light Blue one. Name it 'Foreground'. Select the Lasso tool and set it to Add to Selection. Carefully select the area in the foreground between the bridge and the trees. Open up the Gradients palette and select Gradient Mover from the top-right menu.

17 **Loading and applying custom gradients** In the pop-up window, hit Open and search for 'woodcut.grd' on the CD. Click on the three swatches and drag them to the left pane, then click Done. Select the new swatch called Ukiyo Ground, and have its angle set to 90 degrees. Use the Paint Bucket (Fill: Gradient) to fill in the gradient, then apply the Dye Concentration effect. If you haven't got Painter X, you will need to create your gradients from scratch, using these screenshots as reference for how they should look.

Importing paper textures

Scanned papers are a great way to quickly add an air of realism to digital artwork. Because many of these prints are one or two hundred years old, they tend to have a slightly yellow tone from age. To simulate this, you can scan or download paper textures and then use the Edit>Place command to import them into your artwork. You can then use the Free Transform command to scale the paper to the right size. Check out the following sites for some free paper textures:

www.imageafter. com (search Textures>Fabrics)

http://veredgf. fredfarm.com/ textura/index.html

www.texturearchive. com (search Paper)

www.texturextras. com/ (click Free Texture Paper)

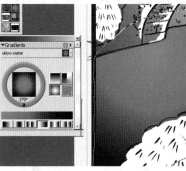

18 **Adding the sky** Choose Select>None. Create a new layer below Foreground and name it 'Sky'. Select the sky area with the Rectangular Marquee tool, choose the Ukiyo Sky swatch from the Gradients palette, use the Paint Bucket tool to fill in the gradient, then apply the Dye Concentration effect. Hit Select>None.

19 **Adding the water** Delete the protruding corners with an Eraser. Create a new layer called 'Water; and move it below Sky. Use the Lasso tool to select the water under the bridge on the left. Select the Ukiyo Water swatch from the Gradients palette. Use the Paint Bucket tool to fill in the gradient. Hit Select>None.

20 **Completing the water** Use the Lasso tool to select the water area on the other side of the bridge. Use the Paint Bucket tool to fill this in with the Ukiyo Water gradient. Hit Select>None, then apply the Dye Concentration effect to the layer. Hide the original sketch by clicking the eye icon in the Layers palette.

21 **Falling snow** Create a new layer called 'Snow'. Move it below the Border layer. Select the Gouache>Fine Bristle 10 brush, white for your Main colour, then paint in the falling snow against the dark sky. Use the Size slider in the Property bar to vary the size of the snowflakes. Avoid painting in the upper-right section though.

22 **Final touches** Select your Canvas layer, and hit Select>All. With the Paint Bucket tool set to Current Color, change your canvas to white. Import in a paper texture (see far left) and resize it to fill the entire canvas. Make your paper the topmost layer and set it to Gel. Add a couple of personalised signature seals in red boxes to complete your artwork!

RODRIGO DIAZ

TITLE | Mara Hernandez
WEBSITE | www.mouseypapel.cl
JOB TITLE | Illustrator

Chilean illustrator Rodrigo Diaz often mixes contemporary subject matter with a 17 Century twist in his commercial work, adding period costume, hair styles and makeup to his portraits. Here however he has painted a more traditional image of South American politician Mara Hernandez – although he's still made use of his signature antique elements in the background.

eShop
Visit the *Official Corel Pain...*
online shop at
www.imagineshop.c...
for back issues
and subscriptions

Visit us online at **www.paintermagazine.com**
reate your own art gallery for **FREE** • Meet other
rtists on the forum • **Subscribe and save money!**

Create with brushes

Painting from scratch might seem an impossible task but Painter's brushes can do most of the hard work. We take inspiration from Bob Ross to show how anyone can have a go

Tutorial info

Artist
Cat Bounds

Time needed
50 minutes

Skill level
Beginner

Though Bob Ross (29 Oct 1942 – 4 July 1995) might well have been the first to say his art would never hang in the Louvre, this gentle man in blue jeans, with the childlike sense of humour and fluffy afro, introduced legions of artists around the world to his wet-into-wet oil painting style. In more than 400 *Joy of Painting* television episodes, he still entrances even non-painters as he completes an entire painting in 28 minutes and entertains with his familiar musings about "friendly little trees" and "happy

accidents". He is best known for his landscapes and was influenced by the years he spent in Alaska.

Few painters have managed to equal the adept flick of his palette knife into a mixture of Phthalo Blue and Titanium White to create, as if by magic, a stream in the foreground or a mountain in the distance. And yet he never nagged us to paint according to rules, but transported us back to the innate creativity of childhood where, whatever we create from our imaginings, our art is wonderful because it is ours. Bob Ross

made painting accessible to everybody and made us all believe that we too, could paint!

In truth, the only way to make a Bob Ross painting is to use Bob Ross brushes, gessoes, knives, paints and canvases, and to study with a Bob Ross instructor. In this walk-through we are not going to attempt to copy his technique, but will instead draw inspiration from his imaginative, spontaneous style for our digital brushes and reveal how simple marks can suddenly blossom into recognisable forms.

First steps

Pick your colours and start blending them

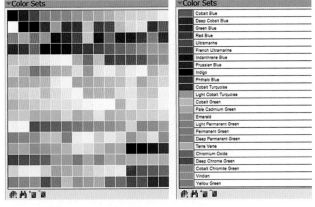

01 Choose a colour palette Load up the Artists' Oils Color Set and make sure that the Display Name option is enabled. This lets you pick out colours according to their familiar name (Colbolt Blue, etc). Decide on the colours you want to use and brush them onto the Mixer Pad. When you have them all, you can save it for future use.

02 Painting wet-into-wet Bob Ross painted 'wet-into-wet', meaning he didn't wait for the oils to dry before painting over them. A similar effect can be achieved by lowering the opacity here and there. Dab on blues for the sky, covering two thirds of the canvas. Use a dark and light blue and the Oils>Bristle Oils brush.

03 Blend until it's just right! We used the Just Add Water Blender brush set to a large size and 29% Opacity to soften the random brush strokes, being careful not to lose the variations in colour, hue and light. Use quick strokes, exactly as you would move a traditional brush in blending wet paint.

To texture or not to texture

That is the question...

If you're printing your painting on canvas, you may not want to add a texture in Corel Painter. However, if it's to be exhibited online or printed on a smooth surface, there are a number of ways to achieve canvas surface effects. We'll look at a few of these techniques.

01 **Apply Surface Texture...** When our painting was complete, we chose Coarse Cotton Canvas in the Papers palette, then went to Apply Surface Texture and played with the sliders. It's best to turn off Shine – and the rest is experimentation unique to each painting. After you've clicked OK, you can still Edit> Fade the effect.

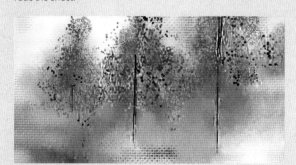

02 **Grainy texture effects** This technique works beautifully using brushes with 'Grainy' in their names. We selected Gessoed Canvas, applied it faintly to the canvas we were working on and made painterly strokes with a Grainy Hard Crayon. A traditional canvas will show deeper canvas texture in places where the paint is thinner.

03 **Texture with Impasto** Impasto Depth adds texture, interest and character to your brush strokes and to your oil painting, and most of the Painter brushes have a Color and Depth option under the Impasto tab. We chose a bristle brush here, and by varying the Depth percentage you will find the buttery oils are amazingly touchable.

From clouds to rivers
Begin creating your landscape

04 **Bring in some clouds and light** We can now splash on some pale yellow that will read as clouds and highlights against the sky. This step can result in some of those happy little accidents, because we haven't determined yet just how the landscape will be laid out – so think in organic, irregular shapes and enjoy spreading the light.

05 **Knowing when to stop can be the hardest part** We continued to blend with Just Add Water and decided to blend away most of the cloud features, but of course you may want to leave some fluffy edges and later add more shape and drama to them. The main thing here is to create interesting shapes rather than ending up with a monotone expanse of sky.

06 **A simple sketch** We don't recall Bob Ross ever making a preliminary sketch, but we've made a quick sketch on a separate layer so our illustrations will show up better. In traditional painting you would paint over it, but in digital art it's just as easy to delete when it has served its purpose, and we can ignore it whenever we decide to paint something different.

07 **Paint a mountain** You could begin painting the mountain shapes with almost any wide brush, including airbrushes, oils, acrylics and chalks. We chose to use the Thick Wet Camel 20 Oil Brush set to Color and Depth, varying the colours from terracotta to light pink. We like the realistic way this brush feathers at the end of a stroke.

08 **Maybe a few more mountains** We've ended up with three mountains in the distance. The dark one will mostly be lost behind the trees, but we'll know it's there! Remember to place warmer colours in front of cooler colours to indicate depth and distance. We're still painting under the sketch layer, not directly onto it.

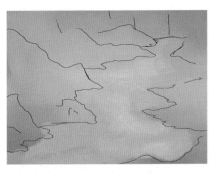

09 **A watercolour stream** In traditional painting you would never paint watercolours onto your oil canvas. That's part of the fun of painting digitally – we can combine all mediums, sometimes on separate layers, giving us even more freedom to explore the possibilities. We used the Broad Water brush to block in the pale blues for the stream.

10 **Friendly little trees** The Oils, Thick Wet Camel 20 brush set to 50% Opacity, and Impasto Depth set to Color works well for small areas like the tree trunks where we just want a base colour on which to build. You might want to use this versatile brush later in the painting, set to Color and Depth at 100% Opacity.

11 **Block in some grassy shapes** And again, back to the digital watercolour brush – this time for the grass. Most of this layer will be covered up, but we want some variation in the opacity, and this will even help us decide where to make shadows and highlights later. These decisions aren't big, but they must be made somewhere along the way.

Bob Ross colour palette

Bob Ross typically painted with a basic set of tube oil colours, including Cadmium Yellow, Sap Green, Phthalo Blue, Alizarin Crimson and Titanium White. Select these in the Artists' Oils Color Set and mix your own colour palette in the Mixer Pad, then save your new colour set. We digital artists can become spoilt by the range of colour possibilities at our fingertips. Starting with basic colours and mixing your own is a rewarding experience. We learned in kindergarten that mixing blue with yellow makes green. Now amaze yourself with your own colour expertise!

Light and shade
Add shadows, glints of light and some texture

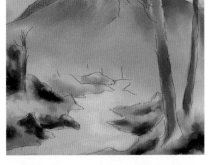

12 **Now for a few shadows** Using the same brush in a deeper green/charcoal, we'll now lay in a few shadows. It seems like magic, as you find shape and dimension in the foreground, and the whole painting begins to take on life and interest. Don't overdo it. We want more light than shadow.

13 **I can't draw a straight line** When you tell people you paint, chances are their reply is, "I can't draw a straight line". Well, even for those of us who paint, straight lines are a challenge, but Corel has thought of that too. Click the 'V' key, touch your brush to the canvas twice, and you'll get a perfectly straight line between two points. Click the 'B' key in order to turn off this function.

Learn more about the joy of painting

Bob Ross Workshop videos are still widely available. If you're interested in this gentle, intuitive style of painting, you may want to order a video and watch his process from beginning to end for yourself. Pay a visit to **www. dickblick.com/ vendors/bobross/ #videosanddvds.** (You can also order traditional painting supplies here.) You'll learn techniques that will translate into your digital painting – and who knows, you might even decide to add traditional oil painting to your talents. But you will have to deal with having paint under your fingernails and on every piece of clothing you own. Digital paint is far less messy!

14 **Some watery glints of light** For the glints we'll bring out one of the F-X brushes, appropriately named Glow. Set it to a small size, Color to White and Strength to about 6% – higher where you want brighter glints. You can also add more opaque strokes with the Thick Wet Camel brush.

15 **The beginnings of texture** Once you've laid down some random colours in the grassy area, choose the F-X Shattered brush to stir them up a bit. Leave it at 81% Strength but reduce its size to around 20. This gives some nice, unstructured texture to this area and others, such as tree trunks and rocks.

Mountain greenery home
Create foliage and rocky shapes

Happy little accidents

Bob Ross was fond of saying, "We don't make mistakes – we just have happy little accidents". Isn't that a beautiful philosophy for what we do? If we take anything from Bob's teachings, we should embrace this ideal. As digital artists, we're prone to reach for the Delete or Undo button too quickly. In your next painting, make a deal with yourself not to reject anything that happens on the canvas. So that brush stroke looks really strange? Leave it – and it may become your favourite part of the painting. In painting this way, what we do becomes art rather than a craft.

16 Sponge in some foliage Our favourite Sponge brush is the one called simply Sponges and left at the default settings, its texture is beautifully suited to blocking in foliage shapes in the distance. Vary the look by changing colours from dark to light as you paint in the shapes. This one is really fun. You'll find yourself dabbing all over the canvas.

17 Begin to define some rocky shapes Use the Chunky Oil Pastel 30 to lay streaks of whites, beiges and charcoal, and then, as we did in the grass, use the F-X Shattered brush to texture them. Vary the size of the brush as you go. Our mountain is taking on personality.

18 Shadows and highlights for crevasses Rather than painting with a loaded Palette Knife, it's best to paint in the rocky mountain colours with other brushes and then use the Smeary Palette Knife 10 set to Color and Depth at only 5%, to spread them and give them shape and dimension. The paints spread like soft butter.

19 A Fan brush for foliage Here's a Fan brush variant we created, beginning with the Smart Stroke brush, Chalk Textured: Size: 70, Opacity: 95%, Grain: 35, Jitter: 29, Spacing: 48, Impasto Color and Depth: 85%, Squeeze: 7%, Angle: 183, Color Expression: Direction. We also sprinkled in some Leaky Pen strokes for added texture.

20 Leaky Pen to the rescue again As you might guess, we like this brush, and when we wanted to add some more scattered and opaque texture to the distant trees, it fitted the bill. Vary the size of the drippy dots it brushes on and don't worry about anything but the overall shape of the trees. You can go back in and soften them a bit with the Sponge brush.

21 A brush for grasses And here's the Leaky Pen again, but we came up with another variant we like a lot. Set the Spacing to 4% and under the Angle tab set the Squeeze to 8% (for now), and play with the brush angle so that you can paint grass growing vertically and at angles. If you set Color Expression to Direction, you'll also get some interesting colour variations.

22 A brush for small branches This is the most interesting variant that we came up with for this painting, and it begins with the F-X Gradient Flat Brush 20. Warning: you'll enjoy this one so much your trees may become very branchy! Set it to Size: 4, Opacity: 100, Jitter: 20, and set Color Expression to Pressure. Vary Size and Pressure as you go.

A soft touch

Keep some areas of softness and add one or two finishing touches

23 **On the rocks** We need some outcroppings of rocks to balance out the softness of our grasses and water. Play with the Palette Knives to determine which ones give you the hard, sharp rock edges that work best for you, and if you create a variant that works well, don't forget to save it.

24 **Keep some softness** Bob Ross didn't fill in every nook and cranny with a tree or rock or mountain. Part of the beauty of his art was that there were also areas of softness where our own imaginations could play. If you've lost the softness, you can always go back in with Just Add Water and find it again.

25 **Finishing touches** Now it's time to step back and see what's missing. Maybe it needs a waterfall cascading down that mountain, some highlights on the tree trunks and foliage, or more splashes of colour in the grass. This painting is about experimentation and non-judgemental creativity. That's how Bob would've done it…

Know your brushes | Find out how we created our effects

Sponged foliage
These trees illustrate the lacy effect of the Sponge brush. It can be squeezed into different shapes using the sliders under Brush Controls>Angle tab. It's good for blocking in shapes of bushes and trees, and varying colours gives preliminary highlights and depth.

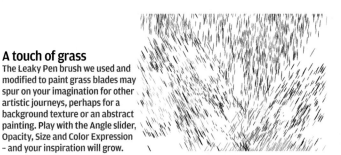

A touch of grass
The Leaky Pen brush we used and modified to paint grass blades may spur on your imagination for other artistic journeys, perhaps for a background texture or an abstract painting. Play with the Angle slider, Opacity, Size and Color Expression – and your inspiration will grow.

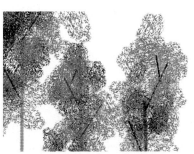

Painting with light
The F-X Glow brush is ideal for highlights. Play with the size and opacity to get awesome effects. With Color set to White, you get glowing highlights that are easy to use. Change to a vibrant colour, and it behaves like a soft airbrush that paints in neon.

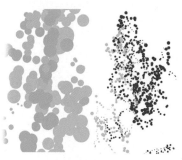

Splashes of creativity
The first time we tried the Leaky Pen brush we wondered how it could be useful, but it soon became a favourite. We like it because in its default setting it looks like paint dripping from a wet paint brush and adds a painterly look wherever we use it.

Fan brush effects
This is the variant we used to make some of the foliage. Traditional fan brushes have limited uses, but every painter has at least one. Ours is versatile – it can paint transparently or with Impasto Depth and change the Size/Squeeze setting etc, for any number of variants.

Watery mist
The Tiny Spattery airbrush lends a misty, watery appearance to rushing water, whether it's down a mountainside or tumbling over rocks. Many of the Brush Controls sliders are greyed out for this, but you can get some great effects via Feature, Flow, Spread and trying the tip shapes under the Size tab.

Tutorial info

Artist
Wen-Xi Chen

Time needed
3 hours

Skill level
Intermediate

On the CD
Start sketch

Watercolour landscapes

We get to grips with a style that's been popular for over 200 years

Watercolour painting is an art form that has been around for a very long time, but has often been viewed as a hobby medium. However, among the users of watercolours, there are a considerably large amount of famous artists including Van Dyke, Constable and Turner.

In England, watercolour painting got a popularity boost in the 18th Century because surveyors, map makers and engineers valued it for its usefulness in illustrating technical works. It also helped that the literati and aristocratic classes at the time saw it as a sign of a good education, so it was commonly taken up by women in their leisure time.

Although they were popular, watercolours still didn't quite hold the same esteem as oil paintings and were in fact largely used by artists to create the sketches that would then become oil paintings. It took the work of three English artists: Thomas Girtin, Paul Sandby and JMW Turner, to establish the medium as an independent fine art paint in its own right. They showed everyone that watercolour could be as refined and as powerful as any other paint, while having an unpredictable streak that made the results so exciting.

Some artists call watercolours an 'unforgiving' medium, due to the transparency of the paint. It really requires the artist to think about their painting and how to build up the colours; techniques like masking often need to be employed to achieve the right effects. Other artists call it a 'liberating' medium. The difficulty in controlling the paint is in itself one of the factors that draw people to watercolours – the loosening of inhibitions and letting the laws of physics run its course to create unexpected and beautiful pictures.

Begin your own watercolour landscape
Take the dive into digital watercolour

Make the commitment

Turn your Watercolor layer into a normal layer that can be modified using non-watercolor brushes. Right-click on the Watercolor layer and choose Commit. Now you can use all the different Digital Watercolor blenders to achieve cool diffusion effects and more!

01 **Sketch** The foundation of a painting is the sketch, and in a medium like watercolour where you can't cover up mistakes easily, it's important to get a sure footing at the start. Here we're focusing mostly on composition.

02 **Masking** Traditional watercolour artists use masking fluid to preserve the colour of a part of the painting. We're going to mask some of the painting by using the Liquid Ink tool to fill in the trees, bridge and some grass. Once you've done this you can make the mask layer invisible.

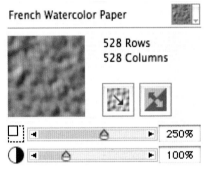

03 **Paper set up** Paper texture is crucial to a realistic watercolour look. Go to Windows>Library Palettes>Show Papers. In the Paper window, select French Watercolor Paper and set the Scale to 250%. This paper grain will appear every time you use a brush with a grain property.

04 **Sky** Create a new layer and select the Digital Watercolor category in the Brush Selector. Use the Flat Water Blender at 5% Opacity, 100% Grain, 10 Diffusion and 0 Wet Fringe to quickly wash in the blue for the sky. Notice that the paper grain has shown up.

Patch it up!

Paint will run with wet watercolour. This applies to both the normal and Watercolor layers. To prevent this type of interaction, dry the watercolour by bringing up the drop-down menu on the Layers window.

05 **Dry Digital Watercolor** Once the sky is looking decent, it's time to dry the watercolour. Select the sky layer and click on the little arrow at the top right of the Layer window. Click on Dry Digital Watercolor and viola! Your Digital Watercolors are now dry and fixed.

06 **Mountains** Create a new layer and fill in the land mass with the Broad Water Brush from the Digital Watercolors. Use a yellow. Now select Watercolors and the Soft Runny Wash. Using this tool will automatically create a new Watercolor layer with a little waterdrop icon. Angle the brush so that the mid point of the cursor is at the top of the mountain, and the cursor is tilted up, which will create a graded stroke.

07 Atmospheric perspective We continued to colour in the mountains with the Soft Runny Wash and the Wash Bristle. Due to the amount of atmosphere we have to look through to see objects in the distance, the mountains at the back are of a blue hue.

08 Dry Watercolor layer Painted something you particularly like and don't want any more wet on wet interference? Just like the Digital Watercolor, you can dry a Watercolor layer by selecting the Dry Watercolor Layer option from the menu in the Layers window.

09 Foreground Moving on from the mountains, switch back to the layer that has the yellow wash on it and use a variety of tools from the Digital Watercolor, including Round Water Blender and New Simple Water, and mix it all up with the New Simple Diffuser.

💡 ~~painter~~

Stroke designer

If you're not an artist, using the Straight Color can feel very intimidating as it is much harder than cloning. However, it is much easier than painting on a blank canvas, as you have the photo right there as a reference tool to guide you through the whole process. Remember to keep sampling the actual colour on your photo as you paint, including the subtle tones between the shadows and the highlights, as this will make your painting much more 'alive' and keep it from looking too flat. This takes practice, but it pays off !

10 Rocky ground On a Watercolor layer, use the Fine Bristle from the Watercolor brushes to add definition to the rocks on the ground. Just go over one of the sides for a sense of depth and shadow. Grass detail can be created conveniently with the Dry Camel brush. Play around with the tilt of your stylus for the best effects.

11 Shadows For the sake of realism, the trees need to have some nice long shadows. We chose a light source somewhere in the middle and on a new layer, used the Digital Watercolor brush (New Simple Water) to mark in the shadows. Remember that shadows are darker closer to the object, and lighter when further away due to light diffraction.

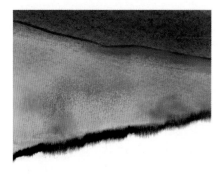

12 Take two Now for the other side of the stream. Very much the same principles as before really: make sure to keep the colours and lighting consistent. On the edge of the stream, paint a dark line on a Watercolor layer and then run a Runny Wet Bristle just above it. The colours will mix to a lovely mossy texture.

13 Masked Once you're satisfied with everything so far, it's time to bring up the invisible Mask layer again. Go to Select>Auto Select>Imagine Luminance. This will select all the black areas.

Phase two
Dealing with the masked areas

Pooling effect

To get the look of paint collecting at the edges of a brush stroke, select a Digital Watercolor brush and turn the Diffusion to 0 and Wet Fringe to 100% or similar. The fringes of the stroke should now look distinct enough to emulate the effect seen in traditional watercolours.

14 Fill in Create a new normal layer set to Default blending mode. Use the Fill Bucket or an opaque brush to fill in the mask selection with a warm yellow colour.

15 Tree bark With the selection still on, use the Round Water Blender from the Digital Watercolors to colour in the tree bark. For birch trees, the Broad Water brush, brushed from side to side, makes an effective birch look. Use the Splatter brushes along the lighter side of the tree to add a natural looking texture.

16 Leaves The Fine Palette Knife from the Watercolor brushes is great for painting leaf details, thanks to its flat shape. If you have a stylus with tilt sensitivity, be sure to experiment with using this for great effects.

17 Water Almost there! The water reflects the sky, and so should be about the same colour. We used the Flat Water Blender for the blue and Gentle Wet Eraser to create the pale highlights in the middle of the stream.

18 Reflection The New Simple Water brush with the New Simple Diffuser is a great combo for reflections. Reflections in the water include the banks of the stream, some of the trees and, of course, the bridge. We added some purple highlights to reflect the background.

19 Bridge The final flourish. We used primarily the Simple Water brush from the Digital Watercolors range. With some final adjustments here and there, we reckon we're finished with this painting.

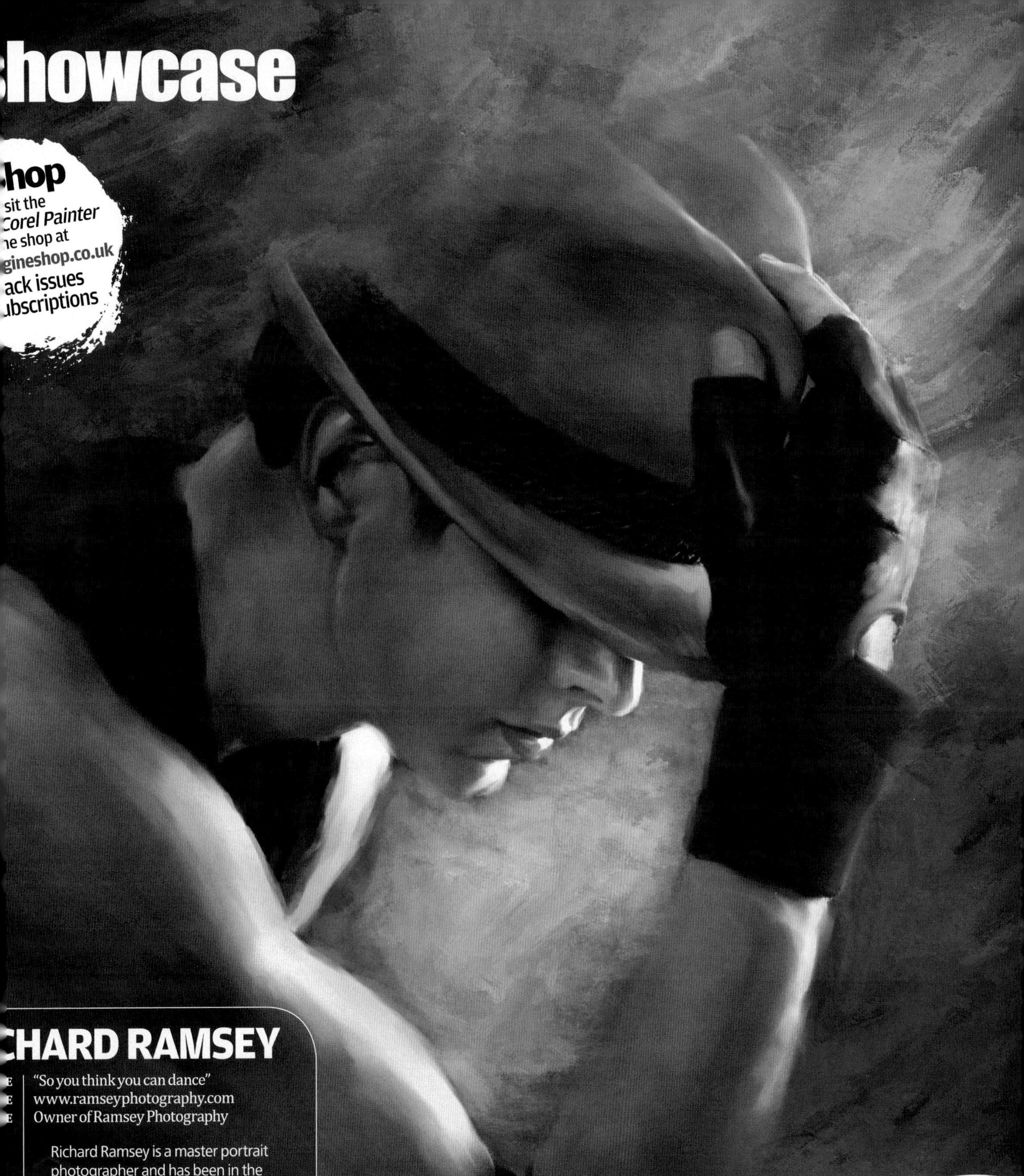

howcase

hop
sit the
Corel Painter
he shop at
gineshop.co.uk
ack issues
ubscriptions

CHARD RAMSEY

"So you think you can dance"
www.ramseyphotography.com
Owner of Ramsey Photography

Richard Ramsey is a master portrait
photographer and has been in the
industry for over 30 years. "I found
Corel Painter to be a vehicle to take my
portraits to a new and higher level," he
says of his unique paintings of people.

sit us online at www.paintermagazine.com

ate your own art gallery for FREE • Meet other
ts on the forum • Subscribe and save money!

Techniques covered

Dry media   pg 150-151

Use traditional pastel methods
Blend colours
Enhance an object's shape
Mimic the look of graphite
Re-create Conte effects

Wet media   pg 152-153

Build up layers of wash
Perfect watercolour surface
Achieve believable edges
Get a wet-in-wet effect
Make Salt effects

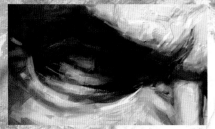

Thick media   pg 154-155

Create thick paint
Make tonal studies
Work with under-painting
Using Impasto brushes

Traditional art effects

Giving your digital artwork the feel of traditional media is a great way of improving the final product. **Jeff Johnson** shares some top tips for emulating traditional effects in Corel Painter

R eal art media is at the heart of Corel Painter and we all know that the brushes, papers and options are set up to mimic real materials as closely as possible in the computer age.

It is, quite simply, a digital art store nestled right on your hard drive for you to pick up and paint with anytime you like. And with features such as the RealBristle brushes in Painter X, and Painter Essentials 4, the ability to fool a viewer into thinking that a digital painting has been created with traditional media is higher than ever.

But there can always be improvements. Play around with the options and tools a bit more and you can start to add little touches that elevate your digital art into a whole

new arena. By calling upon traditional techniques, you can use your tools in a new way and get the very best from them, which is the whole point of this feature.

Over the next six pages, we are going to look at how you can manipulate the tools available to you to get the best results you've ever got. Divided into wet, dry and thick media, you will learn tricks such as mimicking wet-in-wet techniques, getting the look of thick oil paint, building up a graphite sheen and working with pastels.

You might be familiar with a few of the techniques already, but we're sure there'll be a couple of useful tips that will give your painting the final touch you've been looking for.

Happy painting!

Dry media

Painter has a perfect set of brushes which can be used to emulate pastels, so we will stay completely within the Pastel Brush Library for this little foray, save for a trip to the Blender Library to snag a Soft Blender Stump. Natural media pastels are gloriously easy to manipulate and Painter's pastels share this advantage. When handled using traditional methods like the ones employed here they look a great deal like the real thing, with little or no adjustment.

Stump the band | Just like real life

The basic approach here is no different than that you'd employ with actual pastels on paper. Basic forms are blocked in using middle tones and smoothed to taste with a stump. This process is repeated as you gradually work from midtones to the final lights and darks.

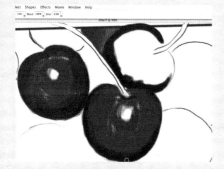

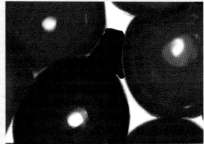

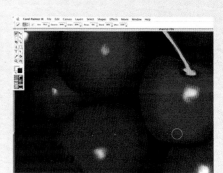

01 **A quick start** The border was drawn with a Soft Pastel brush using the Straight Line option. The cherries were sketched-in using a Sharp Pastel pencil. Then the Soft Pastel brush was used to begin blocking in values. It is best to pick values that don't extend too far past midtones in either direction.

02 **The darkening** Once the basic values are blocked in, switch over to the Round X-Soft Pastel brush (always use the largest brush possible in order to simplify rendering and make modelling easier). Work towards the darkest values with directional strokes that enhance the sense of volume of the shapes.

03 **Rounding things out** The canvas is set to Basic Paper. Grab the Soft Blender Stump, which is found in the Blender palette. Size it very large (about twice the size of your largest pastel brush for each area). Blend the strokes and values together, taking care not to over-blend and lose the nice gestural strokes you have been using.

Getting graphite to look right

Getting digitally created marks to look like graphite involves, among other things, having a firm grasp of the tonal range of the medium. Graphite is very slick and shiny, and there is a subtle sheen that lightens any marks, even those made by a very soft pencil. There are a few ways to emulate this. One is to use Painter's pencils and dial down the opacity, or work on a separate layer with its opacity adjusted. Another is to use a different tool altogether and select an appropriate range of greys. This drawing was done with a small Digital Airbrush using a slightly greenish grey, which we found best emulated graphite.

Conte brushes

One of the best ways to practise emulation is to try to re-create the style of artists whose technique you admire. Here we decided to emulate the look of one of those beautiful anatomy studies by Peter Paul Rubens. The picture was based on a photograph provided by professional model Ben Miller. Painter's Conte brushes are excellent to work with and handle much like the real thing, so the actual rendering was pretty straightforward.

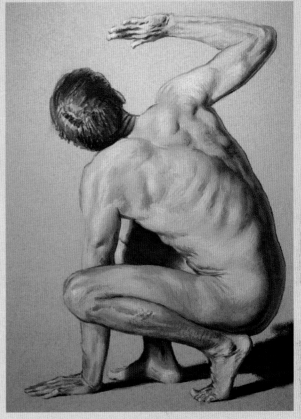

Rubens used toned paper, so start out with a medium-grey as the canvas colour. The Variable Spatter Airbrush loaded with the paper colour and used on a Gel layer set to 40% Opacity was applied to the canvas.

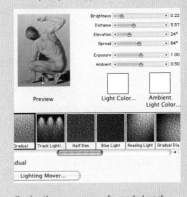

To give the appearance of a graded wash, open Apply Lighting via Effects>Surface Control. Using gradual lighting with the settings shown, apply the effect and adjust it a bit via Fade in the Edit pull-down menu.

04 More, more, more Working with the Round X-Soft Pastel brush, continue rounding out the form with strokes of varying thicknesses and direction. Start with short thick strokes across the form to model rich darks. Then you can switch to a smaller version of the same brush and break up the transition of values with some cross-hatching.

05 Smooth over everything Now for some final smoothing. Using the Soft Blender Stump, made very large, gently nudge things towards the kind of finish you desire. Some folks like things much more gestural than others, while others are oriented towards a smoother surface. Watch what you're doing and react to what looks right to you.

Getting texture and volume the easy way

Outside of eggs and a few other things, organic objects are never too uniform. Pastel, when applied in certain ways, can create a lively, varied surface without a lot of effort. One of the best ways to make your pastel works as energetic and realistic as their natural media cousins is to incorporate gestural strokes in every aspect of the rendering. The X-Soft Pastel brush stands out as being easiest to wield in this manner, delivering an experience startlingly similar to the highest quality pastels.

Wet media

Watercolour is an art form unto itself with an overall look that has a great deal of charm. To emulate good watercolour technique, paint should be applied with a large brush, and with an economy of strokes. Many of the attributes of the medium are built into Painter's Watercolor brushes and this is one instance where simply sticking within this brush set will make marks look satisfyingly like watercolour. The Digital Watercolor brushes are easier to use and more forgiving than their real counterparts, so they're a favourite.

Glazing | The perfect technique for a landscape

Glazing with watercolours works just like it does with oil paints. A very thin layer of pigment is applied over an area of dried paint to modify that area, either to change the colour temperature or darken the area. This is a perfect technique for a landscape, as you simply start with the background and work towards the foreground elements with a series of glazes.

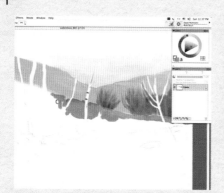

01 First things first After making a light preliminary sketch to help set up the composition and clarify some of the major details, the background can be loosely painted in with washes. The Digital Wash brush is perfect for the job and can be varied in size as needed.

02 Middle ground The middle ground can be painted on a Darken layer, which makes rendering a snap. One of the toughest things to handle with watercolour is overlap, as the additive nature of the medium makes a noticeable line, and the two colours once combined get darker, making basic rendering an indirect and patience-testing effort!

03 To the fore The foreground can also be painted on a Darken layer. Darker objects tend to come forth, so this whole process is one of moving from light to dark. The dark scrub trees were painted on a Gel layer. Things like the birch trees can be handled either by painting over them and erasing with a wet Digital Watercolor eraser, or by painting up to them. Both methods were used here.

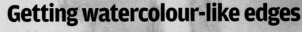

Painted textures

Watercolour can be one of the most effective mediums in evoking a sense of the many facets of light we associate with landscape work. Ways to achieve this can involve interacting with paper texture and by various brushes and techniques to vary surfaces and add life to otherwise flat passages. Let's look at a couple of useful tools: Salt and Airbrush, which are especially good at creating convincing effects.

Salty

Salt has a lovely effect on watercolour and can add great variety to surfaces with just a few light strokes. Here it has been used to diffuse the edges of the values in the sky during the initial stages of the painting. It was also used near the end to add reflective facets to the water.

From Atomizer to Airbrush Painters used to use Atomizers to flick the tips of their brushes, to apply specks of paint to their watercolours. Now many painters use Airbrushes. In Painter, one of the best to work with is the Variable Spatter Airbrush, as its effect gives a very nice emulation of the real deal and can be scaled to fit. Here some nice textures were added to the water by painting on a Gel layer.

Getting watercolour-like edges

Edges are everything in watercolour and to get something to look like the real thing you have to study the edge-work of a variety of watercolourists' styles. The beauty of the medium is also the bane of many a practitioner, as there is little room for error. Digital emulation is a lot more forgiving and you only need to use a few simple techniques, paired with a good choice of brushes, to get the wide variety of edges found in the genre's most representative works.

01 Using the Lasso tool If a watercolourist wants a sharp edge, they have the choice of applying a masking agent to one side, or both in turn. Here the Lasso tool was used to select the horizon line and foreground. Once one side of the edge is painted, invert the selection and work on the other side.

02 Wet-on-wet Getting Digital Watercolor brush strokes to appear to mix lightly with one another, and to mimic the classic wet-on-wet technique, involves some blending. The tree line was painted using a Soft Broad brush, and softened with the Soft Round blender. Use the Wash brush for the background foliage.

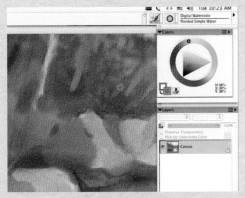

04 Smaller and smaller Now the details can be added. Stay within the Digital Watercolor palette and choose brushes like the Pointed Simple Water, and choose the Pointed Wet eraser to modify passages and to add details. Keep those authentic-looking simple strokes going, even as things get really small. Zoom in a bit and increase the length of your stroke for better control and smoothness.

05 Period of adjustment A watercolour is rarely perfect after the first pass and digital emulation is no different, just easier to fix. 'Digital purist' sounds like an oxymoron, but so as long as the final product has an authentic look, the means are up to the artist. In this case a little contrast was added to the whole painting and an Airbrush on a Gel layer deepened the values of a few passages in the woods.

Paper texture

It is often easier to apply paper texture to a work after the rendering is done. Here is an easy method for doing that, which provides maximum control. Select your preferred texture as a base paper. For this image, Italian Watercolor paper is a good choice. Copy the image and Paste it onto itself. With the bottom layer active, add the Watercolor paper texture via Effects>Surface Control>Apply Surface Texture. Simply dial back the opacity of the upper layer a bit to let as much of the paper texture show through as you like.

Thick media

Thick wet oil paint conjures up images of expressive, directly painted work. Brushstrokes and paint manipulation become partners in helping to express motion, form and energy. Direct painting is perhaps one of the hardest ways to use an otherwise forgiving medium and artists help themselves by solid planning. Getting the colours and values right while trying to manage brushwork is a tough balancing act. So here is a technique that effectively separates those elements and makes each aspect of the process much easier to control.

Easy street | Express yourself through your brushes

Here is a way to make expressive brushwork with thick paint easy to do. And fun! It involves building up paint in layers and leaves you a great deal of flexibility at every turn. Perhaps the most important thing this approach adds to the effect is that it allows you to build up the image rather quickly, with a great deal of control throughout the entire process.

01 Value first A common way to separate out the values and hues of a painting is to complete a monochromatic value study. Try to get a strong, simple rendering that reflects the scope and thrust of the piece you are planning. Don't worry about finer details at the moment.

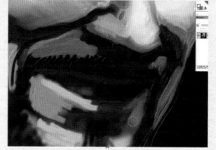

02 Paint by numbers Pick a palette of several values and map them in appropriate spots, sort of like paint-by-numbers, using the greyscale values of the drawing as a guide. Here we have used a low contrast, greenish hue to act as an under-painting of sorts that will enhance the range of skin tones. Stay loose and make sure your brush strokes enhance form.

03 Layers of texture and hue Now that the basic values are mapped in, it is time for another go-around, this time bringing the colours closer to the desired range. This next foray will mix imperfectly with the under-painting, creating nice variations in hue. Also, another pass with the various Impasto brushes will add dimensionality and surface detail that can't be achieved any other way.

Oops, too thick (or too thin)...

Okay, so you got a little sloppy and glooped on a bit too much paint. Or maybe you dug a deep hole that needs filling. The Impasto palette has the perfect tool at your disposal to help you either take a bit of excess depth away, or even fill in a divot. There is also a nifty way to easily raise the overall depth of the painted surface.

01 Too much Things have got a bit out of hand around that eye, with sloppy brushwork starting to really get in the way. Simply grab the Depth Equalizer and run it gently over the troubled areas. Vary the pressure applied and the opacity of the brush, for maximum control.

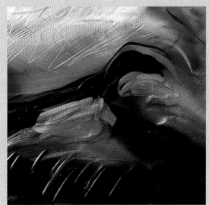

02 Double up All the brushwork looks okay, but might seem a bit flat. An easy way to preserve your brushstrokes and enhance their dimensionality is to copy the image onto itself. You will notice that the depth is now doubled. A bit too thick? Just dial back the opacity of the upper layer a bit, or do a little work with the Depth Eraser.

Add molehills to mountains

Okay, so everything seems to be hanging together. But the longer you look at the image the more it seems just a few things could be done to really make it work better. Some of those things you would like to deal with are independent of the Surface Texture, so you need to get a bit tricky. Here we have a couple of easy solutions to common painting problems.

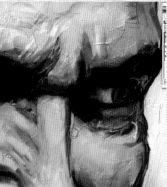

01 Simply darker If a detail or passage is too light, a little colour applied on a Gel layer will do the trick. As it's on a separate layer, making corrections is easy. Here we have opened a Gel layer at 50% Opacity and added a thin glaze of dark grey paint to the right side of his face and underneath his nose.

02 Changing hues Sometimes the values and details are fine, but a few of the colours aren't quite where they need to be. A Hue layer is an excellent tool to use to adjust colours in a painting, leaving brushwork undisturbed. Here we experimented by adding red to the skin around his eye, and some green for the eye.

04 Zoom in Go ahead and start working in the delicious little details, but keep things expressive. Simply use smaller versions of the brushes used up to this point to ensure continuity of brushwork and style. Note how varied the surface is close-up. Liberal use was made of the Palette Knife as a blender and texturizer. It is a tilt-sensitive brush that is easy to wield with minimal practice, leaving very authentic-looking marks.

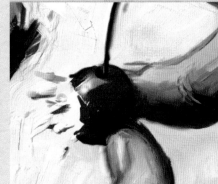

05 Pulling it all together The last adjustments to the image don't need the Impasto brushes. The Tinting brushes work very well for adjusting smaller areas, and many of them will even pull a little canvas back. Here the Tinting Oily Round 35, loaded with a slightly darker value than the background is used around the hand, to give the appearance of the canvas showing through.

Bottoms up

One of the most interesting and counter-intuitive things you can do to gain control over brushwork is to copy the canvas onto itself, reduce the opacity of the upper layer to 80% and make your adjustments with Impasto brushes on the bottom layer. The textures produced by the brushwork pop up through to the next layer (imagine you got the image perfect and would like to improve the brushwork in a passage, without disturbing the image with hard to handle thick paint). Due to the reduced opacity of the upper layer, the paint applied to the lower layer effectively mixes into the upper layer, acting very much like a glaze or scumble.

Bottoms layer   *Top layer*

Paint like: **Edgar Degas**

Famous for his images of the Paris ballet scene, Degas was an Impressionist with a difference. Learn which tools to use in order to create a Degas-inspired masterpiece

Tutorial info

Artist
Hannah Gal

Time needed
4 hours

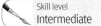

Skill level
Intermediate

On the CD
Start sketch and final file

For more on Degas' life and works, visit www. expo-degas.com

Dance Class

D egas was born in 1834 in Paris, France, to an aristocratic family and started painting very early in life. His well-to-do family was supportive of his talent; his banker father did expect the young Edgar to go to law school, but when this path proved fruitless, his chosen career in art was nurtured.

Degas studied art in France and travelled to Italy where he lived for three years, mastering the works of the classics including Raphael and Titian. His hard work and passion for Renaissance art created a highly accomplished and skilled painter, who continued to evolve throughout his career.

Although part of the Impressionist movement, Degas employed a somewhat different approach and style. He favoured drawing with more control and less of the spontaneity that typified Impressionism. He painted a great deal from sketches and notes made 'at the scene', as well as from memory – unlike some Impressionists who preferred an immediate transfer of their impression of light to canvas.

Like fellow Impressionists, Degas had an interest in modern city life with its dance halls, cabarets, racetracks, opera and, of course, ballet stages. Racing track and ballet dance life provided the disciplined movement that fascinated him. He recorded the gestures, nuances, ambience and atmosphere of the ballet scene, producing art pieces that have fascinated the world ever since. It is worth noting, however, that this versatile artist also studied the everyday life of milliners, dressmakers and laundresses. He did so with great passion, to produce immaculate paintings that are distinctively different from the pastels of later life.

Degas' technique is both unique and highly accessible. It is the result of a 'photographic eye' and experimentation with unusual art methods and materials. Among other techniques, Degas would mix pastels with liquid fixative to make a colourful paste and transfer the excess of pigment from one drawing onto a clear sheet to make an inverse proof of the original.

When etching, he inked the unetched plate and drew with a brush in this layer of ink, then he removed all the ink in places to obtain strong contrasts of light and dark. The multitude of experiments gave birth to richness of surface effects and a great variety in style.

Degas often combined pastels and oil in a single work but the mid-1870s saw him

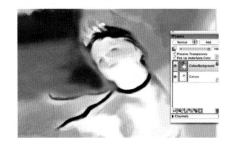

We imitated Degas by using pencil and charcoal, using the Smudge variant of the Blend brushes on the latter

working increasingly in pastel, eventually abandoning oil completely in favour of pastel for which he is best known. Pastels gave the work qualities of lightness, which complemented the subject of dancers perfectly. He handled this delicate medium with confidence and created a body of work that includes some of the most famous art pieces ever created.

We will create *The Star* using a mixture of oils and pastels. Like Degas, we will start with a drawing, move to oil paint and pastels, and explore variants including the Square Pastel and Smooth Pastel.

The pastels are used with a chosen textured paper. Unlike the original, our ballerina is placed on a white background. For colour reference, we will create a colour background on a separate layer that can be turned on and off when needed.

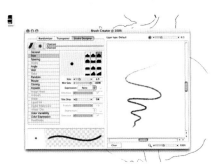

Our ballerina is placed on a striking white background, which affects our judgement of colour. In a separate layer, we created a colour background which can be turned on for reference

Degas often mixed oil paint with pastels. Over our layers of oil paint, we applied pastels to add a quality of lightness. Soft Oil Pastels give a smooth feel, where the Square Hard Pastel brings texture and grain

Outlines and layers
You'll feel the benefit of the layers later on

Brush to blend

Painting with pastels involves blending layers and areas with one another. You can use any of the Blenders brushes for this purpose. Alternatively, turn any brush with Resaturation (Resat) option into a blender. Once you select your brush and variant, go to the Options bar (Property bar) and simply drag the Resat slider to 0.

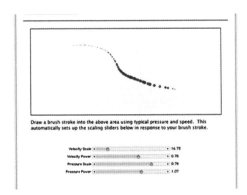

01 Brush Tracking The sensitivity of the stylus is crucial to the making of this piece. Open a new image and set the background colour to white. Before you apply paint to paper, set Brush Tracking by going to Corel Painter>Preferences>Brush Tracking. Try several strokes before deciding, considering the pressure and speed of your application.

02 Paper At the bottom of the toolbox, click open the Papers menu. Out of the list of surfaces, choose Thick Handmade Paper. This surface can be changed at any point of painting so if you find it is not to your liking, reopen this list and choose another. Alternatively, from the Papers palette choose Launch Palette and adjust paper settings.

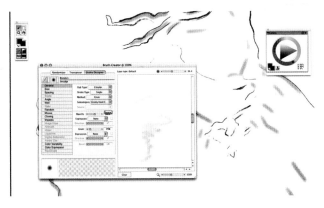

03 Drawing Degas often started work with a detailed drawing. Go to Window>Show Brush Creator and select Pencils>Thick and Thin variant. Draw the ballerina and select Charcoal>Soft Charcoal for thicker textured lines. To complete the drawing, choose Blenders>Smudge to soften some of the lines. Alternatively, load the sketch from the disc!

04 Layers This image is made of many layers. This might slow down progress considerably, but is essential for control at this stage. In the Layers palette create a separate layer each for the dress, face, skin, drawing, original for reference and colour background. A refinement layer is optional at this point, as this is the very last stage of the process.

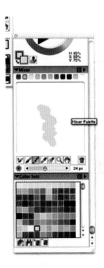

05 First oils As you work, be sure to have your Mixer palette and Color Sets open. Remember to select the right layer as you apply paint to different parts of the image. From Brush Selector or Brush Creator choose Artists' Oils>Bristle Brush and set Opacity to 6-8%. Choose Draw To Colour and Depth and set Depth to 10%. Start applying colour to the sketch.

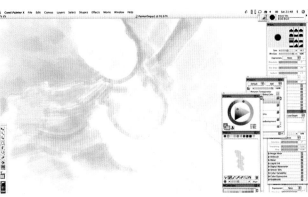

06 Darker shades Use the same brush to add detail to the ballerina. Increase Opacity and adjust brush size as you progress. Observe the original and use the Color palette or Mixer to create the desired shade. Alternatively, double-click on the foreground colour and move the slider slightly towards the dark end.

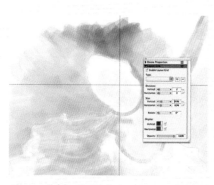

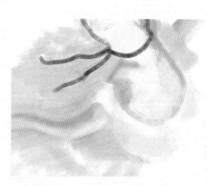

07 **Grids** The features on the face might prove a challenge due to the effect of perspective shortening. Use the grid to help you get proportions right. In the main menu choose Show Layout Grid>Enable Layout Grid. Set your vertical and horizontal lines across the face to guide you.

08 **Face** Once the main lines are in place, you can disable the Grid lines or reduce their Opacity. Use the Bristle Brush at a low 8% Opacity to apply first details to the face. Add more horizontal and vertical lines for further help if needed.

09 **Skin** Staying with the Bristle Brush, set Opacity to 20% and use the Mixer palette to create the right shade for the skin. Click on the Skin layer to select it and apply long strokes to arms and leg. Start with long strokes of the dark shade and use the Color palette to find a lighter shade. Repeat until you reach a near white shade.

Customise

Instead of reaching for the Brush Creator or Brush Selector each time, customise a palette to include all the brushes. Start a new palette by choosing Pastels from the Brush Selector bar. Choose a Pastel variant, drag the variant thumbnail from the Brush Selector bar and release it. You will see a new palette titled Custom appear. Enlarge it by grabbing the lower-right corner. You can now add variants to your palette by dragging a variant's icon onto the Custom palette. The icons on the palette can be moved around by pressing the Shift key and dragging the icon to a new position.

Colour and tone

Bringing the drawing to life

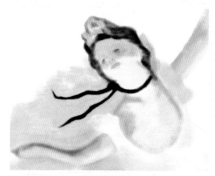

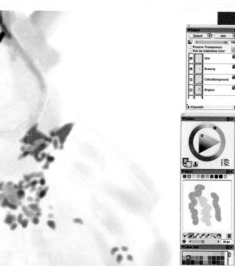

10 **Darker tone** Adjust brush size and Opacity value as you paint and continue to apply Bristle Brush strokes. If you feel confident, apply high opacity strokes. Otherwise, build layers up gradually. You can start with one end of the canvas and work your way using the Move tool to progress, or cover one layer at a time.

11 **Add in the flowers** The flowers add vibrancy to the dress. Their shape can be a little hard to see from reproductions. Use the Artists' Oils>Bristle Brush or Smooth Pastel within the Pastels category, to apply dabs of these spots of colour. We will refine their shape and tone later on.

Texture

We added texture to our complete painting by using Surface Texture. We also used texture while creating the image, within the Pastel brushes and the Papers palette. It is important not to mix too many different textures and scales within one painting. Try to use the same texture for a more natural look and feel.

Bear in mind that the paper you worked with while creating your piece would still be chosen in the Paper Selector, so at any point you can open it and see the settings used. Choose Paper from the Apply Surface Texture dialog box, and adjust settings to complement texture applied so far.

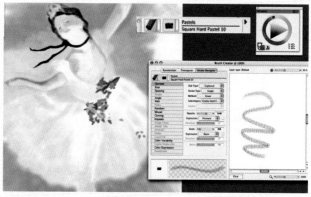

12 **Colour background** Earlier on we created a separate layer for a colour background. This layer, bearing the background colours similar to the original, serves as a guide for correct sense of the colours of the ballerina. Select this layer and apply paint strokes using the paint and brush used for the main figure.

13 **Pastels** Once we have our oil colour layers in place, we can start concentrating on the pastels. These give the piece a feeling of lightness and texture. Choose the Pastels brush and select the Square Hard Pastel variant, subcategory Grainy Hard Cover. Set Grain to 8% and Opacity to 50-55%.

Using pastels to add texture
Offset shade to bring the character to prominence

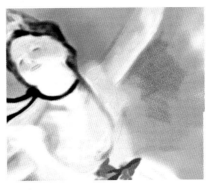

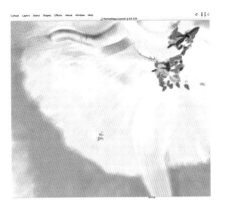

14 **Paper texture** The Pastel brush works with the paper selected earlier. Work at 100% zoom level and judge the texture. If you feel it is not grainy enough, go to the papers list within the toolbox and adjust paper choice or settings. Alternatively, use the Brush Creator's pad to test a stroke at different Grain levels.

15 **Darker shades** Apply the first layer of Pastels, sampling colour off existing colour as you progress. Increase opacity and apply a second layer using the Hard Square variant. You should see the textures of the paper mix with the oil you applied before.

16 **Oil Pastels** In the Oil Pastels category, choose the Soft Oil 20 variant. Choose Grainy Flat Cove and set the Expression to None. Go over the pastels already applied at a 20-30% Opacity.

The Degas effect | Make an 'impression' like Degas

Pastels>Tapered Pastel 10

Thin lines
In some reproductions the thin lines on the fabric is bright white, where in others it is a striking yellow. Pick what works best with your preferred tones. The thin lines are applied as short strokes from the waist down and outwards.

Blenders>Grainy Water

Hint of yellow
The light is facing the ballerina and is slightly yellow tinted. It falls dramatically on the skin of the face, arms and leg. To add a touch of drama and accentuate the highlight on the skin, we used a smoother brush. The hint of yellow would not be as effective on its own. It is meant to complement the white layer underneath.

Pastels>Square Hard Pastel

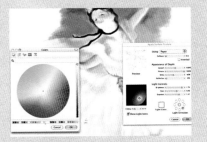

Square Hard Pastels covering Oil Pastels>Soft Oil

White lights
The dancer's raised head shows her neck and chest beautifully. The light is reflected from the light skin and calls for a bright, high-opacity, white colour. The top white layers of paint add drama and clearly show where the light is coming from.

Fabric effect
The light filters through the thin fabric of the dress. Layers of green, pastel peach and white paint have been applied to cover the dress with a Oil Bristle brush. The layer of white pastel paint is less opaque than the thin lines on the right. The stroke is wider and longer.

Lighting
To set the Light Controls according to the light falling on the image, choose Apply Surface Texture>Light Controls. Direct the light to face the dancer from her bottom left by clicking Apply Surface Texture>Light Direction. Control the colour of the light with Apply Surface Texture>Colours.

Oils and pastels
Bring out the richness of the image

Mixer palette

The Mixer palette is an essential tool. Take a few minutes to familiarise yourself with the tools at the bottom of the palette. Dirty Brush Mode, Apply Color, Mix Color, Sample Color, Sample Multiple Colors, Zoom, Pan and Clear are all incredibly useful. Some use it continuously while working, others only turn to it when the Color palette fails to provide the shade they need. Most handy are Apply Color which applies colour to the pad, Mix Color tool to mix the colours, followed by Sample Colour to sample exactly the right shade you were after.

17 Background oil

The background is made of heavy brush strokes that are loaded with paint. As this is only there for reference, apply colour loosely without paying too much attention to detail. It is the feel of the layer we are after. Use Artists' Oils>Bristle Brush at 35-40% Depth to apply paint.

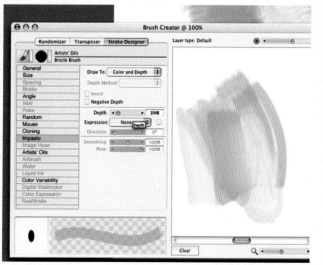

18 Colour background oils

In the Layers palette, select all layers besides the colour background. Click on the top-right triangle to open a menu and choose Drop to create two layers: Colour Background and Canvas. Choose Blenders from the Brush Selector and use the Grainy Water variant at 10-15% Opacity to smooth paint. Go over an area, repeatedly, with the same stroke for a smooth blend of colours.

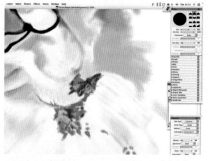

19 Adding layers of Hard Pastels

Go back to the Hard Pastels as in step 13 and apply another layer of this at 8-10% Opacity. Applying a single high-opacity layer will not achieve the multi tones that several low-opacity layers do. It lengthens the process but is essential to getting the airy feeling. Use light strokes and vary their length according to image details.

20 Detailing using Hard Pastels

Use the Hard Pastels brush at a low opacity to apply light strokes around the edges of the dress. These are short to medium length strokes that go from the outside in to hint at folds in the fabric and add fluffy feeling to the ends.

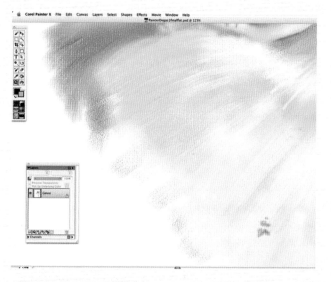

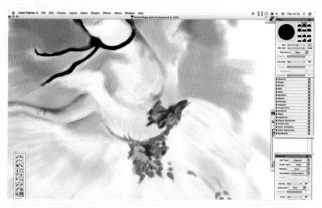

21 Darker Hard Pastels

Zoom in to 100% and create a new layer. This is the final Pastel layer and is meant to concentrate on variations in tone within areas of the image. This is time-consuming but creates the effect of richness. Examine the original to spot the many shades along and around her left arm for example, and apply.

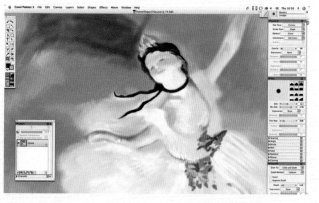

22 Blacks

When you feel the image is well covered, layered and is looking rich in tone, select black from the Color palette and spot the darkest points in the image. Apply dark black to these areas. If unsure, add a layer titled Blacks first. Alternatively, go to Preferences>Undo and increase the number of Undo levels.

Refining the image
Rounding it off with emphasis

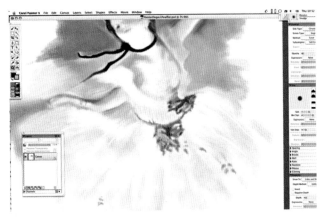

23 **Whites** The very top layer of Pastels on the dress is made of high-opacity white colour. These are short to medium strokes that go from the dancer's waist down the dress. Choose the Tapered Pastels variant at a high 90-100% Opacity and a small brush.

24 **Refine** Go over the image at 100% magnification level for refinement and add details to every part of the image. Darken blacks, whiten whites, add fabric folds where needed, add shadows or highlights and so on. Create a new layer for your refinements and drop it when done. From Pastels, choose Pastel Pencil 3 and use a dark shade to deepen shadows in places like waist, under and along right arm and so on.

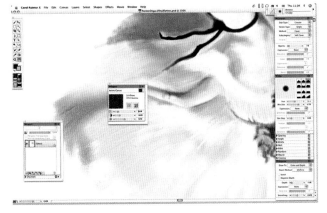

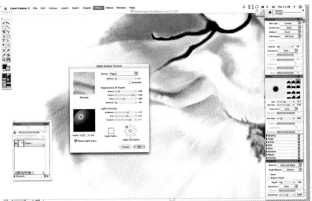

Soften and blend

Pastel paintings are made of many tones blended into another. The mix of colours and shades creates a rich palette.

You apply colour to several areas, and then blend these together for a softer overall look.

There are several ways to achieve the softening effect. You can use the Blender brushes with their multitude of variants, or any of the Oil Pastels variants. We used Blenders' Grainy Water here, working in the direction of the painting. Don't worry about over-smoothing an area as you can easily add texture to it later on.

25 **Canvas** In the toolbox, click on the Papers palette. Choose Artists' Canvas and launch the palette. Adjust settings to 224 Rows and 224 Columns. The texture of the canvas here is highly visible but it is a matter of personal preference how prominent you want this feature to be.

26 **Canvas – texture** Go to Effects>Surface Texture>Apply Surface Texture. Select Using Paper, Amount to 30-35% and Picture to 80-90%. We set Shine to 40% and Reflection to 0%. Apply and view at 100% zoom. Undo and adjust Canvas settings if needed.

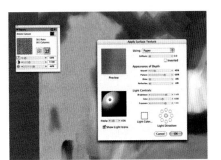

27 **Turn background layer on for a true Degas effect** The dancer's Canvas texture needs to be applied to the background. To match, open the paper texture and adjust the settings. Go to Apply Surface Texture, place the Preview window at the meeting point of the dancer and background layers and observe while adjusting settings.

28 **Fade and erase** Open the Fade dialog box. Observe the Preview box while adjusting the Fade amount to reach the level of effect you are after. Go to the tool box and choose the Erase tool. Use at low opacity to remove some detail around the dancer and reveal more of the texture of the background underneath her.

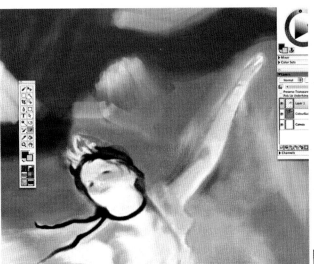

VICTOR LUNN-ROCKLIFFE

TITLE | Tree
WEBSITE | www.pbase.com/victorlunnroc/galleries
JOB TITLE | Retired

Despite using Painter for much of his artwork, Victor sketches every day and says "Everything that I have done has its roots in the knowledge I have gained from drawings in my sketchbooks and from life in the studio."

eShop
Visit the
Official Corel Painter
online shop at
www.imagineshop.co.uk
for back issues
and subscriptions

Visit us online at www.paintermagazine.com
Create your own art gallery for FREE • Meet other artists on the forum • Subscribe and save money!

Paint like: **Edvard Munch**

The Scream is an iconic image of modern life, referenced in highbrow and lowbrow culture alike. We reveal how to recreate this artistic epitome of human angst

Tutorial info

Artist
Hannah Gal

Time needed
3 hours

Skill level
Intermediate

On the CD
Sketch

E dvard Munch is Norway's most famous painter. He was a troubled, multi-talented artist whose dream was to create "art that gives something to humanity. Art that arrests and engages".

With *The Scream*, Munch managed to fulfil his dream to an extent even he would have dreamt was beyond reach. This iconic painting has become one of the most recognisable works of art ever created, with a passion that transcends time and geographic boundaries. To many, it is a truthful rendition of human angst, suffering and the human condition in general.

A particularly strong image, it lends itself clearly to a multitude of uses. From commercials and film, to children's TV, not many works of art can include *Beavis and Butt-Head* as well as Wes Craven's *Scream*, Looney Tunes and *Courage the Cowardly Dog* in their credit list.

Munch has created several colour versions of the piece using different media. He also produced a striking lithograph in an attempt to generate extra income.

The original title given to the picture by the artist is *The Scream of Nature*. The ominous name goes some way towards explaining the story behind its creation.

It is set in the scene of the erosion of Krakatoa and most possibly inspired by the powerful volcanic eruption there in 1883. The ash ejected from the volcano is

said to have created a red tint in the sky that was to last for months. "I sensed an infinite scream passing through nature," Munch has said.

Munch's troubled personal life was a source of inspiration. The paintings are disturbing, a touch twisted, unusual and telling. They are emotionally charged with a unique and unusual sense of colour.

The ability to transfer feelings to canvas with such great accuracy is perhaps Munch's greatest gift and the reason he remains a source of reference to contemporary artists.

Munch is considered to be a key influence on the Expressionist movement in Europe. This particular piece is part of the series *The Frieze of Life*, in which he delved deep into the human psyche with the themes of love, fear, death, life and melancholy.

The artist has attributed his preoccupation with these themes to a childhood laden with sadness. As a child, he experienced the loss of his mother and older sister to tuberculosis. Troubled adulthood followed with alcoholism and unhappy relationships.

1892 was an important year for Munch when the Berlin Artists' Association invited him to exhibit his work. The

paintings caused such an outrage, that the exhibition had to close. The entire episode, however, brought with it a wave of publicity, which benefited Munch's career and he chose to remain in the country. This is where he started work on the monumental *The Frieze of Life*, exhibited for the first time in 1902.

In 1894 Munch began printmaking, bringing the work to a greater audience. Motifs for this more 'marketable' art derived from his original paintings. In 1908, Munch suffered a nervous breakdown and a year later returned to Norway for what was to become an isolated and prolific life. He passed away in 1944 leaving behind 1,000 paintings, a staggering 15,400 prints, 4,500 drawings and watercolours, and six sculptures.

We will create *The Scream* using a combination of media including Acrylics, Oil Pastels and Colored Pencils. We start with a drawing and continue to create a lithographic effect using Charcoal. The application of paint is important in any work of art, but doubly so with *The Scream*. The piece is made of long strokes that would be best applied in one, without lifting the stylus. We will mix long, bristly strokes with gritty texture and use surface texture for a touch of 3D depth.

[BELOW]
Grainy texture
Instead of using a filter or texturiser for the texture in this painting, a highly textured brush is applied to add realism, as in the Grainy Hard Build-up from the Oil Pastels seen here

"This iconic painting has become one of the most recognisable works of art ever created"

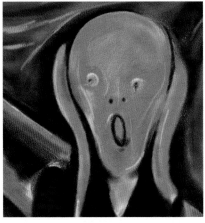

Multi-tone face
Besides drawing the features on the face correctly, we need to place shading and highlights in the right place

Direction
The stroke application varies throughout the piece. Different areas call for different length and pressure

Take a deep breath and begin

Follow this guide and you won't be screaming...

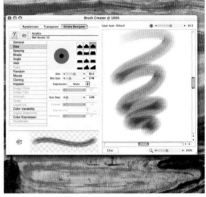

01 Layers Open a new image size and copy the provided 'scream' drawing as a separate layer. For reference, we kept a small copy of the original piece as a layer that could be turned on and off. A third layer seen here is of a Munch lithography, which we'll get on to.

02 Lithography effect To familiarise yourself with style, create a lithography. Go to Brush Creator>Choose Charcoal >Dull Charcoal Pencil 3. Make black your main colour and set Expression to None. With the Drawing layer visible and the Charcoal layer selected, cover the blank image with this solid black medium. Adjust the brush size according to your need. You don't have to do this, though.

03 Acrylics Select Acrylics from the Brush Creator. Real-life acrylic is fast-drying and can be diluted with water. It can tend to look like oil paint or watercolour, depending on the level of dilution. Now choose the Dry Brush 30 category.

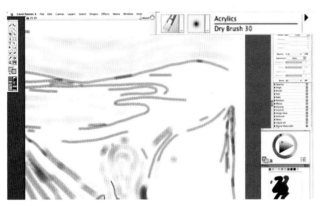

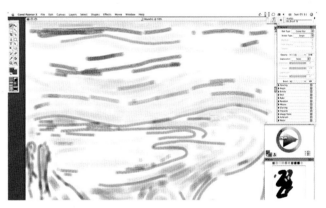

Museum and art history

The Munch museum was created as a tribute to Norway's famous artist. Besides information on the artist's troubled life, it takes an analytical look at his work. Go to **www.munch. museum.no** and delve deep into the life and work of a particularly prolific artist.

Under Life and Work is a section called Munch's Paintings. It looks at different paintings including *The Scream* in detail, speaking of the inspiration to the piece, when it was created and what its importance was in the greater scheme of the artist's life.

It also highlights influences on Munch's life that have inevitably had an impact on his work.

04 Application Create a new layer called 'Colour' and make it the top layer. Use the Color Mixer or Color palette to create the colours you need and apply strokes of black and light brown. The strokes are long and should look bristly and airy. Set the Opacity between 10 and 12% and set the Expression to None.

05 Build up Zoom in and apply brush strokes in the direction of the original. Make these strokes as long as possible and try to keep your stylus on the tablet from the start to the end of each stroke. Pay attention to changes in lightness and try to reflect that in your application from this early stage. This all contributes to a more sensitive and less rigid look.

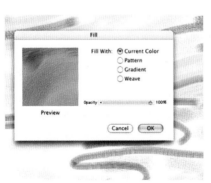

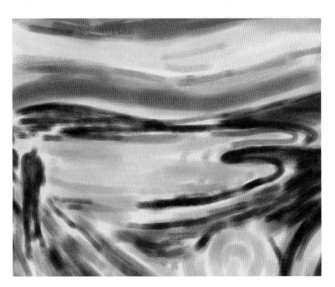

07 Build up close Keep the Acrylics brush at a maximum Opacity of 40%. Continue to slowly build paint. You could choose a prominent shade like orange, cover one area, and use the Grabber to move the next area to apply all strokes of that colour. Or you can concentrate on just one area. The colour builds on previous strokes beautifully.

06 Fill Create a new layer and open the Color palette. Sample a light brown/dark mustard colour. Click on the new blank layer and Select All. Go to Effects>Fill in the main menu and select Fill With Current Colour with the Opacity set to 100%. Place this layer beneath the Colour layer.

08 Drop
The basic strokes throughout the painting should be in place now. Before moving to a different media, zoom out and look out for any overly bare areas accidentally missed. Go to the Layers palette and choose Drop All. You should now have the Canvas bottom layer and Layer 1, which includes the colouring done so far.

09 Use an Oil Pastel
In the Brush Creator, choose Oil Pastels>Oil Pastel 30. This brush brings a totally different texture and is lighter to apply. Under Color Variability, pull the G slider to 20 and see the effect on the stroke in the brush preview below.

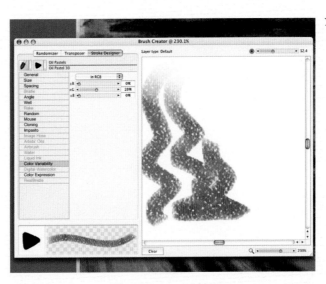

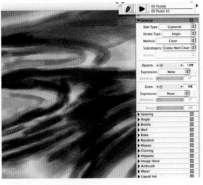

10 Blending oils
Create a new layer and name it 'Oil Pastels'. Set Method to Cover and Subcategory to Grainy Hard Cover. With a 10-12% Opacity and Expression set to None apply light strokes over the previous Acrylics. The two textures should blend together well.

11 Oil Pastel sky
The sky in *The Scream* is nothing short of amazing. It is made of a multitude of shades of orange, mixed with turquoise, cream and yellow. The strokes here need to go horizontally from one side of the canvas to the other. Sample a shade, apply your brushstrokes, sample the shade next to it, apply and move on.

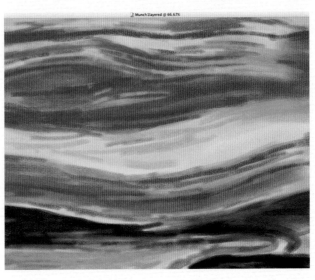

Fill in the person's details
Monster Munch anyone? (Sorry!)

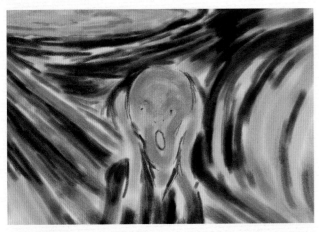

12 Face
Pay particular attention to the person's face. Note the different shades that make it. There is brown, beige, a hint of orange and green. Lightly apply colour to create the features. These are loose at this stage.

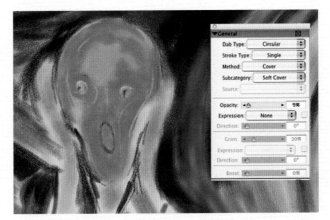

13 Face build up
Zoom in on the face and in the Brush Creator choose Airbrush>Soft Airbrush 40. Set the Method to Cover and the Subcategory to Soft Cover. Use this soft brush at an Opacity between 10-12% to fill in any light areas that have escaped the Acrylics and Pastels.

Color Variability
In real painting, colour is applied using brushes loaded with paint. This paint mixes with colours around it and you often get a single stroke made of two colours.

To mix colours this way, open Brush Creator, select Stroke Designer and choose Color Variability.

Now select in RGB and apply a stroke of your clean paint onto the pad. Drag the R slider to 50 and see the effect; then to 100 and see how the new colour blends in.

Try this with other colours and even two together. Apply your stroke and drag the magnification level at the bottom of the Brush Creator to 200% and see the stroke close-up.

Randomizer
Brush Creator's Randomizer was originally created for those unfamiliar with the brush's controls. It is, however, a useful tool regardless of level of expertise. The idea is simple, you give the Randomizer any stroke and it creates a selection of new variants for you.

Open Brush Creator and click on Randomizer. Fourteen variations of the strokes are available for you to choose from. Click on one and it will display in the preview window below. For a low level of variation, keep the Amount of Randomization slider to the left. Drag it to the far right to see it in full action.

14 Gaining texture from strokes
Increase the Opacity to 15-16% and vary Opacity to apply a layer of this tool all over. Reduce the brush size, sample your colour and apply some yellowy type streaks to the face and body.

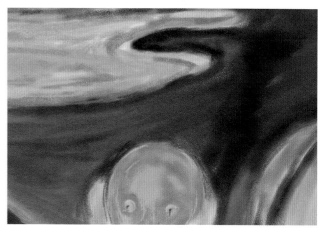

15 Area fill
The low opacity of the brush lets previous layers shine through and remain intact. The textures are working together. Use the Airbrush to cover areas such as the face and area above it.

Build up the textures and colours
Go for thick and luscious strokes

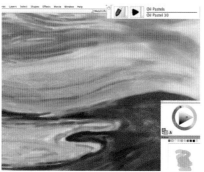

16 Grainy Hard Cover
In this part of the process, you skip from one brush to another as you see fit. Apply Airbrush to fill in an area nicely and move on to the Oil Pastels to add texture. Save your brush so you can come back to it instantly.

17 Rich in feel and tone
Build up the variety of shades slowly to create a rich feel. There is no strict method at this advanced stage. The image should by now be covered with a mixture of Airbrush and Oil Pastels. Zoom in, sample a shade you wish to enhance in order to echo the artist's original and apply both media.

18 Ground detail
The bridge is of pivotal importance to the composition. Its straight, angled lines add to the feeling of discord. It is best to apply these lines in one go, again keeping the stylus on the tablet from the start of the line to the finish. Apply colour in the same way as previous steps, filling in an area and enhancing with texture.

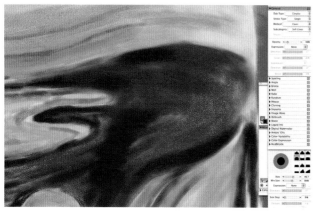

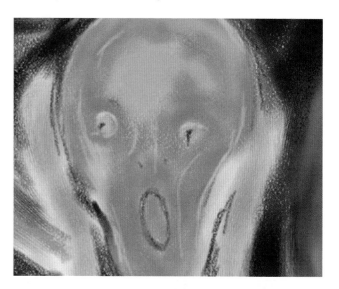

20 Airbrush detail
Set Airbrush to a small 4-6 size brush and a 5-7% Opacity. Observe the thin streaks that are spread throughout the image. Zoom in on the face, sample a light brown/yellow shade and lightly apply in short to medium strokes. Apply once and zoom out to see the effect before applying an additional stroke on top.

19 Airbrush
Use the Airbrush at 18-22% Opacity to start building the darkest blacks in the image. If you are not certain of the level, start at an even lower opacity or go to Preferences and increase the number of Undo levels. Alternatively, create a new layer and drop when it's finished.

21 Oil Pastels revisited Go back to Oil Pastels and methodically go over the entire image to apply texture to the painting. This is in preparation for the next stages where we add definition to elements.

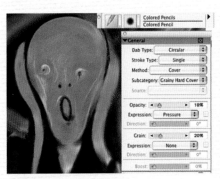

22 Pointed crayon Zoom in on the face, choose the top left brush tip in Brush Creator and set black as your main colour. Slowly go around the face to add a contour line to it. This border adds an edge and overall feeling of sharpness to the piece. It is of paramount importance on the face.

23 Colored Pencils Open Brush Creator and choose Colored Pencils>Colored Pencils. Set Method to Cover and Subcategory to Grainy Hard Cover. Use a Grain of 20% to lightly enhance existing browns on the face and add shades of light green. The textured strokes should be clear and not blended in.

Research

For a seriously deep look at Munch's technique, go to the Munch museum site (**www.munch. museum.no**). You can find out about what canvas Munch chose for a piece, and how it was primed and stretched prior to painting. There is an extreme close-up on details which will give you a great insight into his work.

Another eye-opening feature there is the look through a microscope at the artist's paintings. 'He used a limited palette, and concentrated mainly on relatively clear, bright pigments.' One paint sample interestingly shows 'various layers that contain organic reddish paint, and ultramarine, chalk and lead white paint'. In another real gold was found.

24 Blue streaks The thin streaks are vital to the piece. In step 20, we applied light brown/yellowy streaks to the face and here we apply blue/turquoise ones above it all over the dark lake. Use Colored Pencils this time at 40% Opacity and Expression set to Pressure. Grain should be 20-14% with light and quick strokes.

25 Blue strokes and streaks Zoom in to 100% and observe the streaks. They should be thin but full of gritty texture. Go over lines where there is a group of streaks together to enhance them. Take notice of those streaks to the side of the face as well. Some are slightly lighter than others, so choose a lighter shade to randomly cover some of the streaks existing there already.

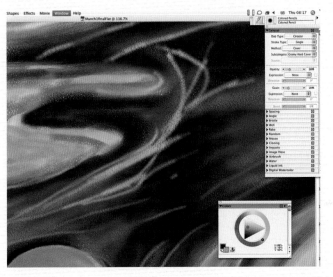

Adding the finishing touches
The bridge over troubled water...

26 Colored Pencils bridge Stay with Colored Pencils but use a 40% Opacity and a thick Pencil to add texture to the vertical lines on the bridge. Keep the stylus on the surface as you go over the area. The colour will build up.

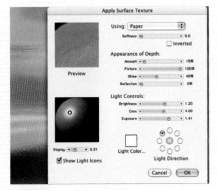

27 Apply Surface Texture Go to Effects>Surface Control>Apply Surface Texture. Set Using to Paper (Basic Paper) and the amount to 15%. This is a slight effect to add overall sharpness to the image and a slight touch of 3D realism.

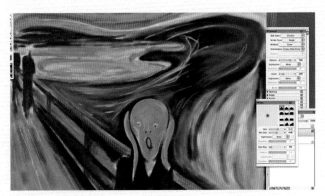

28 Refinement We earlier mentioned the option of creating temporary layers for different uses. Here we created one for general refinements where you zoom in to a 66% magnification level or higher, and make final corrections and adjustments. Start with one area and using a dark black pastel, accentuate the darkest areas in the piece. Use a light shade to highlight the brightest.

Sketch like
Leonardo da Vinci

Polish isn't everything when it comes to fine art! Here we explore how you can create an antique da Vinci sketch

For Leonardo da Vinci, like many other great artists, drawings and sketches were a vital component of both his progression as a great master of his art, and also to the planning and progression of his greatest works. These sketches, or cartoons as they were once known, could be either sketches made on the spot and spontaneously, as a kind of aide memoir or visual note-taking, or they could be a quick study to plan the tonal scheme and composition for a full-blown painting. Da Vinci was really not too concerned about the actual medium used for these sketches, and would often combine pen and ink work with shading, applied by using brown and black chalk and even touches of semi-opaque white paint to indicate highlights. Of course, these sketches looked far different when they were first created and the sketches we see now have been transformed simply by hundreds of years of wear and tear. So here we're going to re-create a da Vinci sketch, complete with all the signs of the ravages of time. To start with, we need to artificially age and abuse a piece of paper, and as you'll see, this is a fairly low-tech technique involving lots of cold tea, the odd blast from a hairdryer and even a few minutes under the grill! With the paper suitably abused, it's then scanned and forms the base of the digital sketch.

At this point, we can start sketching with a number of suitable inky and chalky variants on a suitable paper texture. This is an exercise where less is most definitely more, as we don't want this to look like a brand-new drawing. So turn back the clock and become Leonardo!

Get inventing!

Like the great man himself, get creative with what's around you

Tutorial info

Artist
Tim Shelbourne

Time needed
1-2 hours

Skill level
Intermediate

On the CD
Paper, sketch and final image

01 **More tea, Vicar?** Here's the fun bit! Take your sheet of paper and prepare to abuse it! Dunk a tea bag in warm water, then drip and dribble over the surface. The odd scrub with the tea bag works wonders too. Sprinkle a few grains of instant coffee to produce a little foxing.

02 **A good grilling!** Dry the paper off with a hairdryer, spreading the stains around as it dries. Now scrunch the paper up a little before shoving it under the grill for a minute or so. This will dry the paper out so that it will crack easily if you fold it, giving the whole thing a real antique feel.

Sketch in the outlines

No need to crack da Vinci's code – we've done it for you!

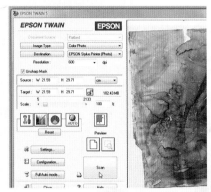

03 Scanning
Scan the paper in the normal way, as an RGB image. Scan the whole thing at a resolution of 300dpi so that you get plenty of detail. Open in Painter and you're good to go! If you don't fancy creating your own, you can use the supplied one on our disc.

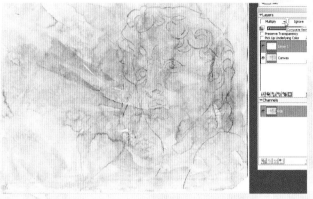

04 Paste the sketch
Open the paper file. Now open the 'Line Sketch.jpg' from the CD. Go to Select>All, followed by Edit>Copy. Close this file and return to the paper image. Go to Edit>Paste to paste the sketch on top. Now set the composite method for this layer to Multiply in the Layers palette.

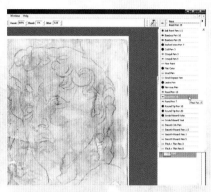

05 Pen variant
We'll start by creating a simple outline to establish a framework for the drawing. Choose Pens from the Category picker, and then select Reed Pen 15 as the variant. From the Color Wheel, choose a midtone red/brown.

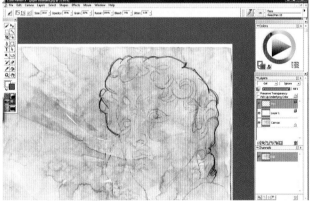

06 Start sketching
Click in the Paper Selector menu and choose Hot Press. Add a new layer to the drawing, naming it 'Pen'. Increase the size of the pen to around 20 pixels. Set the composite method to Gel and begin to roughly sketch over the underlying guidelines.

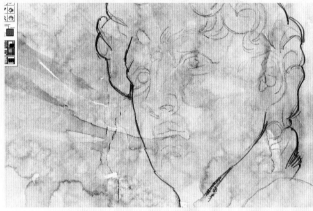

07 Loose outline
Keep this stage of the sketch nice and loose, just a mere indication of the detail we'll add later. Every now and then, it's a good idea to add a few small hatch lines here and there. This stops the outline looking too perfect and mechanical.

Shake it up!

Oddly, these sketches really do benefit from looking fast and spontaneous. Don't concern yourself with creating perfectly smooth curves and absolutely straight lines. Sometimes shaky, spidery lines and marks actually add to an image, and that's most definitely the case here!

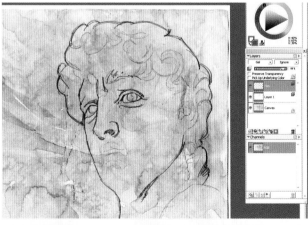

08 Fine lines
Reduce the size of the pen by a couple of pixels in areas of detail, such as the eyes and nose. In these areas, you can start to establish the dark shadow areas by using some more fine-hatching.

09 To taste
The penwork in the hair can be very loose, adding movement and vitality to the sketch. These areas need to be very simply indicated. It's a matter of personal taste how much penwork you add at this stage, but because this is all drawn on its own layer, any unwanted lines can always be erased later.

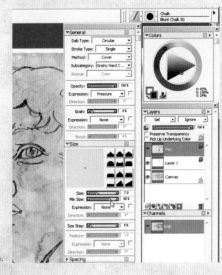

11 Chalk variant

Add a new layer to the image. Choose Chalk for the variant category and select Blunt Chalk 30 as the variant. Go to Window>Brush Controls>Show General. Set the Opacity Expression to Pressure and the Grain Expression to None. In the Size properties, set Minimum Size to 80%.

10 Hatching

In a few areas where there will be less detail in the finished sketch, reduce the size of the pen to ten pixels and use long, spontaneous hatching lines to indicate tone and shadow. We'll modify the Opacity value of this layer later, so don't be put off by the intensity of these drawn lines.

12 Establishing mid-tones

In the Property bar, set the Grain amount to 7%. Increase the size of the brush to around 40 pixels. On a new layer, start to establish the midtones in the image (a pinky-brown). Use a gentle scrubbing motion to establish the shadow areas around the eyes and within the eye sockets.

More or less... less is more!

Vary the size of your brush, ignoring precise details for now

13 Broken shading

Remember, to help with the antique feel, we need a nice broken surface to these areas of shading, so you need to use a hit-and-miss style of shading here, applying more chalk in some areas than in others. Don't attempt any detail at the moment – simply establish areas of tone.

14 Size for size

Adjust the size of the brush to suit the area you're shading, such as using the brush at a large size over the main planes of the face, and use it at a smaller size to add the shading to the eyes, nose and mouth.

Leonardo brushes

Get by with a little help from these friends

It's important to use suitable brush variants for this project. We need to combine fine, spidery pen lines with chalky shading and some smooth highlights. As well as using the correct variants, it's important to set up their properties properly, particularly when it comes to the Chalk variants as we need them to make the most of the chosen paper texture. Remember to set up your Brush Tracking before you start, so that the chosen variants respond properly as you draw. Do this via Edit>Preferences>Brush Tracking. Simply make a representative stroke on the scratch pad within the Brush Tracking dialog.

Pen
We used this variant for all of the penwork and spidery scribble. Opacity was set to 15% and Grain to 22%.

Blunt Chalk
This is the main shading brush, Blunt Chalk 30 from the Chalk variants. Grain was set to 7%. It's important to set the Expression Control to None in the Brush Properties.

Fine Soft Glazing
The Fine Soft Glazing variant from the Oils category was used for the subtle white highlights. Opacity was set to just 2% and Grain was set to 10%.

Sharp Chalk
The Sharp Chalk variant from the Chalk category was used for a little defining sharp-hatching in the final stages of the sketch. Set the Grain value to around 15%.

Scribbling, shading and sharpening up

Add scribbling and shading to form a con-Vinci-ng image

Stand back!

It's often tempting, especially when painting digitally, to continually work with your nose virtually pressed up against your screen. This really can be a mistake. Particularly so on a project such as this, where the whole is much greater than its component parts, it's vital to stand back from your screen regularly to get an impression of the entire sketch.

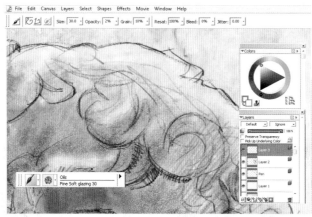

15 Hatch and scribble Reduce the size of the brush to around ten pixels. Now, using the brush at this size, add some areas of diagonal, loose hatching to the hair areas. Some loose, spidery lines in this area will also help with the sketchy feel of the piece. You can do this on a new layer if you like.

16 Highlights brush Add a new layer. Ensure that the composite mode for this layer is set to Default in the Layers palette. From the variant categories, choose Oils. Now choose the Fine Soft Glazing 30 variant. In the Properties bar, set the Opacity to 2% and Grain to 10%. Choose a near-white from the Color Wheel.

17 Subtle highlights Use this brush at around 30 pixels to add a few highlighted areas here and there. Use the finished image as a guide for this. These highlights need only be very subtle, so they appear to have faded over time. Also, add a few highlighted lines to the top outline of the hair.

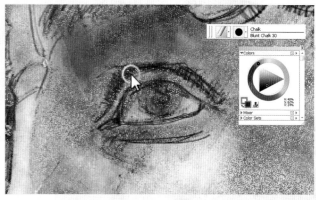

18 Darker shading Add another new layer. Choose a dark brown from the Color Wheel. Now return to the Blunt Chalk 30 variant you used earlier. Use this brush at around 20 pixels to begin adding some darker shadows around the eyes to define them a little. Use quite a tight, random sketching motion for these areas.

Don't fade away!

Obviously, over hundreds of years, light itself has a fading effect on drawings and this applies especially to inks. With this in mind, it's best not to leave your pen-line layer at 100% Opacity, but to reduce its Opacity towards the end of the project. Because of the colour we've used, and the Gel setting of the Pen layer, the lower opacity will adopt a pleasing, antique golden shade, with some overlapping lines being a little darker than the rest.

19 Broader shadows Use the brush at a bigger size (around 40 pixels) to add some broader areas of shadow tones, again using the finished image as a guide. Don't overdo these or make them too dark, as we still want to keep the antique, broken feel.

20 Sharpening up A change of variant now. Click in the Variant selector and choose the Sharp Chalk variant. In the Properties bar, set the Grain to 16%. Now, using the same dark brown colour, and the brush size set to 11 pixels, add some tight diagonal-hatching to the darker areas in the main features.

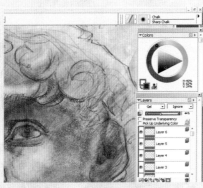

21 **Hatching a plot** It's also a good idea to use the Sharp Chalk variant to add some broader hatching to the areas which have little or no shading around the outer regions of the head and hair. Place these hatching lines close together, and make sure to draw with your wrist rather than your hand to give these lines vitality.

22 **An eye for detail** Now you're nearly done, you can use any of the previous tools and techniques to add subtle areas of shading to clarify the main features, and also include some subtle hatching around the outside of the head to add a little more interest.

23 **Careful adjustment** Remember, because we've placed each stage of the sketch on a separate layer, you can always adjust the intensity of each stage simply by playing with the layer's Opacity value in the Layers palette. Here, we've reduced the opacity of the midtone shading layer a touch for a more subtle effect.

Nearing completion
Finish the leftovers as if it was your Last Supper

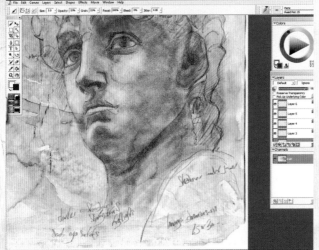

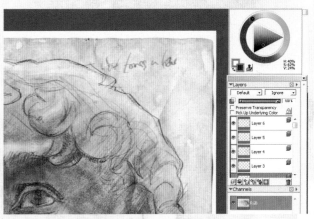

24 **Spidery scrawl** Just as the great man himself did, we're going to add some spidery notations to the finished sketch. Choose the Reed pen variant again and reduce it to a very small size. Add a new layer and zoom into the image.
Using the same brown colour, add some scribbled notes in a shaky, da Vinci–like hand.

25 **The da Vinci code** It helps, although the notes are barely readable, to make the notes relate to the sketch in some way, such as describing tones or colours. Make sure to place the notes in a random manner. When you're happy with your masterpiece, go to Layer>Drop All.

Can't draw, won't draw!

The advantage of creating this image digitally is the fact that you don't have to be able to draw, as you can easily trace your initial drawing from a digital photograph. Once you've opened the paper file in Painter, open the image you want to use for your sketch and go to Select>All, followed by Edit>Copy. Close this image, return to the paper image and go to Edit>Paste. This will paste your copied image as a reference layer above the paper background. Use the Layer Adjuster tool to position this layer and stretch it to fit by right-clicking and choosing Free Transform. Just drag on the handles around the image to resize it. Reduce the Opacity value of this layer. Now add a new layer and trace over the image with one of the Chalk variants. Once you're done tracing the outlines, simply delete the reference layer.

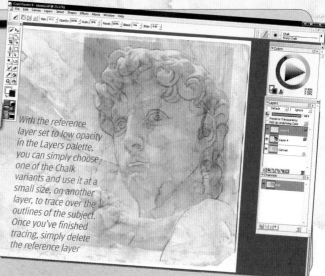

Don't panic if drawing isn't your strongest ability! Copy and paste your photograph onto a layer above the paper layer and reduce its Opacity to easily set up an image to trace from

With the reference layer set to low opacity in the Layers palette, you can simply choose one of the Chalk variants and use it at a small size, on another layer, to trace over the outlines of the subject. Once you've finished tracing, simply delete the reference layer

Paint like: **Tamara de Lempicka**

Tamara De Lempicka's sleek, high-society style is the epitome of the Art Deco movement.
Use Corel Painter's tools to replicate *Jeune Fille En Vert*

Tutorial info

Artist
Hannah Gal

Time needed
Eight hours

Skill level
Intermediate

On the CD
Line drawing and final art

De Lempicka's sleek paintings are a reflection of her lavish lifestyle. Born into a privileged, upper-class background, she was never a struggling artist. This one mingled with the jet-setting elite her entire life.

As a child, she attended boarding school in her native Poland, and spent time in Italy and the French Riviera. De Lempicka did not discover her artistic capability as a child or even in her youth. It was only after marriage and the birth of her daughter that she studied art in Paris, leading to immediate and long-lasting commercial success.

She showed her work in major galleries and sold art for considerable amounts of money, all the while climbing up the Parisian social ladder. She soon became a highly sought-after portraitist for royalty and socialites, who paid handsomely for her artistic interpretation.

Her subjects were of the circles she mingled in, and her work is therefore seen by many as a record of the upper classes of the day. As an artist, de Lempicka is best remembered for introducing a kind of cleanliness to the Cubist period, with bold shapes and great elegance. In doing so, she created a style like no other, with instantly recognised graphic features and simplistic form. This very particular elegance remained her trademark. She befriended the great artists of her time, and adopted a style that would hardly change throughout her career.

The artist's first major solo show took place in Milan in 1925, in the same year she painted the iconic Tamara in the

The look of the original's oil is created here with Acrylics. The medium comes with a selection of ready-to-use brush variants and a unique glazing effect to simulate real-life oil painting

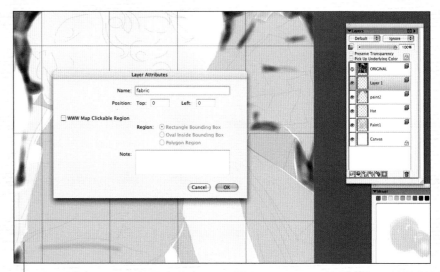
The image is made of many layers, hosting the different elements making the image. Fabric, Hair, Skin and others help maintain control over the painting process

"Her work is regarded as many as providing a record of the upper classes of the day"

Green Bugatti. In it, she is seen as the independent, free-living person that she was in real life. Even her own daughter failed to slow her socially vibrant life, and the little girl was raised in boarding schools and also by her grandmother. She has, however, managed to become the subject of some of de Lempicka's best-known pieces.

The year 1939 marked a move to the US, away from wartime Europe. There, de Lempicka continued her privileged life, moving to New York in 1943. Through these years, she secured her daughter's escape from Nazi Europe, and continued to be in demand.

The period leading up to her 1962 show saw her expanding her artistic horizons and venturing into new subjects, including abstracts and still life. The show was not well-received, and marked an end to de Lempicka's steady professional practice as an artist.

In the same year, which marked the death of her husband and an amazing three resulting round trips around the world, she settled in Texas where she

resided for a time with her now-married daughter's family.

Her travels didn't end there, and in 1978 she moved yet again, this time to Mexico. During this time she is said to have mingled yet again with the international upper-class players of her younger days.

Tamara de Lempicka sadly died in 1980, but has left behind a legacy of iconic and well-loved work.

The trademark de Lempicka sleek finish is time-consuming. It requires patience, a slow build-up of detail and a great number of brushstrokes

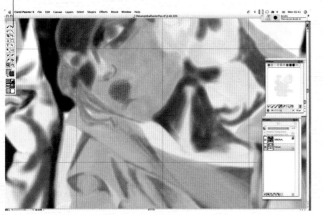

A smooth operation
Picka up-a your brush, and let's begin!

01 **Get ready** Open a new file, and set the size dimensions to 30cm high by 24cm wide. In the Layers palette, create a new layer. Name it 'Original' and place a reference copy of the original in it. This is an optional step, as you might instead prefer to occasionally glance at a separate image of the original.

02 **Drawing guide** Create a new layer and name it 'Drawing'. Copy and paste the provided de Lempicka pencil drawing from the CD. For its creation, we split the screen into sections, which remained useful throughout the painting process. In the main menu, go to Show Layout Grid>Enable Layout Grid. Then under Type, select 5 x 5 Grid.

03 **Drawing** Drawing the image helps to familiarise yourself with its characteristics, and is highly recommended. It is a relatively easy process, especially if you take advantage of the previously created guides. If you choose to draw this yourself, go to the Toolbox and choose Pencil>Thick and Thin Pencil.

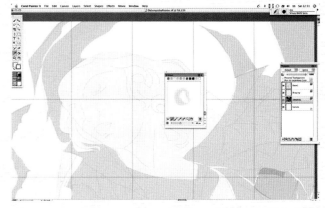

Airbrush

The sleek de Lempicka-look calls for a very smooth finish. The Airbrush is a superb smoothing tool with two main controls. Spread controls the amount of paint spreading out as it is applied and Flow controls the amount of paint actually applied. Be sure to use a minimum of 30-40 per cent. Use the Spread setting for maximum effect. The trick here is to cover the painting with a unifying stroke that creates the illusion of a smooth surface. Hold down Alt+Shift and you can reverse the spray direction as you paint.

04 **Block colour** In the Toolbox, choose the Lasso tool and create a selection around the area of the dress, and to the left of woman's face. Select an olive green as your colour. Go to Effects>Fill in the main menu and select Current Color. Set Opacity to 30-40 per cent. Now select the skin and fill with a peachy colour.

05 **Paint and Mixer** Repeat this process with other areas in the image until you have filled all the greens, browns, blacks and whites with colour. You should now have faint colour over your drawing. In the Layers palette, create a new layer and name it 'Paint'. Now open the Mixer palette.

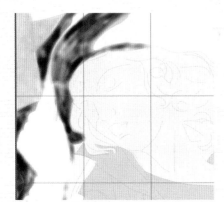

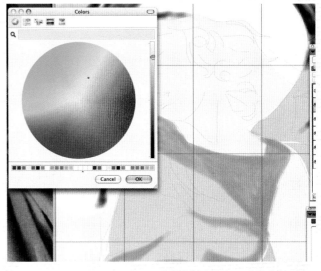

06 **Hat and paint** Go to the main menu and under Window, click on Show Selector Bar. Choose Oils and with a low Opacity, select the Smeary Bristle Spray. Now loosely cover the previously blocked areas.

07 **Fabric** Create a new layer and name it 'Fabric'. Open the Colors palette and try to match the green of the dress. Alternatively, sample the green colour off of the original. Observe the original to see how the fabric falls, and where curves and shadows are. Start to paint the shadows.

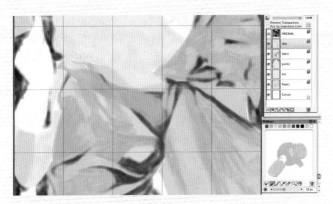

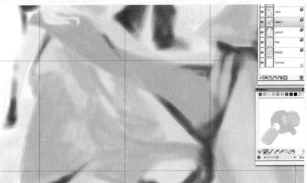

08 Skin Create a new layer for the skin and with the same brush, cover areas of the face and arms. Change the brush size as you progress and vary Opacity at this stage to between one and five per cent. Look at the original to observe where shaded areas are, and use the guides to place them accurately.

09 Acrylics We will build the colour up with the Thick Acrylic 10 brush. Stay in the Fabric layer and continue with the dress. Pick the highlight, midtone and shadow areas and follow the drawing lines to apply the colour. Use a careful and light stroke, keeping with low opacity and slowly building up the layers of colour.

Make Paper, not war...

We chose the Canvas paper texture from the Paper Selector in the Toolbox. You can also access it going to Window>Library Palettes>Show Papers. You can also see your original texture. To do that, on the Papers palette, choose Make Paper. Choose a pattern from the pop-up menu and adjust the Spacing slider. Once you keep the new texture, its name is added to the main Papers list and can now be accessed at any point.

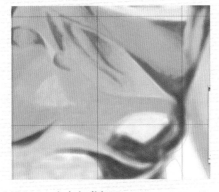

11 Skin and hat Stay with the Thick Acrylic Bristle 10 brush and select the Skin layer. Use sampled colour to apply paint to the skin using medium-to-long strokes. We will refine the transitions between shades at a later stage. Repeat this painting process for the woman's hat. Use a brush at low Opacity and build up colour gradually.

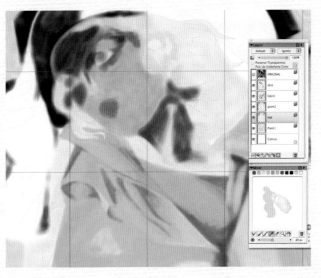

10 Fabric build-up Continue to apply colour to the dress. The strokes here are medium to long, and the Stylus Pressure is set to None. Work with one shade and cover areas with it, before moving to a lighter or darker shade and repeating the process.

Patience will pay dividends
There's no quick way to get the best results

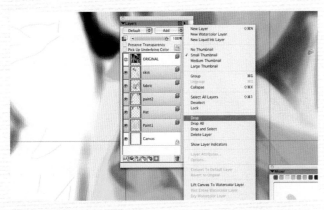

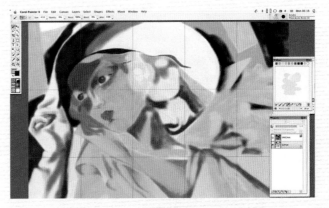

12 Drop Save a copy of your image as a layered RIFF file. Select all layers except for Original, then click on the little triangle on the top-right of the Layers palette to launch the menu and select Drop. The image should now be made of one layer (or two layers if you opted for having Original as a reference layer in the first step).

13 Thick Acrylic At this stage, it is important to refer to the original for getting the fabric folds, shade and overall detail nuances right. As before, be sure to follow the detail that exists, and continuously vary the brush size and Opacity. Strokes remain medium to long, and lightly applied. Now that the image is flat, you can just use the Hand (Grab) tool to move around.

Don't forget about Fade

An oft-forgotten feature is Fade, which lets you reduce the effect of a freshly applied stroke. To do so, go to Menu>Fade. Set the Undo amount to the Opacity level you wish to apply, and drag the image in the Preview window to the stroke area within the painting. This is useful when you are happy with the look of a stroke but wish to reduce the effect.

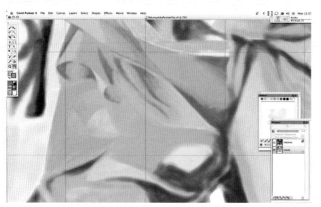

14 Wet Acrylic Under Acrylic, choose the Wet Acrylic 20 variant. Under Bristle, set Thickness and Clumpiness to 0 per cent, Hair Scale to 250 per cent and Scale to 55 per cent. Run the brush smoothly and lightly over the canvas. As previously recommended, it is best to use a very low Opacity of two to four per cent and build up colour gradually.

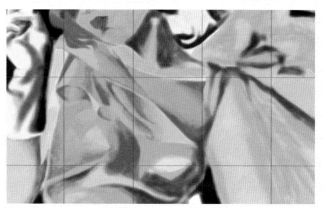

15 Wet Acrylic build This is a time-consuming process that requires patience. The colour builds up slowly as you add one stroke on top of another. Start with one shade; when you have finished covering all relevant areas, open the Color Wheel, move the slide up lightly for a lighter shade or down for a darker one, and continue.

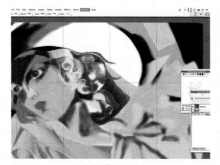

16 Dry Brush Under Acrylics, choose Dry Brush 20 and set Opacity to 20 per cent. Adjust the brush size as you progress using the handy Property bar. To further test and develop your brush, use the Brush Creator. Follow the process described in the previous step, concentrating on one shade, covering relevant area, adjusting shade and moving on.

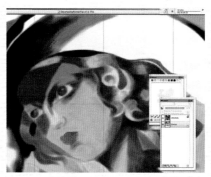

17 Dry Brush 2 At this advanced stage, it is important to apply colour accurately. Follow the drawing lines showing underneath for guidance. Most crucial for the de Lempicka effect is the smooth transition from one shade to the next. For that, you will need to slightly adjust the shade a great number of times as you paint.

18 Wet Acrylic 30 Use the Wet Acrylic 30 brush at 20 per cent to add some depth of colour. Be brave as you commit to darker shades. Under Impasto in the Brush Controls, choose Color and Depth, and set Depth to three per cent. Work with a size 20 brush, again, adjusting the size as you progress.

Lady in green
Smooth the colours to re-create de Lempicka's style

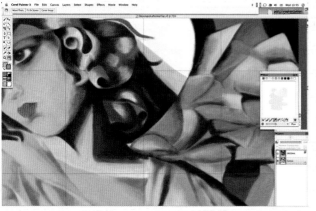

19 Refine green The image should now be fully covered by several layers of paint, but still needs smoothing and refining. Start with the dress, zoom to 75 per cent and go over previously applied paint. Use long-to-medium strokes, adjusting the brush size according to need.

20 Refine browns Work systematically to ensure all areas are fully covered. When you have finished the first round of refining the green areas, move to the browns found all over the image. Observe the original and carefully enhance the painting by increasing Opacity, so adding contrast and depth to the piece.

21 Zoom in
Zoom in to 83 per cent or more, and concentrate on the hair. This is a demanding subject that requires careful observation and repeat applications. Start with lightest shade and use brisk, curvy short-to-medium length strokes. You may want to increase your Undo levels to between 10-15. Your stroke should follow the shape of the hair curls.

Subcategory and Method

Once you choose your brush, you need to set a Method and Subcategory among others. Most Method and Subcategories are covered by Soft, Flat, Hard and Grainy. Choose the right one to refine the brush and achieve the effect you are after. If you familiarise yourself with the Subcategories, you will get better painting results. You can move from Soft with its feathered edges to Grainy brushstrokes that react to paper texture.

22 Blacks
Once the lighter areas are fully covered, move to darker tones around them until you reach the very dark browns and blacks. The darkest blacks give contrast and add a spark to the hair. Build the blacks up gradually, layer upon layer. Use a small brush for areas bordering the hair and in-between curls.

Bask in the glory of your finished piece
Adding the canvas texture

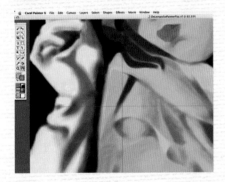

24 Airbrush
For a smoothing effect, select the Fine Tip Soft Air 40 from the Airbrushes. Set Opacity to eight per cent, Method to Cover and Subcategory to Soft Cover. Under Expression, choose Pressure and gently go over the painting underneath. Sample a colour and run the low Opacity brush over the entire area to give it a smooth look. Do not run over areas that are of a different shade. Move between areas until the whole painting is smooth.

23 The glove
The glove is relatively easy to paint. Place the fold lines accurately and you achieve great effects. Use long strokes to apply the lightest areas first and move on to the dark folds. Cover shades in-between the two by moving the slider slightly up or down within the Color palette.

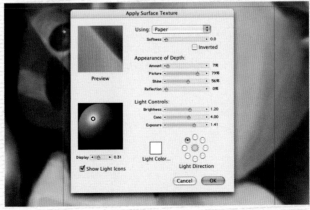

25 Canvas
At the bottom of the Toolbox, click on the Paper Selector. From the long list, choose Artists Canvas. Click on the little triangle top-right of the drop-down menu and select Launch Palette. The settings seen at this stage will be reassessed after we judge the effect of the texture applied in the next step.

26 Canvas settings
Go to Effects>Surface Control>Apply Surface Texture. Under Using, select Paper and set Softness to 0. Set Picture between 70-80 per cent and Amount to five to ten per cent. Look at the effect and adjust the settings according to how textured you wish the painting to be.

Paint like: **Gustav Klimt**

In this tutorial we will show you how to create a portrait in Klimt's style, with the most characteristic features that are associated with his paintings

Tutorial info

Artist
Joanna Michalak

Time needed
Four hours

Skill level
Intermediate

On the CD
Final image

ustav Klimt (1862–1918) was an Austrian Symbolist painter, and a founding member and president of the Vienna Secession movement. While working mainly in the style of Art Nouveau himself, the group he headed welcomed painters of all different styles, from Realists to Naturalists.

Born just outside of Vienna in Baumgarten, Klimt was from a large family of three sons and four daughters. All three sons showed early creative promise, but after an upbringing in which Klimt showed remarkable artistic talent and went on to first study then work as an architectural painter, his father and brother died when Klimt was 30 and so he had to take over the financial responsibilities for both their families. This era marked a change in his style, painting more personal work than following the rigid structure of commissions. This new direction was to shock as many as those who lauded it.

Klimt seemed fascinated by women, both painting them and being with them – he fathered at least 14 children throughout his life. It was his overtly sexual depictions in his work for the University of Vienna's Great Hall in 1894 that led to public outcry and eventually he ceased working on commissions

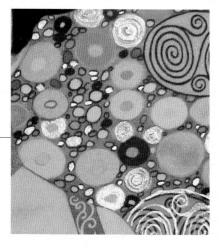
The gold ornaments are very characteristic for Klimt's Golden Phase. Even if created with gold paint instead of gold leaf, it still can give artwork a real flavour of Klimt

The light colours and smooth shading created with the help of Painter's Blenders should re-create Klimt's delicate strokes

Klimt's paintings are famous and well-loved, partly because of the variety of fantastic and stylised patterns used

for the public. But far from fading into obscurity, Klimt flourished under private commissions, and at around the turn of the century, he won widespread praise and respect from critics for his beautiful paintings that often utilised gold leaf.

In the following tutorial, we will try to create a painting that would represent the most important features of Klimt's

Our image was based on the beautiful *Portrait of Adele Bloch-Bauer I*, commissioned by her husband Ferdinand. Adele is the only model to have been painted twice by Klimt, as he depicted her in another portrait five years after the first. At the last count, the original *Adele Bloch-Bauer I* was the third most expensive painting ever to have been sold,

> "The group Klimt headed welcomed painters of all different styles, from Realists to Naturalists"

'Golden Phase' – ethereal but sensual beauty, stylised decorative patterns and the famous gold ornaments – using Painter IX (Pen tools and Blenders) and gold paint on a printed image. His models were made of soft, pastel colours, while ornaments are also one of the most distinguishing and recognisable features of his style.

bought for around $135 million by Ronald Lauder in 2006 to display in New York's Neue Gallerie.

Klimt required lengthy sittings in order to achieve his very deliberate painting style. Whereas it took him three years to complete this painting, we're going to attempt to emulate it in a matter of hours, thanks to the majesty of Painter.

Setting up the sketch
Begin with the figure

01 **Sketch** This is our sketch based on the portrait. You can trace over the final image file on the disc or trace over a photo of a loved-one. We worked to dimensions of 30cm high by 24cm wide. At this point, it's irrelevant what brush you use. However, we knew we wanted darker outlines so we have used dark brown – you can blend it easily with other colours of the picture.

02 **Choosing background colour** Next you need to choose the colours and tones for your painting. We prefer to do it at the beginning, because often the colours are blended with the background. For this one, we chose a darker yellow since we know the final painting will include lots of gold. We started our colouring on a separate layer, with the line art underneath.

03 **Making changes** As you see, we allowed ourselves to make a few changes to Adele's face as we didn't want it to be an exact copy of the portrait. Using your imagination and making your own choices is fine. It can make your work more fun and you can learn from the great masters and create something with your personal touch at the same time.

04 **Choosing colours** It can be hard to pick up the skin colours when you want to re-create a certain painting, because there are always different reproductions. The ideal situation would be to paint it directly from the original, which is, of course, not always possible. We decided to use colours from a lighter reproduction with lively colours. Create this palette on a separate layer, so you don't lose them later on. We have used a pale skin colour and some shading using the Fine Point Pen at 27% opacity.

05 **Skin shading** Next we added a few brighter tones of yellow and blue to the skin. We chose the Fine Point Pen brush as our tool (Opacity set to 27 per cent). Even if it's a Pen tool, you can imitate many different mediums when you use it either with different opacities, or else together with the Blenders.

Shading skin

The bodies Klimt painted are ethereal and seem to be very soft and delicate, yet very sensual at the same time. We tried to re-create this feel by delicately cross-scratching with the Fine Point Pen, while blending different skin tones that we chose. Then we softened the strokes a little bit with the Soft Blender Stump. It's not exactly Klimt's technique, but the effect is similar.

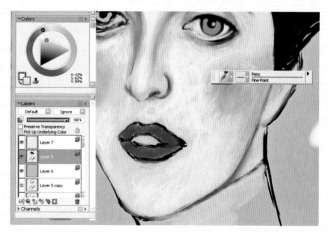

06 **More shading and outlines** Here we worked some more on shading the skin and overpainting the dark outlines with violet (using the Fine Detail Airbrush), trying to make them more delicate yet still visible (soften the outlines with the Soft Blender Stump, Opacity set at 37 per cent). The violet added a nice greyish shade to the dark brown lines.

07 **Rough strokes** Now to work more on the details of the eyes, nose and lips. Keep the painterly feeling by softening the rough strokes a little, with a soft Blender or soft brushstrokes (Opacity at 18 per cent).

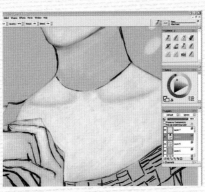

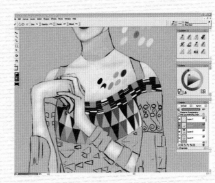

08 Hair We started off with Adele's original haircut, but then decided to make things more dynamic by adding some swirls and strands of hair here and there. To finish, we softened the edges with the Soft Blender Stump again and also used a bit of Blur (from the Photo brush category).

09 More colouring of the skin After finishing the face, we moved on with colouring the skin, still using the same tools and methods as described in step seven and the side tips. Here, you can see what the rough strokes looked like before the delicate softening.

10 Geometrical patterns For the dress, leave the more realistic shading and move to more abstract, imaginary parts of the portrait. The famous geometrical patterns are one of the most recognisable features in Klimt's art. Here we tried to be true to the original. We still used the Fine Point Pen, but this time at a higher opacity.

Banish the blank canvas

One of the most difficult things is starting a painting. Staring at a white expanse of canvas can be very daunting, so you need to get some colour down quickly. One good way of doing this is to flood the entire area with a base colour, as we did here. Pick a colour that establishes the mid-tones and it will make your other colour choices easier.

Absolutely abstract
All hands to the dress

11 Shading the patterns Even if the colouring of the patterns is rather flat and not realistic (like the whole idea of her dress and the background), they still have got a painterly feel to them. We wanted to keep it, adding a bit of shading of brighter tones than the base colour (we reduced the opacity of our brush and softened the strokes with Grainy Water).

12 Hands Adele in Klimt's painting has beautiful hands in a great pose, so we decided to keep them as close to the original as possible. Klimt's shading is very soft, almost invisible, but at the same time it defines shapes very well. We painted the hands using the same technique as for the rest of her skin.

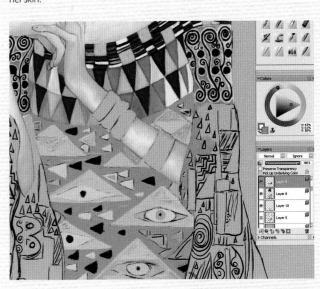

13 Shading hands However, we had to be more careful with the shading and used more of the Soft Blender. The same skin tones have been used, but with more light blue, yellow and orange on the fingers. The outlines were a bit more visible too.

14 The dress The neckline has been done before, so we started working on the middle part of the abstract clothing. First we painted something like a background, using darker and more greenish tone of yellow. We did it on a separate layer under our sketch. When we were fond of the colour, we could draw the yellow, grey and brown patterns over the line art again.

Entering the Golden Phase

All eyes on you

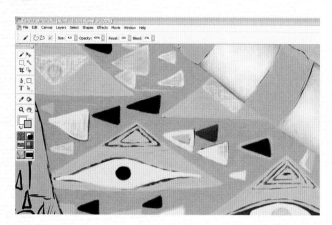

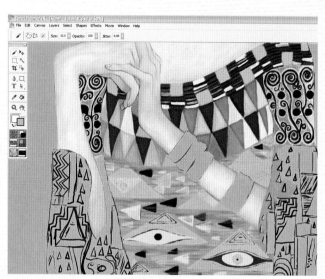

15 More patterns We allowed ourselves more freedom with the patterns this time. And again, they were painted with the Fine Point Pen (Opacity 43 per cent), without Blenders this time, because we wanted the painterly texture to be more visible and rough in contrast with the soft skin.

16 Adding details Here we added the details to the patterns, but still tried to keep them as irregular and rough as possible. You don't have to be very precise while painting such objects, especially when you like to use a big canvas for your paintings. Otherwise, they would get lost after resizing the picture.

17 Adding more details Take a look at the previous screenshot, and you can see that we also added a few darker and brighter random horizontal strokes. We did them on a separate layer again (Fine Point Pen with a lower opacity). Now the parts of them that ran over the patterns have been erased. Then we collapsed the layers – it simply creates less chaos and makes the file much smaller.

18 The sleeves The sleeves have different patterns to the middle part of the dress, but the procedure of re-creating them was the same – first we painted the overall shapes and filled them with colours, leaving the sketch a little bit visible (Fine Point Pen, Opacity 43 per cent).

Photo Blur

Photo Blur is mostly used by artists who are into photorealism, but you can use it if you want to make something look very soft without blending it or changing its shape. Hair is a good example of something it works well on. For our final image, we have used a little bit of Photo Blur on the edges of the woman's hair and for single hairs as well.

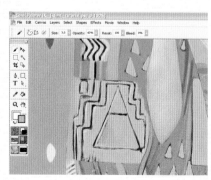

19 Working on details Next we could add the details. All the time we tried to mix various shades of yellow, grey, brown and a bit of olive green in order to create an interesting diversity. The colouring of Klimt's patterns might look flat compared to the realistic painting style, but the colours certainly aren't.

20 The golden elements In some places we also added a bit of brighter yellow. The main problem with re-creating Klimt's painting style via digital mediums are the golden elements. Because we couldn't make them really gold, we chose to mark some of the golden parts with a light yellow tone.

21 Background At this stage, the lady was nearly finished and we could work on the background. Again, we created a new layer under the collapsed layers with the figure and drew a sketch of the background patterns.

22 Sketching swirls We lowered the opacity of our sketch layer and added a new one above it. Using the Fine Detail Airbrush, we drew the swirls on the left and right side of the woman. Then we added some over her head, too.

23 More swirls Next, we changed the brush to the Fine Tip Pen (Opacity at 29 per cent) because of its flow and softer edges. The swirls were softened and smoothed. Then we removed the rough parts using the Eraser at a low opacity.

The Sponge

This tool doesn't look like there would be much potential in it, but sometimes it's the best way to paint something that looks like trouble. Here we used it to paint the background irregular patterns, which could have taken ages if we tried to do them by hand. But we also found the Sponge very helpful by painting more realistic works – you can use this brush to create a wonderful skin texture (on the right side of the image). Just lower the opacity and try it out with different colours and tones.

24 Using Sponge It's a perfect tool when you want to create a lot of undefined splatters. We painted the left border side of the picture brown and then added many yellow Sponge strokes. You'll find that this is one of the easiest parts to do.

25 More background patterns Next up were the yellow and red squares. Again, we used the Fine Point Pen at a higher Opacity of between 43 per cent and 57 per cent to define the figures. Later, we drew a few darker strokes (after lowering the opacity of our brush) in order to create an effect similar to the canvas texture on the real painting.

Now your Gustav is a must-have
Keep going with the patterns

26 And even more patterns The next two steps don't need much of an explanation – we painted the grey and violet figures over her head, lots of little brown, orange, grey and yellow squares around and the oval elements in the middle. We used the Fine Tip Pen at a high opacity for the squares and the Fine Point Pen for the ovals. The swirls inside the bigger ones have been painted once then copied, since they're very much alike.

27 Jewellery The final addition was the jewellery. The bracelets were created the same way as the dress. We painted her necklace with the Fine Tip Pen, mostly by adding more and more short strokes of grey, very bright blue and a bit of the skin tones. As a final touch, you can also add a texture that will give it the look of a real canvas.

Paint like: Johannes Vermeer

Tutorial info

Artist
Anne Pogoda

Time needed
Two to three hours

Skill level
Intermediate

On the CD
Sketch

Do you know that it was "the Sphinx of Delft" who painted "the Mona Lisa of the North"? At least that is how art critic Thoré Bürger referred to the Dutch Baroque painter Johannes Vermeer, because so little is known about him. The "Mona Lisa of the North", ie the Dutch *Mona Lisa*, refers to what the *Girl with a Pearl Earring* is sometimes known as.

It is sad but true that most of what's known about him nowadays is based only on a few official documents, comments by other artists and his paintings themselves. Even the exact date of his birth is unknown.

"Vermeer liked to apply colour to the canvas in loose, granular layers to produce transparent colours"

Vermeer spent his entire life in Delft and it is not sure where he studied, or if his teacher was Carel Fabritius or Leonard Bramer. He joined the Guild of Saint Luke, a trade association for painters, in December 1653, and because the Guild's records show that he couldn't pay the admission fee, we can assume that he had financial difficulties. But since he was elected head of the Guild for four times between 1662 and 1671, it is obvious

By applying the RealBristle brushes, you can emulate the same technique that Vermeer used and gradually build up layers of colour

that he was considered an established craftsman and well-respected artist among his peers.

Vermeer mostly painted domestic interior scenes, which means large genre pieces and portraits, and is well-known for his eye for detail and a great handling of light in his art. This was one reason why David Hockney assumed Vermeer could have been using a camera obscura. According to Hockney, Vermeer's art shows certain light and perspective effects that cannot be achieved without the help of such lenses as those found in the camera obscura.

However, what is known for sure is that Vermeer liked to apply colour to the canvas in loose, granular layers to produce transparent colours that means there is much more variety in the way the colour itself is perceived. This way of underpainting can make a red skirt appear much more lively by working on the shadowed areas with a blueish tone first, which he worked over later with a reddish tone. The fact that the blue shined through afterwards gave it all a much better effect.

It is assumed that Vermeer got his great understanding of light from his studies of Leonardo da Vinci's work. According to da Vinci, each subject reflects light in its colour. This can be observed very well in the *Girl with a Pearl Earring*, which is considered one of Vermeer's masterpieces. Her cheek is lightened by an orange tone, which is reflected light that comes from her dress.

Other than that, the identity of the girl who so innocently glances over her shoulder is unknown, and it is also not known if the painting was commissioned or not. It is also assumed that the painting wasn't

This sketch is a precise tracing made from Vermeer's Girl with a Pearl Earring. *It is on the disc for you to practise with, in both a transparent and a non-transparent version*

even meant to be a portrait, but part of a bigger painting that was never finished for an unknown reason.

This means it is an even bigger task to re-create this painting because it leaves much space for interpretation, and so it may not be such an easy task. First of all, the composition is a typical portrait, which helps us to put it into a category. It has a strong light source and works with massive contrast; the colour palette contains warm reddish tones that are set in contrast to the blue hairband and the white border of the top of her dress, and since the earring is the focal point, it is very important to place it correctly.

These facts made us decide to create a tracing as a sketch of the original painting. Of course, this can also be achieved by using a grid but the result is basically the same – you just spare a lot of time if you trace all the important outlines and work from that.

Start with a sketch

Make an outline of the original to work on

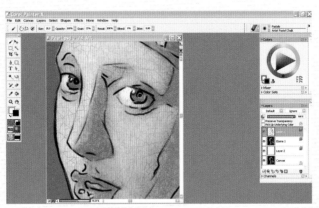

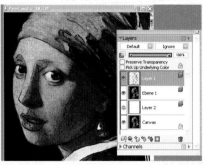

01 **Nailing proportions** First of all, create four layers. The first one that will be our canvas layer includes the original painting. The second one is filled with white and the third one is the painting yet again, set to 60 per cent Opacity. Layer number four is blank and will be used to trace the outlines.

02 **Start tracing** When you are asked to make an exact copy, it is vital to have all the proportions nailed correctly. Therefore, you could just use a grid but you can also just trace everything that is important. The result will be the same. For tracing, we used the Pastel>Artist Pastel chalk, Size ten, Opacity 100 per cent.

03 **Is this all that's needed?** If you are unsure if you have found every important detail, you can switch off the white layer, which will make the painting visible at 100 per cent Opacity and gives you a better chance to see all the details. When you resume tracing, switch the white layer on again as you might have problems to see the black outlines if you don't do this.

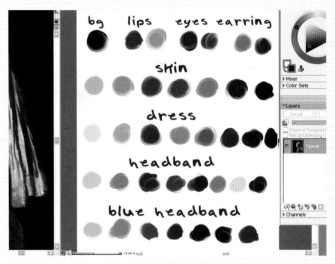

05 **Find the colours** Since the painting we found online is of a rather bad quality, it is important to grab a colour palette, as it will help you immensely to work from it. It also helps to understand which colours were used in special areas that might not be visible at once, for instance, the greenish and reddish spots that were added to the black background.

04 **The sketch is finished** This is the finished result of the tracing we did. We have supplied this sketch on the disc for you to base your work on if you are unsure which details are important to be traced from the original.

Get the info quick

If you want to get great information about an artist quickly and don't know where to take a look, we would definitely recommend going to www.wikipedia.com. The free encyclopedia is updated every day and watched over with much care to provide only the best and finest information about each topic existing (it is even possible to look up a detailed article about the history and meaning of the word 'blah', for instance!). It is also where we retrieved this wonderful large file of Vermeer's *Girl with a Pearl Earring.*

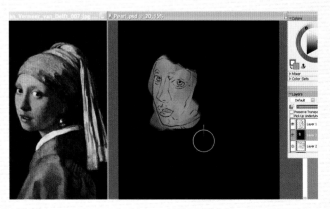

06 **Start painting** Make a new layer located underneath the sketch, and pick the Oily Bristle from the Artists' Oils. You can work with a size that's as large as your machine permits, which meant we mostly worked with 200px in Size and 100 per cent Opacity. Fill the canvas with black.

07 **Start colouring** Now pick one of the orangeish mid-tones from the skin palette, and start to give some basic colour to the face. The brush is still set to a fairly big size (in this case around 170px) and 100 per cent Opacity. Staying on the black layer will make the colours react with each other and create a lovely transparent effect.

08 Colour blocking Continue blocking some basic mid-tones in by grabbing them from either the painting or your earlier-created colour palette. Don't worry if it does not fit correctly into the outlines since you aren't working on refinement yet.

09 Applying shadows See what a big difference it makes to add the shadowed areas to your sketch! It seems much more lively. We are still working on the same layer to make all colours interact with each other, but set the Opacity of the Oily Bristle to 80 per cent.

10 Let there be light Now work on the highlights. You can again pick them from the source painting or your Color Picker. Set the brush to around 20 per cent in size to work on smaller areas like the yellow headband.

Benefits of the Bristles

You may wonder why we didn't start to work with the RealBristle Brushes from the very beginning. The reason why we decided not to do so is because the RealBristle Brushes are very fuzzy and make you feel as if you need an endless amount of pressure to make them give much colour. So it would take forever to create a solid coloured pattern as a base to work from. That is why we suggested an Oily Bristle from the Artists' Oils for this job. It might give the painting a look that is a bit artificial, but the colours are solid at once, thus great to base your work on.

Work over the outlines

At this stage, you should have a painterly version of the original

11 Get rid of the outlines Now time to start getting rid of the outlines. Create a new layer above the outline layer and start to work more precisely on the face. The size of the brush should be set to around 30px here.

12 Blocks This is how the face looked after we had worked over most of the outlines. It looks a bit blocky but clearly defined, especially when it comes to the lighting situation, which is a very good base to work on for later refinement.

13 Massive colour application When you have worked over most of the outlines, you should get a very painterly impression of the overall work, which looks a bit artificial since the Oily Bristle is so big when it comes to applying colours. But we will get rid of that as soon as we continue the refinement.

14 Don't worry about detail When you work over very detailed areas like the headband, don't be worried. Since you will create a new layer for the refinement later, you can always switch off the outline's overpaint layer and check if all that you have applied is where it belongs. And if you still feel irritated, you can also compare it all to the original Vermeer painting to make sure it all fits correctly.

15 How to apply a rough paint effect To get this painting closer to the final refinement, create a new layer and switch the tool of choice to the RealBristle Brushes>Real Round Bristle, Size 35px, 100 per cent Opacity.

Refine the colours and the shape

Blend and smudge your way to success

Use a RealBristle brush to blend colour

When you want to blend colours by using a RealBristle brush, you have to get familiar with its fuzzy appearance, which makes blending colours rather tricky. Here is a way how it works out anyway. Work on a mid-tone coloured area and pull the colour into darker or lighter areas.

16 **Quick colour blending** If you feel that some areas still look too blocky and unconnected, you can speed the whole process up a bit by using the Soft Airbrush 40, sized to around 50px, seven per cent Opacity from time to time.

17 **More detail** We then switched back to the Real Round Bristle and added more detail to the face. We still kept the Opacity at 100 per cent and had the brush size set to nine pixels while working on the smallest parts, like her eyes or the highlights of the lips.

Colour smudging

In step 20, we started to mention how to smudge or blend colours with a RealBristle brush, set to around 200px in size. The reason why you have to work with the Esc button here in order to make the brush stop moving is because 200px is a massive size for such a brush and your machine might take forever to render it, which means that the stroke could eventually become longer than you have planned it to be. To avoid that, just quickly hit the Esc button once the brush has reached the position where it has to stop moving to avoid damaging detail.

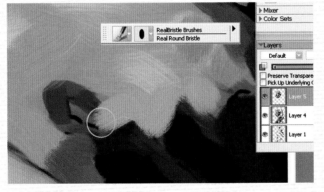

18 **Hairy brush** The headband is a great example to see how hairy the Real Round Bristle really is. It feels hard to apply but is worth all the work. Its size was set to around 35px while working on the headband, and if you feel that it is giving not enough colour to you, move the brush back and forth with pressure until it gives as much colour as you want.

19 **A rough texture** Now when applying the RealBristle Brush to the rest of the figure, you will realise how it will change its surface. The brush has added a lovely fuzzy texture and will push it all away from the artificial plastic digital look and towards something that looks as if it was actually painted with a real brush on real canvas.

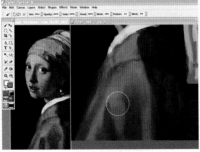

20 **How to create a soft colour blending** To blend all of the colour even more, merge all the layers into one and create a copy of it. On this, work with the Real Round Bristle set to 150px in size and 100 per cent Opacity. Pick the colour of the area you're working on and drag the brush from bottom to top. When you want the brush to stop quickly, press Esc.

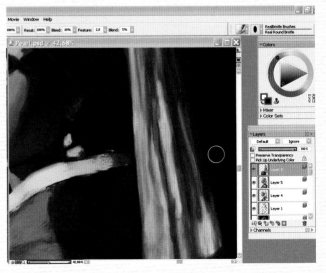

21 **Smudging colours** For the headband, set the brush to around 50px and drag it over the headband in a vertical direction. Hit Esc to make it stop before it hits the black background and you will find a lovely smudged effect. Note that it is important you apply enough detail before you start smudging or else the painting will look totally blurred.

22 **Softening up the headband** Smudge the blue headband by picking its darkest colour and carefully drag the brush from bottom to top again. Taking a look at the most important part, her earring, will show that it looks almost like as it is on the original painting now – which is good! The brush should be set to around 100px this time.

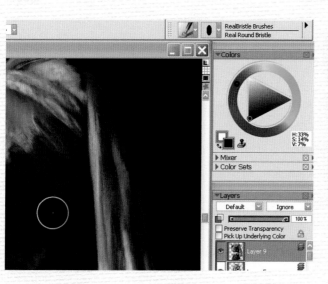

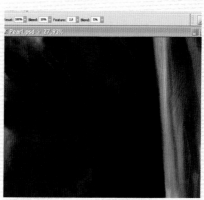

23 **The artificial look is gone** On this close-up, you can see what the blue headband looked like after we smudged it. The artificial digital look is completely gone now, while we have managed to keep most of the detail.

The different brushes used

These are the brushes we used in this tutorial: the Artistic Pastel Chalk, the Oily Bristle and the Real Round Bristle. Painter supplies us with such a huge palette of brushes, and you may find others that you find work best for you. This also means it should generally always have a brush for whatever you see fit for your art; however, we reckon that the current selection is the winning team when it comes to creating a painting that looks like it was really hand-painted.

Finishing touches

Before completing the painting, contrast it with the original to see how it compares

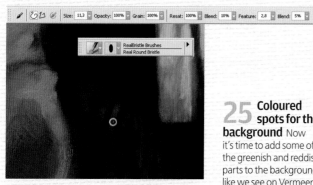

24 **Bringing back some detail** Now that you have smudged all the colours to give them that wonderfully natural look, you can set the brush to around ten pixels and carefully work some more detail into the folds by adding more highlights.

25 **Coloured spots for the background** Now it's time to add some of the greenish and reddish parts to the background, like we see on Vermeer's original painting. You can set the brush to around 100px in size again and scribble around to create a pattern that looks like it is hand-painted.

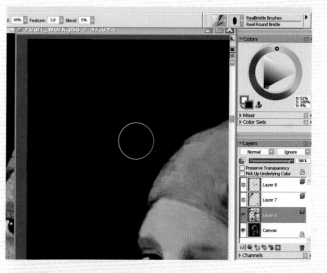

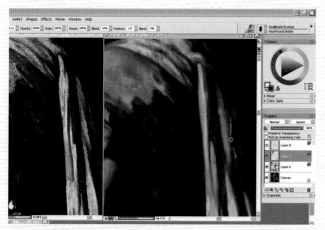

26 **Some last detail** At this point we decided that we wanted some more detail for the blue and yellow headband, so set the brush to around ten pixels in size again to add some more highlights.

27 **Nit-picking** Now it's time for some final corrections. Therefore it is necessary to compare the painting that you've just created with the original again very carefully to spot things that have to be adjusted. In this case, we reduced the orange area at the back of her head.

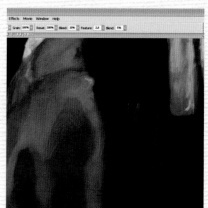

28 **Final corrections** On the very last step, we zoomed in on the dress and compared it to the original to work over the latest detail until it felt good.

Paint like: Toulouse Lautrec

The soul of Montmartre, or child of Moulin Rouge? We capture the spirit of this seminal artist...

Tutorial info

Artist
Anne Pogoda

Time needed
4 hours

Skill level
Intermediate

On the CD
Sketch and final image

The artist with the longest name you may have ever heard, Henri Marie Raymond de Toulouse-Lautrec Monfa, was born in 1864 in Albi, which is located in the Midi-Pyrénées Region of France. He was the first-born child of Comte Alphonse and Comtesse Adèle de Toulouse-Lautrec, who were first cousins. This made him supposedly suffer from a number of health problems, that were possibly caused by this tradition of inbreeding.

Henri fractured both his thigh bones at the ages of 13 and 14 which ceased his legs growing, and so he was just 1.54 m tall. This made it physically impossible for him to follow most hobbies that used to be typical for men of his age by that time, which supposedly made him focus on art. So he became an important post-Impressionist painter, Art Nouveau illustrator and lithographer.

Known as 'The Soul of Montmartre', he used to portray life at the Moulin Rouge were he lived among the women for long periods. He witnessed their most intimate moments, which inspired him to paint many lesbian scenes.

During his lifetime, Lautrec sadly discovered another love, and became an alcoholic. He died in 1901, because of health issues caused by syphilis and complications due to alcoholism.

Even though Lautrec only lived to 36, he was extremely productive during his lifetime. Unlike Vermeer (featured in the last tutorial), who supposedly only produced around 30 paintings throughout his whole life, Lautrec (according to Wikipedia) produced the outstanding amount of '737 canvases, 275 watercolours, 363 prints and posters, 5,084 drawings, 300 pornographic works, some ceramic and stained glass work, and an unknown number of lost works'.

For recreating his work I picked *The Toilette*. This was because it shows a woman in a private moment of her life. And since I know that Lautrec found intimate moments of the women from Moulin Rouge very inspiring, I decided to go for it and try to capture the spirit of his creativity. On this painting we see a woman from behind, who sits half dressed on the floor. Unlike in most paintings where subjects hold eye contact to the viewer by being shown from the front, we can't get a direct connection to her and so have to take a closer look at what is surrounding her to have a chance of understanding the painting.

Her head, with fire-red hair, is clearly put as the focus and is located near a bucket, which is supposedly filled with water. So she possibly just washed herself, but whether she just got out of bed, or if it happened after a show, is something we don't clearly know.

The colour palette is held in bright tones for all that is important, like the woman in the foreground, or the foliage and bucket which stands in contrast to the very dark tones of the chair and the ground that she sits on. The colour palette, which is visible at once, contains black and white, which is supported by several yellowish tones, blues and an eye catching red. The overall appearance of the brush strokes seem loose, but clearly defined enough to understand the painting as a whole without problem. This should be an interesting subject to work on, and hopefully not too hard for you to re-create at home!

"Known as 'The Soul of Montmartre', he used to portray life at the Moulin Rouge where he lived among the women..."

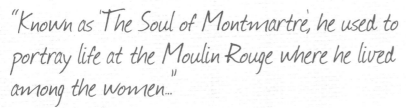

This is a basic colour palette, which I grabbed from the painting for a better overall understanding of the colour scheme

Here we have the sketch that I created from the original painting. As always, you can find it on the disc to base your own practices on

Prepare to paint
Trace to get an exact copy

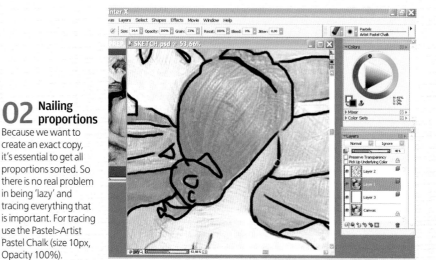

01 **Painting preparation** Start by creating four layers. The first one (the Canvas) will include the original painting, the second one is white, and the third one is the painting again, but set to 40px and 60% Opacity. Layer four, which is blank, will be used to trace the outlines and get the proportions nailed correctly.

02 **Nailing proportions** Because we want to create an exact copy, it's essential to get all proportions sorted. So there is no real problem in being 'lazy' and tracing everything that is important. For tracing use the Pastel>Artist Pastel Chalk (size 10px, Opacity 100%).

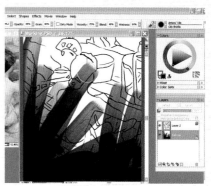

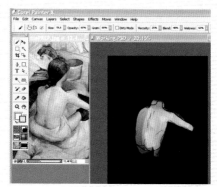

Online museum

This time, side tips will mainly deal with cool places on the web for your old master researches, so that you'll know more websites besides Wikipedia which bear great opportunities to find old masters online. The best example for this is probably **www. artrenewal.org**. The website offers a virtual museum containing every dead and living master you could think of, and also announces high priced competitions and fantastic workshops every year. Besides this, the attached search bar makes it easy to find old masters quick. So as you can see, the ARC is a must for every art friend!

03 **The finished sketch** And here we have the finished sketch of the tracing, which you can find on the disc to base your own practices on. When you are unsure what to trace for your own work, you can switch off the white layer, which will make the painting visible at 100% Opacity, offering you a better chance to see all the detail. When you resume tracing just switch the white layer back on to see the black outlines.

04 **Colouring the background** Create a new layer, which is located below the charcoal sketch, to base your first work on. Pick Black and Oily Bristle from the Artists Oils. The size should be Large, so everything around 200px at 100% Opacity is just fine!

05 **Get started with the colours** To find correct colours while working, you can pick the desired colour by pressing Alt while working with the Brush tool. Releasing Alt will transform the Picker back into the Brush tool, which guarantees comfortable working.

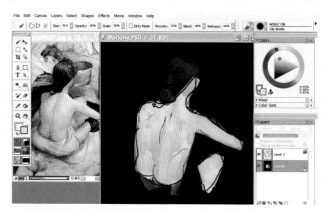

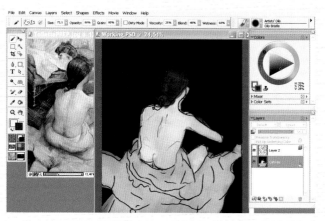

06 **What to begin with** I set the brush to around 60px in size and 80% Opacity and decided to get started with the body and hair first to get a base for the painting defined. It doesn't matter if you paint over the outlines since the painting will be further defined later anyway.

07 **Something to sit on** To get better navigation through the painting set the brush to around 70px in size, keep 80% Opacity, and pick the blueish tone from the blanket she sits on.

Define everything

Use different brush sizes to define the sketch

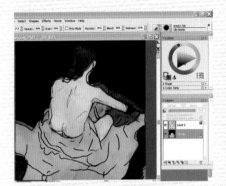

08 **More definition** Setting the brush to around 28px in size, I continued to define the shape around the figure. Don't worry if the colours you start with look like basic blue, green and yellow, since this will be overworked later anyway.

09 **A whole basic definition** Continue to work on your basic colour palette by picking more colours from your reference and adding them to your basic painting. You can set the brush back to around 80px in size now.

10 **More definition for the base** To get the background more defined it works best to add some lighter tones to the basic tones, which you have applied. While doing this you can stick with the Oily Bristle from the Artists Oils.

All about old master copies

Another interesting address is www.1st-art-gallery.com. The website basically deals with the reproduction of old master copies, but done with real paints on canvas. They also offer a service to transform customer's photos into wonderful traditional oil painting. Take a look around and you'll find interesting information about old master copies, including a wonderful copy of the *Girl With a Pearl Earring* from our workshop last issue. Scrolling down the frontpage also reveals a must-see, which is an interesting video that shows how an old master copy is created by hand.

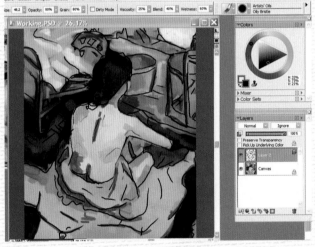

11 **Under the outlines** Just continue adding highlights and some other tones which you feel are important for the overall understanding of the painting until you think that it is defined enough to start working over the outlines.

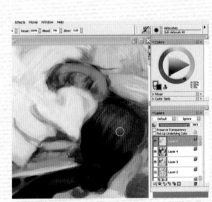

12 **Over the outlines** Now it's time to start working over the outlines. Create a new layer and start to carefully work out some areas – you can keep your current brush settings for this. On this screenshot you can see how I started to overwork the foliage on the left chair, and the chair itself.

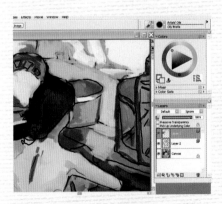

13 **More painted structure** Continue to paint over the outlines carefully to achieve a more painted look for the background. You can size it down to around 30px for the smaller blueish lines if you want to.

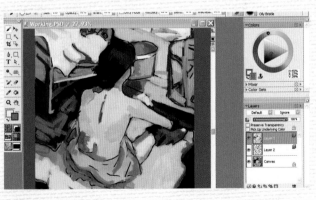

14 **Painting over continued** Here you can see how I continued to paint over everything until I had the feeling that it was all defined enough to disable the Outlines Layer. Please note that I also added darker tones to the painting at this point to have a good base for the refinements which I had planned to apply later on.

15 **Refinement without outlines** Now disable the Outlines Layer and choose the Airbrush>Soft Airbrush 40, set to 20px in size and 25% Opacity to work on specific detail, like strands of the hair or chair structure.

Finishing touches
Use little strokes to refine the details of your painting

Find stock photos to improve

Besides the very chaotic stock photos category of DeviantART, you will find a great and well-sorted collection of stock photos at **www.sxc.hu**. As soon as you have signed up an account most, if not all, photos on this site seem to be available for free in good resolution. As soon as you click on a desired stock photo you can see the terms of usage on its right side, which can be set up for each image individually by the image owner.

Find great anatomy books online

If you are looking for great anatomy books you might often figure that there aren't many good ones on the market. But who needs to buy books when you can find some of the best at **www.fineart.sk**. The website offers a free collection of all Andrew Loomis anatomy book, since the original books are too old to be found on book markets. They were scanned and put on **www.fineart.sk** together with some other literature regarding anatomy, and extremely self-explanatory anatomy, for artists' photos.

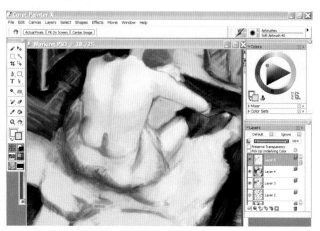

16 Sexy back The same refinement technique as step 15 was used for the back and the foliage she sits on to make all colours blend together, which makes it possible to work on the rough painted look in step 17.

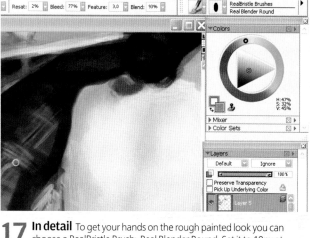

17 In detail To get your hands on the rough painted look you can choose a RealBristle Brush>Real Blender Round. Set it to 10px at 100% Opacity to paint some lines for the ground structure.

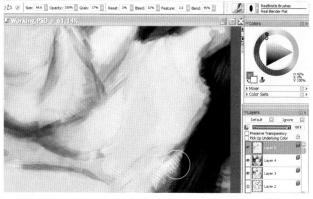

18 Little strokes As you can see on the original painting, there are many little strokes. Because painting every stroke by hand would take forever, it is a wise decision to go for the Real Blender Flat from the RealBristle Brushes, and set it to around 60px in size with 100% Opacity.

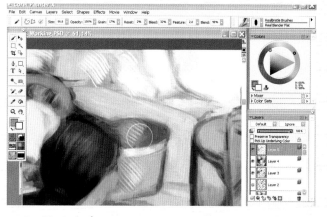

19 More strokes Here you can see how I continued applying the strokes to the painting. If you feel that the strokes stick out too much you can carefully reduce them with a Soft Edged eraser.

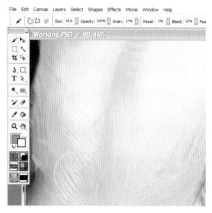

20 Back to the back Go on painting the strokes on her back now. If you figure that they are standing out too much you can gently push them back with a Soft Eraser.

21 More for the floor Here we are in the left corner of the floor again, but this time with a Real Tapered Round set to 5px in size and 100% Opacity, to give the lines more fuzziness.

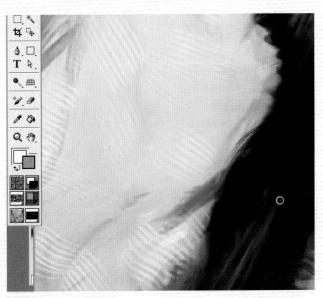

22 The floor again The same procedure as on step 21 should be continued with all floor areas now to achieve the same loose look, as seen on the original reference.

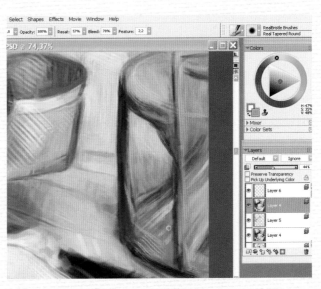

23 Strokes for the table structure To be honest I'm not sure what this structure is – it could be some sort of yellow table or a big hourglass. But whatever it is, it surely looks much better now some smaller strokes have been applied!

Learn online from other painters

The best forum thread I have ever seen to learn and see great examples of speed paintings is possibly Sijun's speed painting thread. The almost a 1000 page-long thread is located at **www.forums.sijun. com** and offers a chance to see great talents like Craig Mullins at work every once in a while! But the other work that is posted there every day is worth a look, and will help you to learn a lot about painting – especially when it comes to colour palettes and composition.

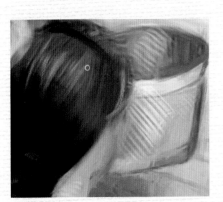

24 Hairstyling Keep the RealTapered Round and get yourself an orange tone from the reference painting to apply more strokes for the hair. When you're done you can repeat the same procedure with a dark red.

25 Final refinement Now it's time for some final detail! For that you can pick the RealBlender Flat. Set it to 50px size and 100% Opacity. Add tiny brush strokes wherever you see fit, and where you have the feeling that something could be missing.

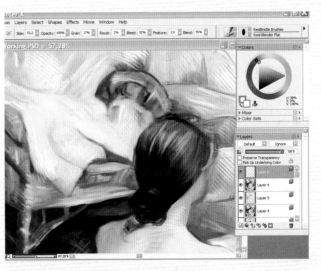

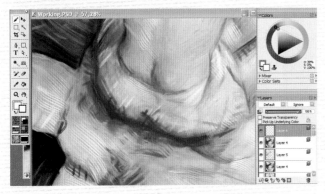

26 Some last more detail Here you can see how I applied some final tiny strokes to her back and the foliage. I switched between white and blue to do this. It really isn't necessary to try to have every brush stroke at exactly the same position as on the reference painting, since nobody will notice this anyway. As soon as the overall feeling of the painting is captured, it's perfect!

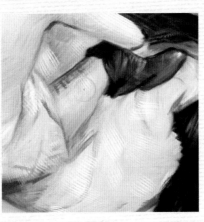

27 Nitpicking I wanted to have some more tiny strokes on her overall body, and so worked over the leg once again until I was satisfied with the result.

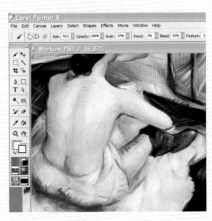

28 And here we are The leg was the last thing that bothered me, along with some other little strokes applied here and there. The master copy is successfully finished now!

Paint like: **Art Nouveau**

With curved lines and floral patterns we invite you into the world of Art Nouveau to create an autumnal piece of art...

Tutorial info

Artist
Joanna Michalak

Time needed
5 hours

Skill level
Intermediate

On the CD
Source files

A rt Nouveau, also known as Jugendstil, is an international movement and style of art, architecture and applied art – especially the decorative arts – that peaked in popularity at the turn of the 20th century (1890–1905). It was a reaction to academic art of the 19th century, and is characterised by organic, especially floral and other plant-inspired motifs, as well as highly stylised, flowing curvilinear forms. The origins of Art Nouveau are found in the resistance of William Morris, to the cluttered compositions and the revival tendencies of the Victorian era, and his theoretical approaches helped to initiate the Arts and Crafts movement. Around the same time the flat perspective and strong colours of Japanese woodcuts, especially those of Katsushika Hokusai, had a strong effect on the formulation of Art Nouveau's formal language. The wave of Japonisme that swept through Europe in the 1880s and 1890s was particularly influential on many artists with its organic forms, references to the natural world and clear designs that contrasted strongly with the reigning taste. In painting and graphic design, two-dimensional Art Nouveau pieces were painted, drawn and printed in popular forms, such as advertisements, posters, labels and magazines.

Japanese woodblock prints, with their curved lines, patterned surfaces, contrasting voids and flatness of visual plane, also inspired Art Nouveau. Some line and curve patterns became graphic clichés that were later found in works of artists from all parts of the world. Leading practitioners included Alphonse Mucha, Aubrey Beardsley, Gustav Klimt and the American glassmaker, Louis Comfort Tiffany. Art Nouveau remained popular until around the time of World War I, but was ultimately replaced by the modernist Art Deco style.

"Art Nouveau pieces were painted, drawn and printed in popular forms, such as advertisements"

Stylisation
Art Nouveau artists gave up the realistic approach and used stylisation instead, especially when it came to hair. It becomes another ornament that's unrealistic, curvy, and marked with a bold outline. But it's not only hair - flowers, plants, branches are used as a part of stylisation, as well as long, flowing fabrics.

Pattern
Floral elements dominate the pattern designs too. They are used as backgrounds, sometimes as part of clothing and jewellery, but mostly as sophisticated or simple borders. They can be replaced with parts of Byzantine mosaics, or complicated and dense curvy lines.

Flatness
Art Nouveau served a decorative and practical purpose; it had to be eye-catching because it was used in advertising. The artists replaced loose brush strokes with flat colours to complement the clean, strong lines of the drawing. While the drawing itself becomes more complicated, the colouring has to be simplified.

Creating the figure

We show you how to stylise a figure with Art Nouveau features

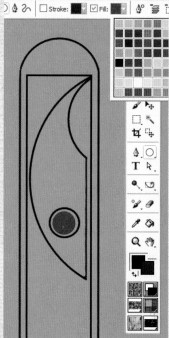

01 **Sketching the pose** If you have problems thinking of a pose, use a photo. We start with a loose sketch in blue. Choosing a different colour for the sketch will help you draw the actual line art later. You can modify the hair and add some stylised attributes.

02 **Background motif** Using motifs from nature is typical in this style of art. Flowers, branches and all kinds of plants can be drawn realistically or turned into graphic forms. Here we've chosen a tree with some leaves to illustrate the autumnal mood.

03 **Sketching the border** Stylised borders are one of the most significant parts of Art Nouveau. We chose a rather closed, simple, arc-based border. At the moment you don't have to worry about details – they will be more important later (when you work on the actual line art).

Creating a border with shape tools

If you have problems drawing straight and clean lines, shape tools can be helpful

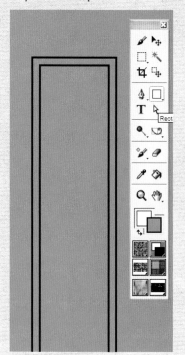

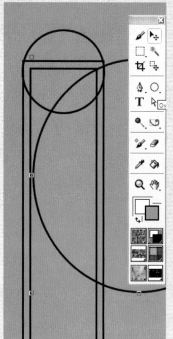

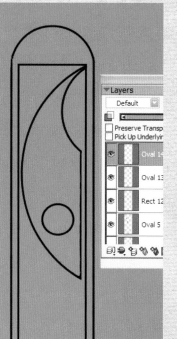

RECTANGULAR SHAPES

If you want to create border columns choose Rectangular Shape from the side menu, then mark Stroke. Now you can decide the size and shape of the object you want to draw by stretching it (hold the left mouse button or the button in your tablet pen).

OVAL SHAPES

Now you can create a pattern inside your column by adding a few oval shapes from the same menu. Every shape will be automatically created as a new layer, so you will be able to move them around later and construct your pattern more precisely.

EDITING THE SHAPES

In order to remove parts of the shapes that you don't want, simply choose Commit from the Layer menu (right-click on the shape layer). Now you can just erase those parts of the shapes that are unnecessary for your pattern or incorrect.

COLOUR FILL

If you want to make the pattern more varied and complicated you can also add shapes that are filled with colour. Choose the shape you want from the side menu and mark Fill this time instead of Stroke. Now pick the colour you want to fill your shape with.

04 Start with the line art When you are happy with your concept sketch you can start with the line art. Add a new layer above the sketch and start to draw following the lines. We're using Pens>Fine Point at 100% Opacity and size 4 in Black here.

05 Stylised hair Another very important feature of Art Nouveau is the highly stylised hair. You don't need to draw every single strand of hair, just use a few curved lines to mark its flow. At this point we don't draw the jewellery, leaving the finer details for later.

Art Nouveau in modern form

When you want to use Art Nouveau stylisation it doesn't mean that you have to limit yourself only to pretty women and floral ornaments. The Art Nouveau stylisation can be used in any kind of work you wish – from a portrait to a comic book. All you need is to try to turn the reality around you into a stylised decoration. Experiment with modern objects and try to incorporate Art Nouveau elements into your own style!

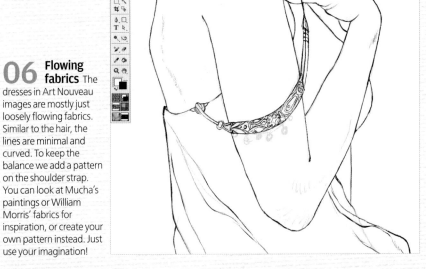

06 Flowing fabrics The dresses in Art Nouveau images are mostly just loosely flowing fabrics. Similar to the hair, the lines are minimal and curved. To keep the balance we add a pattern on the shoulder strap. You can look at Mucha's paintings or William Morris' fabrics for inspiration, or create your own pattern instead. Just use your imagination!

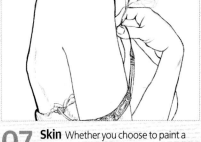

07 Skin Whether you choose to paint a fully shaded body or keep your colouring flat, the only thing your line art needs is the outlines of the body. You have to mark the body's curvature on the skin, and you can additionally draw few delicate lines in places like shoulder blades and shoulders.

Draw the outlines
Strong lines are a characteristic feature

08 Strong outlines One of the most characteristic features of Art Nouveau is its strong outlines. We draw them around our figure, but we thicken only the external lines – they will make the remaining lines appear finer and thinner. You don't have to worry about keeping the bold lines the same size as making the thickness variable will make it look more natural.

09 The tree We apply exactly the same rules while drawing the line art for our background tree, but instead of thickening the external lines, we keep them rather thin and delicate. It is also better to draw this on a separate layer, because we will need to change its opacity later on.

Stock photos

If you don't have a model to draw from live or an idea for a pose, stock photos might be a big help for you. Some stock artists will provide you with great and very inspirational photo sessions, with great poses and even equipment and fabulous clothing. Examples of great and useful galleries are **www.lockstock. deviantart.com** and **www.faestock. deviantart.com**.

Jewel colours and rich patterns

We show you how to mix a Color palette for an autumnal Art Nouveau image

Smooth line art

Did you ever wonder how the Art Nouveau artist created their smooth and clean lines? When you look at the reproductions in art books they seem perfect. But in fact they are far from that – if you could take a look at the original Mucha posters you would see many irregularities. So don't worry if your line art doesn't look very smooth – when you resize your picture, it will look perfect.

10 **More hair** Now that we've drawn the tree we're going to change the composition a bit, and balance the right side with a few strands of long hair. Again, we draw curved lines, which cross each other at the ends. We round the endings and remove the crossing lines to get the characteristic Mucha style of hair.

11 **Border pattern** We now fill the upper part of the border with a floral pattern (on a separate layer). We chose to draw leaves and little round fruits as these will correspond best with our subject. We will only one side (left or right) of the border with the chosen pattern.

12 **Repeating the pattern** You don't need to reproduce the pattern by hand to fill the centre part of the border. Just copy a part of the previously drawn leaves and paste it into the centre part. Remove the redundant areas. Group the pattern layer with the border layer and collapse them. Now it's time to take care of the other side.

13 **Symmetrical border**
It's hard to draw a symmetrical border, but thanks to the copy and paste option you don't need to worry about it. Select the border and choose Edit>Copy, then Edit>Paste. Select the new layer again and pick Effects>Orientation> Flip Horizontal. Put the two halves precisely together and drop the two layers. Your perfectly symmetrical border is now completed.

14 **Choosing colours** We want to create an autumnal mood, so we choose warm colours based on yellows, reds and oranges. Add two new layers underneath the line art (keep the figure, border and tree on separate layers in case you would like to change anything later). With such precise colouring it's better to have different layers for the figure and the background.

15 **Blending colours** We hide the layer with the foreground for a better overview, and blend the sky colours. We use Blenders> Grainy Water at 80 per cent Grain and 29 per cent Opacity here to get the irregular gradient effect.

16 **Colouring the tree** The tree shouldn't draw too much attention and stand out, so we choose light olive greens for the colouring. You can also add more texture with lighting and shading here. At the end of the whole colouring process we will set the Opacity of the tree line art to 60 per cent.

17 Skin shading We pick a light tone for the skin and colour it in a flat tone. Later we use a slightly darker tone and Airbrushes>Fine Detail Air on a low opacity to add some delicate shading on her cheek bones, throat, fingers, back and elbow. You can also blend it with Grainy Water or Soft Blender Stump.

18 Painting the face Now we need a new layer above our line art to paint the lips, nose and eyes. Even if the rest of the colouring remains flat, those elements can be modelled more realistically, yet still quite simply. Our main goal is to make them look softer. We use the Fine Point Pen on a lower opacity and a lot of different blenders.

Textures

Applying a texture to your drawing or painting can take it to a new level. You can add an antique feel to the picture, create a new mood or turn a simple drawing or sketch into old-looking sepia artwork. Some sites where you can find many great textures to experiment with are **www.cgtextures. com, www.resurgere. deviantart.com** and **www.sanami276. deviantart.com.**

Sprinkle with Nouveau dust
Adding iconic flavouring

19 Hair colours We use a greenish brown for the hair that complements the rest of our Color palette. We use flat colouring for the hair; just add a darker or lighter tone to some strands to create some eye-pleasing diversity. You can use any brush you like here, just remember that hard edged brushes are more precise and better for colouring within lines.

20 Colouring the border We fill the gaps between the leaves with the darker of the tones used for the hair. The leaves are red to complement the dress, with dark shading along the inner lines (you can blend it a bit with Blenders>Grainy Water). The fruits are yellow to make them stand out and add a bit of variety to the other colours that are dark and similar.

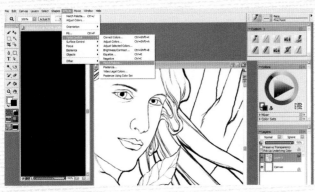

21 Changing line art colour Our line art is black and stands out a bit compared to the warm palette of the picture. We can change it using the Effects>Tonal Control>Match Palette option. The easiest way is to create a new file and fill the canvas with the desired colour (we used dark brown), and then match the line art colour with the other file's colour.

22 Texture If you want an extra touch-up for your newly created Art Nouveau piece to give it an antique look and increase the flatness, use a texture (we used a Fine Paper texture here). After you have saved your file with all layers, drop them and add the texture on the top. Now just play around with the layer settings and opacity until you get the texture result you desire.

Paint like:
Cézanne

Post-Impressionists don't come any better than Paul Cézanne. We demonstrate how to re-create a classic Cézanne still life painting...

Born to a wealthy family, Paul Cézanne was in the fortunate position of being able to devote his entire life to painting, giving him the opportunity to develop a unique style and visual vocabulary. Along with many other works, Cézanne painted over two hundred still life studies where he concentrated on the distillation of form and colour into their essentials. Cézanne found perfection in natural forms, and concentrated very much on the essential shapes and hidden geometry in a scene. He maintained that everything in nature could be distilled into cones, cylinders, cubes and spheres. Cézanne was also a bit of a magpie when it came to taking different influences from his artistic contemporaries; in all of his paintings you can see the strong forms and line work of Manet, the light and colours of the Impressionist school, and the balance and compositional harmony of Poussin. In fact, Cézanne once said that he wanted to "paint Poussin from nature".

We're going to pay homage to the great man here by creating a still life painting that reflects his style and aesthetics. For this we're going to be fairly strict and paint directly on the canvas. To use a photograph as a start image here would rob us of the chance to convey the essential shapes of the objects within the composition. In order to achieve this look properly, you'll need to concentrate on how you work with colour and line.

We'll start by very loosely sketching in shapes, and although you can do exactly as Cézanne did by studying the objects in reality, don't be afraid to manipulate and simplify the shapes as you go. Concentrate on luscious colours, the expression of form and making the shapes look good on the canvas, rather than slavishly describing each individual element.

Tutorial info

Artist
Tim Shelbourne

Time needed
5 hours

Skill level
Intermediate

On the CD
Sketch

Start the still life

Set up a still life. Observe, simplify and sketch

Get drawing some more!

Because we're painting from scratch here and keeping well away from any tracing or cloning, becoming practised at observation and drawing is vital to make the end result convincing. Carry a small sketchpad around with you, and even if you've only got a few minutes, use them to grab a quick, simplified sketch of a nearby object. Every bit of practice helps!

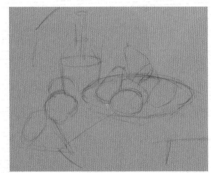

01 Create the canvas Go to File>New and create a landscape orientation canvas at 300dpi. Here we've made the canvas 15x11 inches, which gives a lot of room to work and allows you to use the brushes at quite a large size. But you can always make yours a little smaller, which will put less strain on less powerful machines.

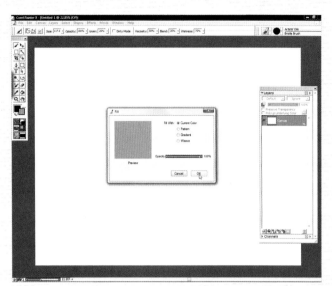

02 Midtone fill It's a good idea to establish an overall midtone across the canvas, which makes judging tones easier than working over a stark white space, so choose a midtone warm grey from the colour wheel and go to Effects>Fill. Choose Current Color and click OK.

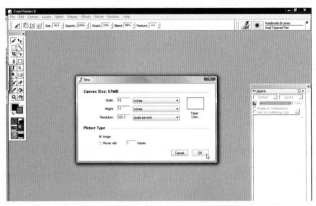

03 Initial sketch Choose the charcoal set of variants and select the Soft Vine Charcoal 30 brush. Choose a very dark brown colour and start to indicate the main shapes within the scene. Remember that here you're just concentrating on the essential overall shapes, and the placement of these within the canvas area.

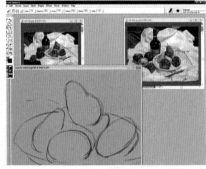

04 Essential observation It's important to bear in mind that you're drawing completely freehand, either from reference photos you took or directly from your still life set up nearby. Here we're interpreting and simplifying shapes, adjusting their placement to make a pleasing composition.

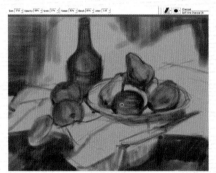

05 Block in the shadows Once you have the main shapes and forms indicated, increase the brush size and roughly shade in the darkest shadow areas in the scene. Don't bother with the midtones here as the filled canvas represents them, but it's useful to get an approximate tone map established at this stage.

Hidden geometry

When you're setting up your still life for this painting, try to look for the hidden geometry in both the scene itself and the individual objects within it. You'll soon start to see cones, spheres and cylinders that will add harmony and structure to your painting. You can even sketch out these shapes over your painting on a separate layer as you work to give yourself some reassuring guides.

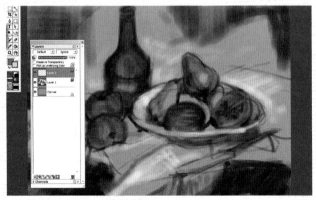

06 Tone mapping By changing your foreground colour to white you can block in the lightest parts of the image. This tonal sketch will help you a lot throughout the painting process, and will act as an underlying foundation for the tones, colours and modelling you apply later. When you're done, add a new layer.

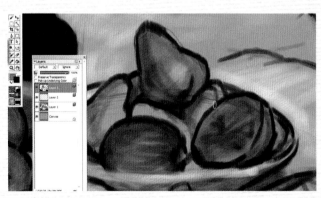

07 Brush for outlines Now that you have your tonal framework complete, we can get down to the business of painting. Start by adding a new layer. Now select the RealBristle category of variants. Choose the Real Oils Short variant. Set the Feature to around 5 and the Blend to 10%. Now, using a near black colour, start to add the enclosing outlines to the objects within the painting.

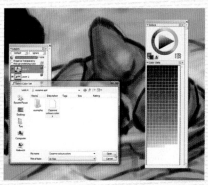

08 Underpin the composition This is a characteristic of the Cézanne still life, and these outlines need to be quite sketchy and loose. In the finished painting they will serve to unify the painting as a whole and emphasise the natural forms and shapes. As you paint these outlines you can adjust and refine the geometric shapes of the scene's component objects.

09 Set up a color set You have a few choices when it comes to picking the colours for your image. We set up a special color set, but you can easily use the default version and pick colour from there. You don't have to be exact with this – pick the colours that feel right for you and the scene you are painting.

10 Establish the shadows Add a new layer. Now choose the Real Oils Soft Wet variant. Set the Feature to 5% and Blend to 10%. Go to Window>Brush Controls>Show Size and set Min Size to around 75%. From the Papers Selector at the base of the toolbar, choose Coarse Cotton Canvas. Now start to paint the very darkest tones in the painting.

Cloning no-no!

It can't be stressed enough that your job here is to interpret rather than copy. Just as Cézanne would not have carefully painted over a photograph, it would be pointless to clone this painting from one. By drawing and simplifying the objects in your scene you will develop your own personal and unique language.

Colour composition
Start adding shades and tones to your still life

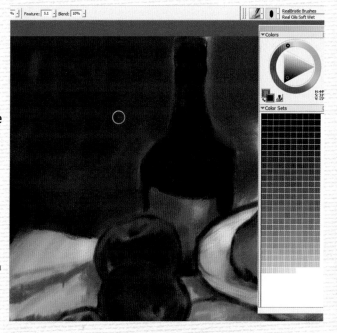

12 Establish the balance At this stage, it will also help to roughly establish the background. We've used some nice dark greens here, which complement the fruit and really push the still life itself forward. Also, make sure to establish the dark areas beneath the cloth at the bottom of the painting and start to block in the rich reds and russets in the fruit.

11 Essential darks Remember, we're just establishing the darks here. You can make your brushwork quite free here, using short strokes at different angles to describe the contours and volume of the objects you're painting. Choose appropriate colours from the Color Set as you go.

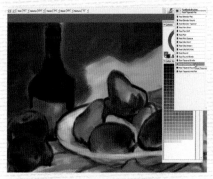

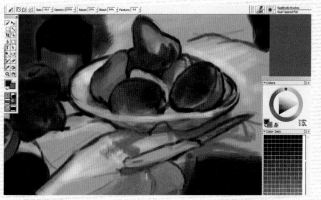

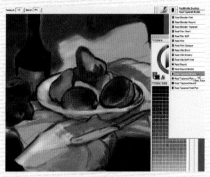

13 Another brush Before painting in the darks of the drapery, it's time for another change of brush. Choose the Real Tapered Flat. Again, set the Min Size to around 75%. In the Brush properties, set the Bleed to a very high value to make the colour feel more liquid, and use a Feature setting of around 6%.

14 Drapery shadows Now start to brush in the warm shadow areas of the cloth. Again, use strokes that follow the planes of the fabric, preferably referring to your still life setup. Establish the darkest neutral tones first, working your way up to the lighter midtones. Your brush work still needs to be quite loose here.

15 Intense colours Don't worry about the lighter areas of the cloth yet, we'll tackle those later. It's time to start adding some areas of quite intense light colours to the fruit. Select the Real Tapered Bristle variant. Set the Feature to 7 and Blend to a fairly low value so that the paint on the brush feels quite thick and dry.

Compositional quirks
Ready for more? Let's bring the scene to life!

Clever texture

Your finished painting will benefit from a subtle canvas texture, but not over the entire picture area. When you've finished painting, flatten your image via Layer>Drop All. On the canvas layer go to Select>All, followed by Edit>Copy. Now go to Edit>Paste In Place. Go to Effects> Surface Control>Apply Surface Texture. Choose paper for Using and adjust the Amount to your liking. Go to Layers>Create Layer Mask. Paint on the layer mask with black to hide the texture over the lightest areas of the painting.

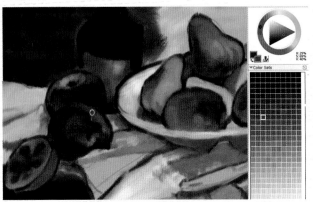

16 **Observe and identify** This is where observation plays a really important role. You now need to identify the lightest areas of the fruit and simplify the shapes within these areas. Choose your colours carefully and apply your strokes following the contours. You can still refine the shape of the fruit here, concentrating on making pleasing shapes on the canvas.

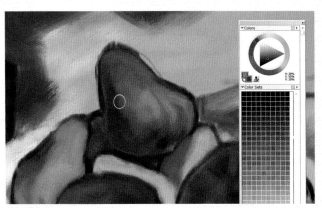

17 **Complex modelling** You can blend these highlights in with the existing midtones simply by increasing the Blend value of the brush and brushing back into them. It's worth taking your time here using slightly lighter and darker colours around the main highlights to develop some rather intricate modelling.

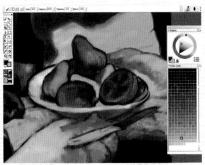

18 **Give the cloth form and body** Now start to add in the lighter areas of the cloth. Don't use bright white here, but a variety of slightly dusky off white colours. Use the brush in short strokes along folds to 'cut in' to them, and give the cloth the very painterly finish that is typical of Cézanne's work.

19 **Shape versus perspective** The very brightest highlights in the painting should be reserved for the bowl itself. Again, use short strokes to form the edges of the bowl rather than drawing careful outlines. The aim here is to convey the actual shape of the objects, not to reproduce the effect of the object in perspective exactly.

20 **Keep it real** Often, Cézanne made objects such as this quite lopsided to describe the essence of their shape better, so don't be afraid of doing this here. Leaving broken areas of background canvas showing through here and there will help with the overall spontaneity of the finished painting.

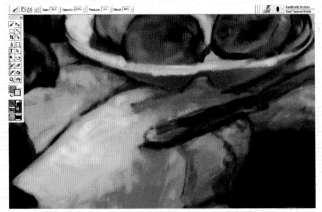

21 **Add highlights sparingly** You can also add some touches of very bright highlights to the cloth, but don't add too many. Again, reducing the Blend value of the brush will result in dry, sticky colour that seems to drag over the surface, just as it would in real-world painting.

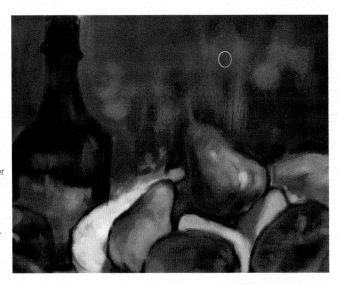

22 **Background interest** Use the brush at a much larger size to add a few lighter greens and neutrals to the background. This will break it up a little and add interest. You can also use these colours to refine the overall outline of the bottle shape.

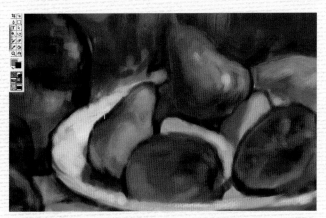

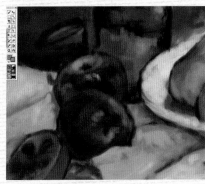

23 **Reflected light** The bottle needs a little light adding to it, without adding too much detail. Do this by adding short strokes of fairly dark bottle greens using the Real Tapered Flat variant. All we're doing here is indicating reflected light and giving the eye somewhere to rest in the top third of the composition.

24 **Take a break** Now take your time to assess the painting as a whole. You can use all of the previous techniques to refine things here and there on another layer. It's a good time now to reinforce the dark outlines around the most important compositional components, and to refine the darkest folds in the fabric.

25 **A few flourishes** Don't forget to add small catch-lights to the fruits as this will give them real solidity. Again, don't use pure white here, but very light blues and mauves. Once you've flattened the painting, try adjusting the colours via Effects>Tonal Controls>Adjust Colors, and increase the saturation for a more vibrant result.

Observation is key | Study your subject

The key element of this tutorial is observation. Take a look at the shapes that your still life forms; look for cones, cylinders and rectangles. We call this 'hidden geometry'. Look at how you've set up your still life or photo reference and make use of it!

HIDDEN GEOMETRY

In the early stages of your painting, it's worth taking your time to think about the hidden geometric shapes within your composition. Here's a very simplified sketch of our composition here, adding weight to Cézanne's insistence that you should paint the essence of what you see.

MAGIC MODELLING

For this kind of painting, rely on modelling with light and shade to create form – not complicated drawing and line work. Here you can see the difference that good light and shade can make. The pear on the right has volume, whereas the one on the left, with too little modelling, looks flat and abstract.

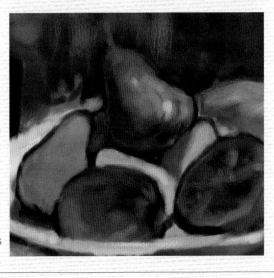

EXPERIMENT WITH COMPOSITION AND VIEWPOINT

To complete this project successfully you need to look, look and look again. Go out and buy some fruit, set it up on a table and be adventurous with your camera. Photograph it from various viewpoints and rearrange the objects. Try to look for pleasing, natural shapes within the composition itself.

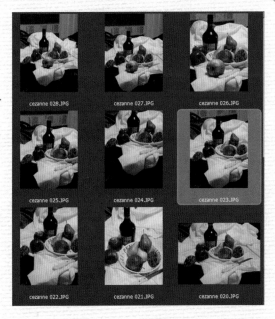

STUDY THE MASTER

You can't paint like Cézanne without studying his work, so do a search on the web. There are hundreds of websites out there telling you everything about Cézanne that you could ever want to know. Study his work closely and it will improve your own painting immeasurably.

Art skills section

222

254

250

242

246

232

214

Artist insight...

How to plan a
painting

1 *Taking the photos*

Planning the composition

2

Getting ready to clone

3

(c) SUSI LAWSON 2008

Before you start throwing digital paint on your canvas, follow **Susi Lawson**'s guide to planning the image and enjoy better results

nless you are blessed with a natural ability to draw and paint whatever is in your imagination, photos will play a large part in the creative process. But just because you are using a photo, it doesn't mean you can't plan beforehand or try out digital 'sketches' to make sure your painting is the best it can be. In this lesson we're going to learn how to go about acquiring that great picture. We are not going to take the lazy way out and scour the internet for free stock photography, we're going to put on our hiking shoes and head to the country!

All you need is a decent digital camera to capture your vision of what will make a beautiful work of art. If you're not a professional photographer and feel a little uncomfortable in this area then this is the time to cast aside your inhibitions and get away from the computer for a bit. This article will give you the information you need to stretch your legs and your digital camera IQ!

I will be taking along the Canon 1D MkIII and a Canon 70-200 f/2.8L IS telephoto. This lens provides a great range for zooming in and out. I also will bring my Canon 24-105 f/4L IS in case I want a good wide-angle shot.

Let me stress that you can use a point and shoot with a good zoom for this task as well, so can still enjoy the fresh air and excitement of taking your own reference photos to use as the basis of some great art.

We've included three photos on the disc for you to see how and why we changed what we did. The file 'Landscape 2' was the main inspiration, but 'Landscape 3' is used, too.

Choosing a composition

As I approached the scene I knew right away that I wanted the little weathered shack to be the focal point and the stark winter trees to be the backdrop, but I also knew that the scene needed more, such as leading lines that help bring the composition together and add more interest to the overall scene. There are actually several such elements in this scene, and the way we frame the image in the viewfinder is essential to a successful composition. Even though cropping and such can be done in software, it's best to get the composition as pleasing as possible in the camera. In these samples, you will see what is included and why.

Location: Ceres, Virginia USA

Portrait
This scene's composition works because I have placed the cabin in the lower left, and the lines of the farm truck path lead the eye from the tree line straight to the cabin.

Taking the photo

Choose the time of day with care – early morning or late afternoon is best

For this shoot we are going to a beautiful valley in the Blue Ridge Mountains of Virginia in a little farming community called Ceres. The back roads of this area are filled with the charm of old abandoned farmhouses and weathered cabins of days gone by, and they make for a great element of interest in a landscape shot. We will be shooting from a hill and aiming the camera at a scene about a mile away, so that's why the telephoto lens is essential in capturing a variety of shots. It is always good to vary the shots from close to far, and from portrait to landscape mode, to enable you to have plenty of variety to play with and choose from, when you get back to the computer.

When shooting landscapes it's best to arrive either after sunrise or just before sunset to catch the best light. But don't let this be a hard and fast rule, as you may never find the time to take pictures! These shots were all taken in the late afternoon around 6.30 to 7.30pm, so it was getting close to sunset. This light gives the long low shadows and pleasing warm light which makes for interesting scenes. (My good friend and budding photographer, Denise Romano, came along and shot the location pictures of me in action).

This area of Ceres is my favourite spot. The little cabin with the sloping landscape and tree lines make for a great composition. I have taken pictures of this scene in every season. It's now coming to the end of winter here, so the colours are not at all vibrant. But we can improve the image during the painting phase. When taking photos, try standing in different positions for a variety of viewpoints. Don't be afraid to squat down, or even take something to stand on!

Landscape
This image has beautiful lines that lead the eye all over, and yet it comes to rest on the cabin. Notice the diagonal triangular shape of the fence coming from the left corner and uniting with the tree upper line – complemented by the 'S' curve of the truck line.

Close-up
Here I capture a closer view of the cabin using my zoom at 200 and walking to the right side. Notice the converging diagonal lines of the landscape connecting all the elements.

Portrait

1

Landscape

2

Close-up

3

Sketch it out

The Rule of Thirds works on the theory that if you place points of interest in the intersections of nine equal squares (or close to them), your photo becomes more balanced. Our eyes usually go to one of the intersection points naturally, so the Rule of Thirds works with this natural way of 'seeing'. Here are some doodles to show how this has worked in our photo.

This composition is pleasing because the cabin is not in the middle of the image, and all lines lead your eye around the image, but back to the cabin.

Notice, once again, the focal point of the image is not in the center – yet the eye is guided by the adjoining lines all leading back to the cabin.

Landscapes do not have to be horizontal. Notice in Portrait Mode, the leading lines work just as well for a pleasing composition.

Painter's composition tools

If you don't fancy drawing out compositions, you can use Painter X's tools. The best are Divine Proportion (Canvas>Compositions>Show Divine Proportions) or the Layout Grid (Canvas>Compositions>Show Layout Grid). These grids appear over your scene and can be modified to suit your needs. Move them around and then crop the image to the desired composition.

Prepping the final photo

It's easy to make a photo bend to your needs. I like the photo I have chosen (Landscape 2), but it could do with some more height. The Resize Canvas tool will add some empty canvas to the bottom. I will also use the Straight Clone brush to add elements from another image and get the perfect scene for my vision.

01 Close-up To resize the canvas, go to Canvas/Resize and add 500 pixels to the bottom of the image as shown.

02 Cloning To clone the foreground area of another image into the empty canvas area you just created, choose the Brush tool and select your Clone brush using the Straight Cloner.

Start your clone source in the left corner of the first image you want to copy, then move your cursor or stylus to the empty canvas and paint the new foreground onto the white area. Now close Landscape 3 as we no longer need it, and use the same Clone tool to eliminate the distracting pole in the foreground by using the grass beside it. Clean up any other debris using this method.

Colour controls

Before we paint our landscape we need to prepare it with simple tools. Now that we have the composition and elements we want to include, we can boost the colours and darken the tyre tracks that add human interest to this weathered and otherwise lonely landscape. The tracks tell the viewer that 'there's life on the farm'. Increasing the saturation will reveal colours that weren't apparent before and help you decide where you want to go with your painting.

03 Burn tool Since the truck path in this landscape is an essential part of the composition, let's make it stand out even more by using the Burn tool and going over this area to really emphasise it, as shown. You will find this tool in the Photo brushes.

04 Adjust the colours Now let's adjust the colours by going to Effects>Tonal Control>Adjust Color, and add more saturation to the landscape to liven it up.

The final artwork

Turn your creation into a masterpiece with a little help from Corel Painter

Now that we have the pictures taken and the composition worked out, it's time to take our favourite scene into Corel Painter and make this into a painting worthy of framing! I know right away that I want to add more colours to those winter trees and bring in some depth and light in the shadows, and just generally add some life to the landscape.

HERE'S HOW...

01 Painting the grass For the grass I chose the Oil>Round Camel brush for its smooth soft quality. Paint over all the large areas left to right, taking care not to paint over the tyre tracks.

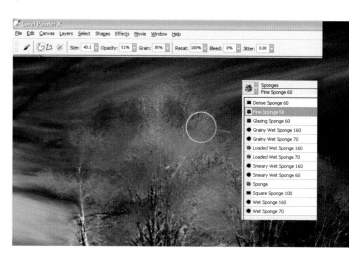

04 Painting the tree tops Now let's use the Fine Sponge brush at 50% Opacity, and brush the tops of the trees using an up and down motion for a really pretty effect that works well for this area.

07 Adding more tree colour By using the Regular Sponge brush and deselecting Use Clone Color, I can add some bright yellow to the top of the trees to suggest the sunlight.

02 Painting the tracks Now I zoomed in using the same brush, and I painted over the tyre tracks following the lines of the tracks with my brush, while adjusting to the curves so as not to smudge them away.

03 Blending shadows Still using the Camel Oil brush, zoom in and paint over the blue shadows and areas between the trees, taking care not to rake across the trees. Don't worry about any small twigs and such-like in theses areas.

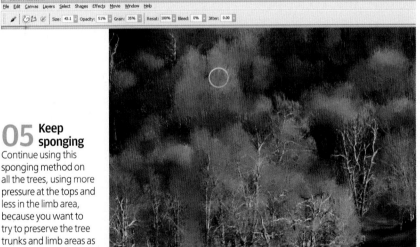

05 Keep sponging Continue using this sponging method on all the trees, using more pressure at the tops and less in the limb area, because you want to try to preserve the tree trunks and limb areas as much as possible. Zoom in where you need to.

06 Tree limbs The tree branches add interest to the painting, but using the Acrylic Capture brush and painting over them by following the lines with a Small Tip brush makes them less 'stark', and makes them blend in more with the rest of the painting.

08 Adding shadow colour Again, using the Regular Sponge brush, I will now add dark purple to the shadow area of the trees to add some depth.

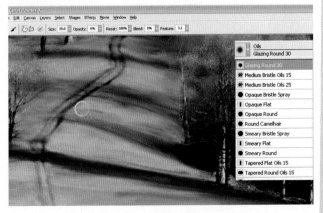

09 Glazing in ground shadows To add more colours I chose the Oil Glazing brush, and added some soft violet shadows to the ground. Be sure that Use Clone Color is deselected.

Things to remember

Be prepared for the shoot

It's always good to have at least two lenses to choose from. If you can bring along a second camera with a wide-angle lens, and one with a telephoto, you will be ready for anything and won't have to worry about changing lenses.

Cautious and courteous

The best place to find beautiful scenery is usually in remote areas of the country that you discover by just driving around and stopping when something catches your eye. This is how I found the 'Kidd Farm' featured in this tutorial. However, when you are on private property it's always best to call or knock on the door and ask permission to be there. Not only is this courteous, but also safe, as you never know when someone might have a watchdog, or just not be too friendly towards strangers!

Don't get too caught up in rules

The rules of composition are good to learn as a guide, but don't let it stand in your way if your scene doesn't fit this rule. Be creative and follow your own heart – you are the artist and the ultimate rule-maker or breaker of your own work!

Finishing touches

Paint the cabin, add a fence and brighten up the overall scene

11 Add a fence

There's a fence in the left foreground that adds to the composition, so I defined it more by painting over it with dark brown using the Acrylic Opaque Round brush. The last thing I always do is pump up the brightness and contrast of my painting by using Effects>Tonal Control> Brightness, Contrast and Adjust to get the most pleasing result.

10 Paint the cabin
Using Clone Color and the Acrylic Capture brush, paint over the entire cabin – taking care to follow the natural lines of the roof and boards.

FINAL CLONED PAINTING

"THE LAST THING I ALWAYS DO IS PUMP UP THE BRIGHTNESS AND CONTRAST OF MY PAINTING"

(c) Susi Lawson 2008

SPECIAL OFFER FOR USA READERS!

Subscribe today and save 62%

For regular digital art inspiration, why not take out a subscription to the **Official Corel Painter** magazine?

Exclusive subscriber benefits

- Subscribe today and pay just $75 for 13 issues *
- Get each issue for as little as $5.77 (usually $14.95)
- Receive the mag before it appears in the shops
- Never miss an issue
- Money-back guarantee on any unmailed issues

Non-US readers turn to page 29

*Terms and conditions
This is a US subscription offer. You will actually be charged £50 sterling for an annual subscription. This is equivalent to $75 at the time of writing, although the exchange rate may vary. Your subscription will start from the next available issue. This offer can expire without notice

To order securely online, visit the website below and enter the offer code **USA**

www.imaginesubs.co.uk/COR

To order by phone, call the number below and quote the offer code **USA**

+44(0)1795 414 611

A guide to...
mark-making

For perfect pictures, you need to pick the right marks for the job.
Read on for a guide to what works well when drawing a great sketch

PARALLEL HATCHING

TONAL SHADING

DIRECTIONAL MARK-MAKING

CROSS HATCH

Drawing reference photos

GO TO www.morguefile.com

Designers and artists are constantly being challenged to become more sophisticated and creative in their approach to grabbing people's attention, and it is the way they use their tools, be it a pen, brush or computer to create marks on paper, that ensure their survival in this high-speed world. The transference of information and the viewer's ability to interpret that information are the two key factors that make all types of art and design successful. But they are on a winner above writers; if a picture paints a thousand words, that's a three-page essay read in an instant, and if you'll pardon

the pun, mark-making is the best way to make your mark.

The suitability and readability of the marks need to be completely appropriate to get the message across. These pages set out to enhance your understanding and your awareness of the power of your mark-making, and how it will make others respond. We are going to expand our own visual dictionary of marks we can use to describe our subject. We are going to think about marks in terms of words; how can we fill the image with information and details that the viewer will 'read' and understand clearly? This takes a lot of empathy and observation

on our part, choosing the right words for an answer is just as hard as choosing the right marks for an image.

But this isn't as esoteric as it might sound. There are tried and tested methods for which marks convey what effect –some are good for shadow, for example, or there's the perfect mark for fur. Using the correct marks for the job will give your drawings that stamp of authenticity. We're looking at the major ones here, along with what they are suitable for.

The reference photos we've used come from MorgueFile (**www.morguefile.com**), but you can practise on anything.

Your mark options
What works and what doesn't

All marks are dependant on pressure (how hard you press it into the page), softness (what H or B the lead of your pencil is) and expression (what is the meaning of the mark? Is it a light cross-hatch to suggest a light shadow on a face, or is it a harsh, brash, speedily drawn cross-hatch that suggests movement, speed or darkness?). These will vary drastically as you might want to portray anything from smoothness, wetness or fluffiness. While a lot is left to what mood you want to convey, there are some tried and tested marks that always work wonders. Here are the best:

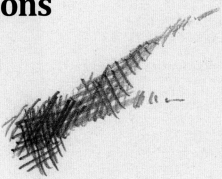

CROSS-HATCHING
Cross-hatching is the fail-safe mark within mark-making; it covers all evils, flaws and errors. You can count on it when you aren't quite sure what mark to use. It can be very effective for furry or fluffy objects.

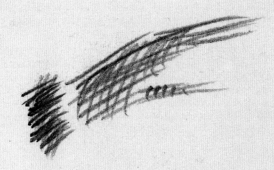

DIRECTIONAL MARKS
Directional shading is a very expressive type of mark-making, a representation of which way and length you feel the mark should be made. It is great for fur and vegetation, such as grassy tufts and tussocks.

PARALLEL-HATCHING
Parallel-hatching is really a response from you as you react to the object in front of you. Look carefully at the surface; do the grains or hairs or cells all go in one particular way? We used it effectively for describing the grain in wood; da Vinci used it to suggest the sky in about two seconds flat.

DOTTING
You can use dots to describe shadows as they graduate away in the same way as cross-hatching. The emphasis is not so much on pressure and meaning, but size, tool and repetition. A sharp pencil creates a tiny delicate dot; oil pastel creates a stodgy, meaty one.

SMOOTH SHADING
Smooth shading... everyone's mark-making nemesis! The temptation to scribble can be overwhelming. Our tip to create smooth shading and avoid stripes at all costs is to use a B lead on its side. Shade with an even pressure, in circles, to avoid stripes. This is very good for metal or shiny, smooth objects with a flat texture.

TONAL RENDERING
Tonal rendering is the epic means of creating subtle tones and shadows on flat or smooth surfaces. Use the pencil as above, but apply pressure for added depth and take the pressure off to lighten it. Always shade at the same speed.

CASUAL STROKES
Casual strokes are the marks used to describe, in the simplest terms, the maximum information as fast as possible. Van Gogh casually marked out the clouds in his drawings. It's perfect for working drawings and thumbnail sketches from imagination or reality.

CIRCULAR STROKES OR CONTOURS
Circular strokes are best employed for watery or moving objects, or if the object itself is circular in nature; curly hair or wool for example. They can convey three dimensions quite beautifully too. If you are looking at a posture or a pot, a spiral description can be very effective.

Drawing 101

Contour strokes

Notice that the swirls are contours like you would find in a tree trunk, concentric circles that follow the form of the shape of each block

MorgueFile ref. no. H432

When you watch water sparkle and move continually, the big abstract shapes and blocks of colour that undulate harmoniously together merge with soft and hard lines. We chose to use curvaceous contour lines that define those emergent shapes with definition. This is not a fluffy texture, it needs structure, which is odd for something so formless. Shading these shapes accurately and observing their jigsaw-piece snugness are your keys to success.

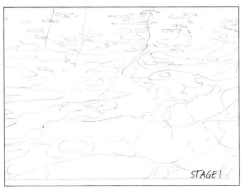

STAGE 1

STAGE 2

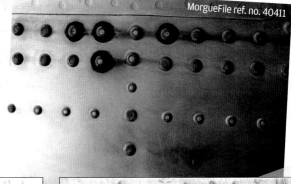

STAGE 3

SETTING UP THE COMPOSITION
First of all you need to break down the picture space loosely, but with care, sweeping light **H** pencil lines across the paper to represent the major sections of the image. Consider areas of light or chunks of dark.

A LIGHT LAYER OF SHAPES
Continue to use your **H** pencil to lay out the outlines of the main shapes that the water makes. As this is a light layer, it gives you a great amount of room to manoeuvre, the flexibility to make mistakes and to estimate how the final image will play out.

A SECOND LAYER OF SHAPES
Use the depth of a **B** pencil to add some tonal variations. Keep in mind the areas at the back which are going to demand more darkness and the front areas which need a lighter swirling description. Use a **4B** or **5B** pencil for the real depths of darkness and an **HB** will do for the swirls in the foreground.

Tonal rendering

Use your magical powers of observation to really look at how the highlights create form and the shadows create depth

Smooth, flat, almost textureless objects such as those made of metal can often be the most demanding in terms of precision and control. Because the surface is flawless and smooth, all scribbles and any out-of-place marks are to be avoided at all costs. The perfect marks can be made with either tonal rendering or a graduated shading. By following the technique below, you can simulate the subtle variations of the shadows as they merge and overlap.

MorgueFile ref. no. 40411

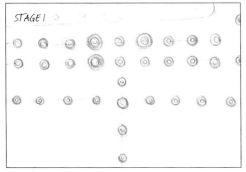

STAGE 1

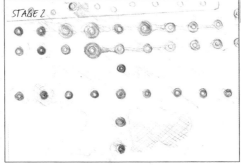

STAGE 2

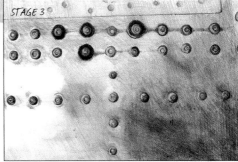

STAGE 3

SETTING OUT THE COMPOSITION AND REAFFIRMING IT
This image is basically a composition of circles along a series of lines; map this out with gestural lines and shapes in an **H** pencil. Go over it carefully to confirm where and what size each circle is, and ensure that all they all relate accurately.

IDENTIFYING THE TONAL DIFFERENCES ON THE IMAGE
Now you are ready to plot the areas of the greatest or least area of tone. Pay real attention and familiarise yourself with all the lights and shadows. Scribble in a layer of expressive directional-hatching to identify them.

SHOWING OFF YOUR AMAZING POWERS OF OBSERVATION
Now gird up your loins to get down to the nitty-gritty. Apply the correct amount of pressure and choose the appropriate weight of lead to create the shadow you want. A blunt edge and the side of your pencil will create smooth shadows.

Directional shading

Nature produces some of the most beautiful patterns in the world, so grab your pencil and draw them

The grainy molecular nature of wood is perfect for exploring marks made in specific directions. The layers and rings and whorls in the wood form repetitive patterns in clear directions. Vary your pencil and the pressure to modulate these in order to express and describe the shape and shadows that the grains and cracks create. Careful observation and analysis of the texture is equal in importance to really nail down the image accurately.

MorgueFile ref. no. 133132

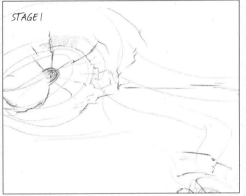

STAGE 1

SETTING UP THE COMPOSITION
Break up the blank paper with a brisk and expressive drawing of the main players of your piece. Use an H pencil to freely describe how the pattern flows across the page.

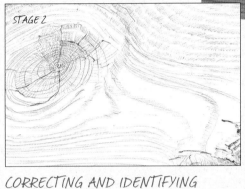

STAGE 2

CORRECTING AND IDENTIFYING MAJOR RELATIONSHIPS
Build up layers of pattern and swirling shapes and add detail where necessary. Correct and tweak with care and accuracy the spatial relationships between the curves and curls in the grain.

STAGE 3

DIRECTIONAL SHADING
On this H pencil skeleton, build up the flesh of your image with short, stubby lines that follow the flow of the grain. Work out how they flow together and use a pencil with more depth (4B) to accentuate the cracks and directions the grain takes. This will add substance and excitement to your finished image.

Cross-hatching

Go to town with your pencil and marvel in the glory of folds, and the fantastic tonal variation that they provide

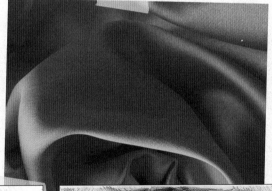

The most fun and satisfying things to draw in our opinion are folds. Folds in anything; clothes, skin, paper. The method is almost exactly the same for each. We generally use cross-hatching, just because it does the job perfectly well, though you can use curvy lines or contour lines to create a certain effect, or even straight lines to contrast with the flow of the line. But for observational purposes and serious drawing, cross-hatching works like a charm.

STAGE 1

SKETCHING THE OUTLINES
Sketch in lightly with an H pencil the main outlines of folds, creases and curves of importance; be gestural and expressive to ensure you get a feel for the movement of the fabric. Then briefly and lightly fill in the areas of shadow so you have a foundation to work on.

STAGE 2

THE FIRST LAYER APPLIED
Now you can really get to grips with a carefully considered layer of light H pencil that you can thoroughly cross-hatch. First follow the curve of the fold with one direction of cross-hatching and then give it a second layer heading in the opposite direction.

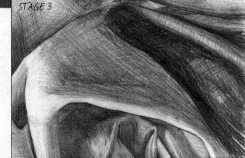

STAGE 3

THE HIGHLIGHTS AND DEPTHS
Finally, and most rewarding, use a 2B pencil to define the shadows and highlights quite beautifully. You are definitely allowed to scribble and build up additional layers in the depths of shadows, but do vary the pressure and speed at which you cross-hatch so you create delicate hatching too.

Understand
Shadows, highlights and midtones

Shadows and highlights are an artist's greatest allies. Forget rulers and erasers, understanding shadows helps you troubleshoot drawing problems...

H ere is your first challenge, which is designed to help you look for and distinguish those helpful, but annoyingly elusive, tonal variations. Look steadily at whatever happens to be in front of you. Any sort of lighting (as long as it isn't pitch black) will do. Now if you can, allow your eyes to go out of focus, and you will notice the tones much more readily as the real objects lose their sharpness. If you can't make your eyes unfocused, half close them so you can almost see your eyelashes. This is easier for some people, but can be a bit uncomfortable for a long time. Notice how that pile of books on the table casts graduated tones on the wall behind it, for example? Shadows that you may not have fully been aware of before can really help with proportions and shapes, and outline problems that you may have with drawing or painting.

We are going to investigate the hues of different tones too in this tutorial. As the French Impressionist painter Monet knew only too well – there is rarely an occasion that finds a truly black shadow. His paintings demonstrate shadows and tones in blues and pinks rather than simple greys, as seen in his snowy landscape *La Pie (The Magpie)*. This observation was made in conjunction with the connections made at the time regarding colour theory and the implications this knowledge of primary, secondary and complementary colours had on tints and shades. For this exercise it helps to know that there is more to shadows than various depths of grey!

Our first task involves breaking a photo down into its midtones, shadows and highlights. You will see how each layer combines to create the final colours. Then we will move on to creating a sepia tonal study on pages 230–231.

Paint the scene

This photo is an excellent example of a wide tonal range. It exhibits dark shadows, bright highlights and has many midtones in-between. We're going to eventually deal with the image as a whole, but for now, we've concentrated on specific parts of it and shown how it can be broken down into the highlights, midtones and shadows. Have a look at our interpretation along with the original photo and you will begin to see how it works.

This photo was taken from MorgueFile (**www.morguefile.com**). It's no longer available, but a similar image can be found with ID 126622.

ORIGINAL PHOTO

SHADOWY PEAKS

The peaks are shadowed by billowing cloud, creating clear and defined shapes. The lighter shadows have a purple tint, and the darkest are very deep and may include black. Begin with the lightest first; the creamy, sunlit stone. Then add a layer of middle-grey, and intensify specific areas by adding one or two deeper greys on top. Follow this format of light to dark with the whole picture.

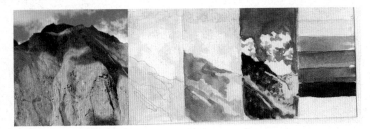

PURPLE PEAKS

This swatch illustrates the colours needed to represent the aerial perspective at work on the distant peaks. It subtly changes the colour of the shadows on these mountains. Compare them with the sharpness of the browner foreground peaks for the right touch of purple and paleness. The distance diminishes their contrast and sharpness.

DISTANT SHORES

The shoreline of the lake is just visible at the top – note the reflection of the mountain and the hills adding a dark green tone on top of the blue-grey. Your greatest challenge is to get a sense of distance. Use your marks, shadows and colours with careful consideration. The light blue should be covered with a layer of graduated ripples that merge at the shoreline.

FOREGROUND RIPPLES

A light base once again brings out the reflected stonework. Now carefully pencil in the general shapes of the dark tones or the highlights (whichever you can distinguish with the greatest ease). Then gradually build up the blue tones with an accurately scaled range of marks; smaller at the back and bigger at the front.

STONY TREE LINE

This is the part of the mountain where the gradient and temperature is too severe for trees to grow. Grass foothills recede to reveal the mountain. The sun hits it, bleaching the stone, and grass clings on to it in patches. Tones are limited and the contrast reduced, so pay great attention to the depth of shadows to create an authentic, yet subtle difference.

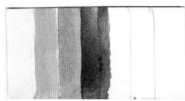

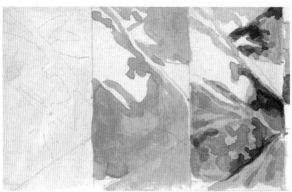

> *"...pay great attention to the depth of shadows to create an authentic, yet subtle difference"*

GRASSY FOOTHILLS

This area presents a challenge to the subtlety and effectiveness of overlaying greens. Consider carefully how you are going to angle your brush, and what size it should be to sweep over the rolling foothills. Accentuate the subtle curves or build up a shadowy, energetic bushiness. This expressiveness contrasts nicely with the structure and control needed to negotiate the house.

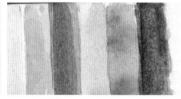

Split an image

Simplify the daunting task of evaluating and depicting tones by having a systematic approach. It's best to work from light to dark, so begin by accessing the image and picking out the highlights. Lay these down first. Then establish your midtone values. If you're using watercolour as we are here, you can usually apply another layer of wash. Finally it's time to bring in the shadows. These really liven up a painting and make it something special.

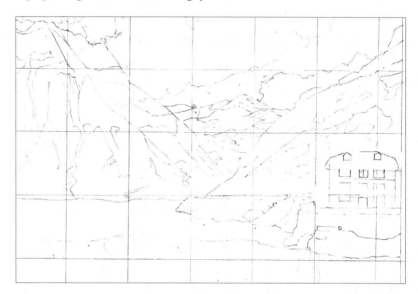

TRACE THE IMAGE

Download the photo we have used for this tutorial and use a grid system like this one shown above to sketch it accurately

PALE WASHES

Imagine you are wearing x-ray glasses, or looking at the photo through a microscope, and choose the lightest colour for each section. Ignore heavy shadows and detail, and select and mix the colour with care. In this example, the mountains have a creamy, pinkish tone, which is picked up less obviously elsewhere: the shoreline, the brick work and in the water, which seems logical since the mountains and the house are reflected in it. Use a Large brush to achieve the least and smoothest brushstrokes. Mix a yellowy-green and a very watery blue for the sky, grassland and the water.

MIDTONES

Half-close, or adjust the focus of your eyes to simplify the complex, detailed shadows that fall on the mountain. Ensure that your drawing is visible beneath your watery highlights, use an H pencil to prevent smudging and allow removal of gridlines used to plot it out. A brief line drawing should guide your **Flat-Tipped Medium** sized brush to represent the shadows on the mountains in a greyish, blueish purple. Then enhance the blueness and flatness of the sky with a middle shade of blue. Pay attention to the general shadows on the water, use a big brush if necessary, and consider the direction your brush is going: would down or sideways be best?

SHADOW

As the shadows get darker they become more detailed and shapely, so choose a smaller brush to sharpen the focus and contrast. Intensify the amount of colour and reduce the water you mix to add greater depth. This should create the desired illusion of depth or realistic three-dimensions. This stage really will test you. Keep looking at the photo, tweak and adjust your marks and mixing where necessary. Remember that the foreground is always darker and sharper than the fuzzy lightness of the background. Be prepared to water down dark shadows, and layer-up to darken weak ones. The shape and direction of your marks is pivotal here too achieve a polished finish.

Use Painter to select tones

Let the software do the work...

Some scenes lend themselves beautifully to working with tones, leaving the viewer in no doubt as to where the shadows, highlights and midtones lie. But for every easy scene, there are thousands of trickier outlooks that need a lot of concentration and a bit of invention. All of which is fine if you are well practised in mentally dividing a scene into tonal values, but what if you've just started out? A trip to the Posterize command in Painter is a good start. This feature will strip away colour information, simplifying the scene so you can get a better idea of where the midtones, shadows and highlights lie, before attempting your painting. It's very easy to use the command. Simply open your photo>Edit>Tonal Controls>Posterize and enter a number of levels. The less levels you have, the more simplified the colours.

01 Information overload This is a very complex scene. There are lots of greens, and the sunlight has distributed the highlights all over the image. You could spend ages gazing at the image to try and gauge where the important areas are, but there is a far easier way. And that way is the Posterizer!

02 Stripping it back Here we've opened the Posterizer command and entered '2' in the Levels field. Notice how the shadows have become a lot more pronounced, and the highlights leap off the screen. The rest is the midtones.

03 More detail You don't have to go to extremes – here we have entered '5' as the number of levels. A lot of detail has been retained, but the various levels have been given a helping hand. A setting like 5 is good if you still want to play about with the midtones.

Drawing 101

ORIGINAL PHOTO

Tonal study

Tonal studies allow an artist to get to grips with a scene and understand how the colours are distributed. Although you can use different colours in a tonal study, limiting yourself to just one will allow you to concentrate on the scene in front of you. The greatest test is to allow tones to build the image for you. Pencil should be a guide only, do not rely on outlines to create three dimensions, use tones. Look at the bright white columns, the outlines on them are invisible and the edges are created by the shadows that lie behind and beside them. Try this for yourself by going to **www.morguefile.com** and downloading image reference 137840.

DETAILED LINE DRAWING OR TRACING

Use an H pencil to draw the shapes accurately, in line. Do not shade or use a ruler to measure out the exact relationships between features. Crucially, draw significant details like the latticework, the weatherboards and the wooden rails at the front. Check your angles to achieve an accurate perspective. Now you have created a solid, reliable foundation to build tones on.

LIGHTEST OF WASHES

There are three things to do here. Mix up a generous, very watery amount of watercolour, just a couple of brush-fulls of dark brown to tint the water. Brush this over your drawing everywhere except the areas of white – namely the left sides of the foreground columns. Use a large brush, as the coverage is more important at this point than control.

A SECOND LAYER

Once this wash has dried, rub out any pencil lines around the white areas. Try to keep the sharpness with watercolour shading only. Use a large brush to give a second layer of the lightest wash on any area of general big shadow. You should be aiming to reveal the diagonal shadow across the back wall, door, window and the latticework.

MIX UP A DARKER WASH TO WORK ON SHADOWS

Now you have a base coat of clear, subtle tones you can start to build up interest focus and detail. Use a smaller, flat-ended brush that can create a thick and a thin mark, a little like calligraphy. Mix a darker wash and test it out on the top of the veranda, just to check that it isn't too overwhelming at this stage.

A LAYER OF MIDTONE

Take your time, work carefully and systematically. I am working from top to bottom so that my hand doesn't smudge or hide my last brush mark. Once again, look carefully at the curved cornice at the top of the veranda, the door, the window and the dark shadows that are cast on the wall.

THE SHADOW OF THE LATTICEWORK

This detailed area deserves special attention. Look carefully at the photograph and notice how the shadows fall. Use your smallest brush to paint in the shadow that fills the diamond shapes, and the shadow on the right side of the latticed wood.

ESTABLISH TONAL RANGE

Now do a third wash. You may need a fourth or fifth as well, to define the variations realistically. Use a medium sized flat-ended brush to layer and define shadows. This image demonstrates the full range of tones from white to dark. The window and the column demonstrate the greatest tonal contrast, and this is an important limit to establish and work within.

DARKEST SHADOWS IN THE BACKGROUND AND FOREGROUND

Once the range is established to your satisfaction, work over the whole image – taking care to keep detail sharp by allowing layers to dry before you work over them. Keep looking at your photo to check the tone and detail.

OVERALL TONAL RELATIONSHIPS

Allow your work to dry and take a break from it for an hour or two. Some people look at their work with a mirror, and that can pick up things that your brain has ignored previously. At this stage the tone of the ceiling was bothering me, so I mixed up my lightest tone once again and swept another layer on top, using a flat large brush.

GAIN ACCURATE SHADOWS

You can leave your image at step nine, all your tonal work is complete and you can feel satisfied that you have produced a realistic, high quality, sophisticated painting. However, you may feel inclined to create shadows with more formality, depth and polish than a brush can achieve. I felt thus inclined and reached for my colouring pencils and ruler.

FINAL DEPTHS

This image shows the completed painting with coloured pencil detail, a mid-brown and dark brown pencil crayon, the brush marks of three different brushes, along with a huge amount of patience! Test your tonal observation with a range of subjects. Start simply with one object, you never know where you'll end up...

The skills of
Still life drawing

Fine-tune your drawing skills with the age-old tradition of still life

Try following our tutorial using the still life photo on the disc

SOURCE FILE ON THE CD!

Drawing 101

The still life genre is one of the most popular vehicles artists use to flagrantly show off. This formula for painting arrangements of everyday, inanimate objects dates from the 17th century.

One of the seminal still life artists is Juan Sanchez Cotan. Cotan's work exemplifies the prevailing taste at the time for all things real and somewhat grubby. The movement at the time was Baroque. Its famously stark lighting and dramatic shadows were a reaction to the previous beautifying period of the High Renaissance, glorifying the dirt and no-frills ugliness of real life. 17th century Spanish painter Velazquez painted *An Old Woman Cooking Eggs* when he was 18. The dark shadows and unforgiving lighting sets off the copper, ceramic and metal objects beautifully.

This style of lighting has been hugely influential throughout the centuries, and can be seen in the *Godfather* trilogy to create a sense of dark, brooding despair. We are going to use this dramatic tone to enhance and enrich our still life setup.

In contrast to this oppressive style, Audrey Flack is a contemporary American artist whose body of work includes some equally stunning work, yet are in total contrast to the Baroque themes of darkness. However, they too have prodigious 'wow' factor qualities. This artist uses air brushing as part of her technique, and creates impossibly colourful, textural and glossy still lifes. Her work is worth examining to illustrate two points about still life. First, her innovative use of composition and unusual viewpoints gives great results. In *Chanel*, her use of a cramped and close-up viewpoint and the mirror reflecting the scene enriches the detail and intricacy of the composition.

Still life scenarios

What works and what doesn't in this genre

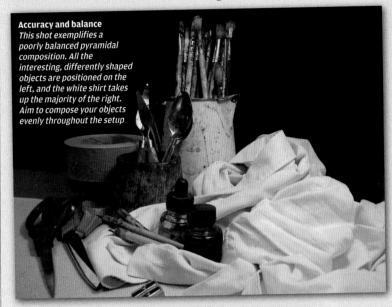

Accuracy and balance
This shot exemplifies a poorly balanced pyramidal composition. All the interesting, differently shaped objects are positioned on the left, and the white shirt takes up the majority of the right. Aim to compose your objects evenly throughout the setup

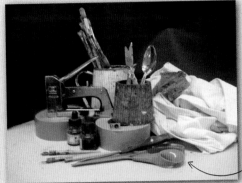

Contrast and definition
Emphasise the visual qualities of your objects. Spotlights create more highlights and shadows than fluorescent light. Make sure your objects show off their best features. Use a good quality image and avoid pixellation and blurring

Ellipses and foreshortening
This unusual shot is not in keeping with Baroque Realism. The scissors and pens loom bizarrely towards you and the circular tape appears flat. The stapler is also disguised by the foreshortening and the brush tips are lost

Chosen composition
All the objects can be clearly seen and are positioned so they enhance each other – large with small, plain with intricate. This provides a fun and challenging set of tasks

Poor composition
The aim of composition is to show everything off and to really give the illusion of casual placement, but to actually arrange things pleasingly with a sense of togetherness. This attempt misses the point, like the scissors

---

Second, Flack illustrates another purpose of still life, which is worth mentioning here because it may influence your choice of objects. In her piece, *Marilyn Vanitas*, she refers to the 17th century theme of still life known as Vanitas paintings.

Objects are chosen and arranged because of their meaning. These paintings were composed specifically so as to subtly remind people that life and beauty is fleeting. Typically, a small or partially hidden symbol would lurk within a stunningly beautiful setup. For example, in Cornelis de Heem's *Vanitas*

Still Life With Musical Instruments, the jam-packed virtuoso performance by this Dutch artist is a picture of disarray and excess, and at the very bottom, if you look carefully, a snail hungrily eyes the fruit.

So now it is our turn to rise to the formidable challenge of still life. Over the next few pages we will break the task down into steps, troubleshoot potential mistakes and list important tips to help you on your way. This tradition allows you to explore the elements of art – line, form, shape, tone, texture and composition – and enhance your skills of observation. We will go through several

different ways to help you 'see' what is really there rather than 'look/glance' at what appears to be there. The next few exercises will help build your confidence to enjoy drawing successfully.

When it comes to setting up your own still life, there are alphabetical pointers to consider: accuracy, balance, contrast, definition, ellipses and foreshortening. The images above illustrate how these principles can affect a still life setup, so try them all and get a good grounding in the principles. We're concentrating on traditional pencils here, but you can apply the principles to any format.

Drawing the scene
Drawing normally

Now you have a still life photo, it's important to consider some of the common hurdles and traps that can occur during this task.

There is nothing more daunting than a blank page, so drawing a grid over the photo and then one on the paper will help you position objects accurately.

Another way to begin is to choose an object near the centre of your composition and use it to relate to shape, size and spaces taken up by other objects. This measurement can be used to ensure that everything is drawn in proportion to that measurement. Keep checking the relationships between the objects and correct them if it goes wrong – don't keep blindly trudging forward.

A really clear line drawing can be sketchy at the outset. Pencil in shapes, but go over the top of this once again to draw a bold confident line for clear definition.

With an accurate line comes accurate tone. Shading needs layering, subtly and an appropriate choice of pencil. But, just as much, it needs really keen observation. When drawing ellipses, draw the bottom curve then turn your paper upside down and re-draw it; it is a much more natural, controlled and even method.

The mantra 'less is more' is always worth keeping in mind. In art, it essentially means that some lines and shades that you think need to be included don't. The paintbrushes best exemplify this. The delicate texture of their bristles can be lost if you outline them heavily; let the background do the work for you, leave the line out, and draw the background solidly but a bit randomly.

When you are making the marks, bear in mind the subject you are drawing. For example, drapery loves curvy, more circular lines to accentuate the contours, but use dots and scribbles for sponge.

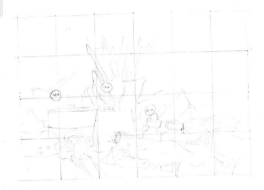

SQUARING UP
This really lets you map out your image without thinking about the relationships, and is excellent for building your confidence. There is no shame in using grids, so don't feel like you are cheating. It's a great starting point and used by many more people than would care to admit it.

ACCURATE PROPORTIONS
Work outwards from the middle using a cross in the centre to start the measurements. The spoon fits about three times into the top half of the picture and one of the brush tips can be spotted two 'spoons' up. Now you know you are not going to run out of space at the top.

LINE DRAWING
Once you are happy with your sketchy 2H workings that quietly outline your objects, use a H pencil to produce a clear and confident shape that sorts out any complex areas you may have secretly put off tackling, for example, the scissor blades or the brushes.

SHADING
With a solid foundation of drawing, use 2H, H and HB pencils for the midtones and greys, and 4B and 6B pencils for the darkest background areas. Check you have a really broad range of contrast from black to white. Circular rather than stripy shading can really improve the smoothness of your shadows.

REDUNDANCY
Look closely at the still life and, where there is a meeting of intense darks and lights, consider how you could use the shadow to make the outline redundant. This really tests your powers of observation, so if at first you don't succeed...

MARK MAKING
Experiment with the marks to show what you and your pencil can really do. The metal sheen is achieved with a rubber, but nothing is impossible. Smudging, scribble, rulers, rubbers and grids all are acceptable in the name of the still life 'wow' factor!

Upside-down drawing

f you can feel yourself bridling at the idea of having a go at the 'serious' high-brow challenge we have just rattled off, here is a welcome break!

This is a really entertaining and quite mind-boggling exercise. It is often far more effective at helping you actually lay out a picture than squaring up or figuring out proportion measurements. We are enchanted by the optical and psychological magic of it, and it once again helps to dispel that age-old procrastinatory myth of 'I can't draw'! So prepare to suspend your disbelief and roll up your sleeves to pull off the best trick in town!

We have included the still life photo on the disc. Turn this upside-down and, starting at either the left or right side, draw what is in front of you. This can be on a larger piece of paper, but it must be approximately the same landscape shape as the drawing. Keep referring to your drawing and then the photo. Hold your nerve and don't turn it up the right way until you've finished! Then, with a flourish, amaze your audience with the accuracy of your work.

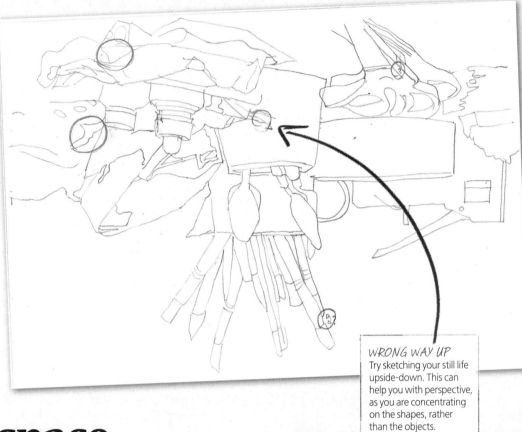

WRONG WAY UP
Try sketching your still life upside-down. This can help you with perspective, as you are concentrating on the shapes, rather than the objects.

Negative space

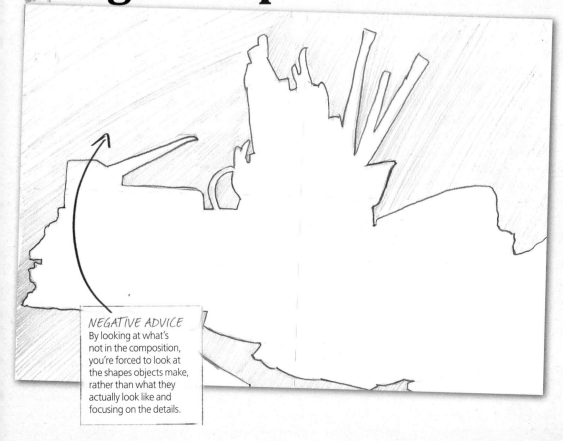

NEGATIVE ADVICE
By looking at what's not in the composition, you're forced to look at the shapes objects make, rather than what they actually look like and focusing on the details.

ne exercise that will definitely increase your understanding of the still life genre and allow you to express yourself a bit more freely is to look at the negative space of your image.

Our brain often fools us into taking the easy option and only recording objects as we expect them to be shown. Think of how easy it is to draw from your imagination as a child. The brain stores its own little visual vocabulary based on past experiences and previous versions, and it's much easier to churn out these than to really apply it. Children's formulaic drawings of houses are intrinsically recognisable as houses.

In the room, the objects themselves occupy positive space and the space around them is negative. For this task, draw lines and shapes to represent the space that the still life does not take up. The best example of this is the space between the handle and jug; it helps you look at the shape of the handle not just take it in and jot it down without thought. Draw as if you have never seen them.

Drawing 101

A still life step-by-step

Break an image down into sections for triumphant results

So, armed with some helpful tips, some interesting ways to test your powers of drawing, and a confident can-do attitude, it's time to try showing off some of your own 'wow' factor. The following steps show a systematic, logical approach to tackling the task, bit by methodical bit.

The setup we have used is a randomly but pleasingly arranged collection of artroom paraphernalia. They have been chosen for their variety of textures, forms and shapes, but are in keeping with the muted colours of the Baroque artists we have looked at.

Working from a photograph is a great way to begin; it's convenient for many reasons, especially because it is flat already, and takes up much less space. When you are confident using photographs, push the limits of your comfort zone and rise to the challenge of drawing a real still life that is right in front of you. Enjoy the experience of fluctuating light conditions and mysterious shifting of objects, knowledge of which will be denied by other members of your household, and the unstoppable passage of time on objects that are perishable! But seriously, the sense of achievement, enjoyment and relaxation is worth it so do have a go.

Tackling the still life

Go from photo to a piece of art

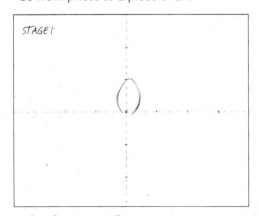

STARTING POINT
Use a ruler to mark the centre of each side and draw a very light or dotted cross with an 'x' at the centre. Draw the same (if possible) on your picture. Measure with your finger the times your spoon fits along the top line (about three times) from the centre; divide this line into about three equally. Draw the shape of the spoon.

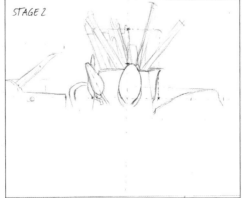

TOP HALF PROPORTIONS
Using your standard measurement of the spoon, work out where the rest of the objects sit in the top half. For example, the top lip of the jug may be two spoons wide with half a spoon on one side and one and a half on the other. Think join-the-dots at this stage.

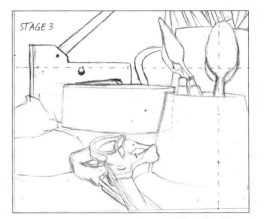

BOTTOM LEFT QUARTER PROPORTIONS
Pay special attention to the foreshortening of the scissors; rely on your standard spoon and be reassured that it will not try and fox you – yes those scissors really are that short! Concentrate on making sure the outlines are clear and confident – there is no need for tone at the moment.

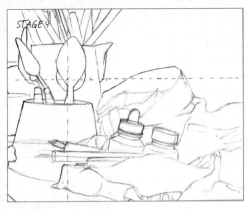

STAGE 4

BOTTOM RIGHT

There is much more detail in these two bottom quarters, so it's important to feel confident that they are accurate. Take pride in providing yourself with a concrete foundation to work with. It's not a myth that you should look more at the still life than your drawing. Keep looking, checking and tweaking it until you are absolutely happy.

STAGE 5

MAPPING TONES ON THE RIGHT SIDE.

Now you have outlined and positioned the shapes, it is time to do the same for the shadows. With a light, unlikely-to-smudge, H pencil lightly draw the shapes of the shadows. Don't worry too much if you don't get them all, the general catchment area will do fine.

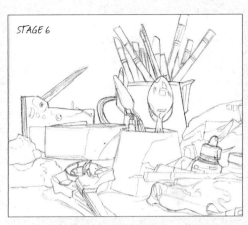

STAGE 6

MAPPING TONES ON THE LEFT SIDE.

At the moment you are using a light, hard pencil that can been shiny and difficult to work into if it's used very firmly, so use it lightly and it's very easy to correct, as well hardly leaving any marks. Draw the outlines of the shadows lightly on the left hand side.

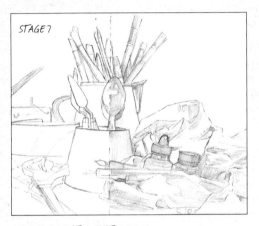

STAGE 7

BASE COAT OF TONE

Shade in the areas you have drawn as shadows. This just needs to be a general shading; don't worry or overwork it, it's simply to give you an idea of how the shadows are going to look so that you can correct their shape and position, but not their intensity.

STAGE 8

AND SOME MORE

Once again, shade the areas you have designated as shadow. Assess the shading in comparison to the photograph; if you are totally happy, move on. Now comes the hopefully foolproof non-smudge tip. I have done this as a right-hander; sway the sides around if you are left-handed.

STAGE 9

MODELLING THE TONES ON THE LEFT

Aim to include the breadth of contrast from black to white in your image, but this stage is all about the full range of greys. Work from left to right to prevent your hand smudging previous shading and really enjoy exploring the marks, shadows and shapes created by overworking with the HB pencil. Use the pencil and pressure to its fullest advantage.

STAGE 10

MODELLING THE TONES ON THE RIGHT

Work up the right side, using the flattest part of the tip of your pencil to avoid scratchy marks, correcting where necessary with a rubber. Enjoy the subtler tones in the shirt and enhance the folds with curved lines. The modelling should really take a while, with lots of checking and correcting.

STAGE 11

THE BACKGROUND LINES AND REDUNDANCY

Look very carefully at the top of the stapler and you will see a thin graceful highlight. Capture this when you fill in your background, and remember the sketch but bold bristle effect too. Solidly colour in the stark background and show off the skill of the foreground. Now treat yourself!

How to...
draw eyes

In day-to-day activity, eyes can betray the spoken word. In art too, they can reveal hidden truths, so it's imperative to master their form

Drawing 101

How many times do we refer to eyes and sight in everyday life? 'The eyes have it'; 'I see what you mean'; 'Seeing is believing'; 'Eyes are the windows to the soul'. It could be argued that these describe the credibility or truth that eyes express. A smile is false because of the crinkle of the eyes, not because of the curve of the lips. It is therefore crucial to try and overcome initial mistakes. This tutorial aims to refine and enhance both your observational and drawing skills.

When we are very small, we make huge assumptions when drawing faces and eyes. We assume we automatically know where the features lie within the ears, chin and hairline. We forget to double-check – we've looked at faces, eyes in particular, all our lives and we think we don't need to look twice. We forget that it's hard to draw accurately from our imagination, which regularly trips us up. So with that in mind, some common assumptions with eyes include missing or seriously linear eyebrows, repetitive,

sparse eyelashes or including the whole of the outside of the iris. Then there is the shape of things. The almond shape of the eye, how far down the hood of the lid drapes, the reflection in the pupil – there's plenty to look into. The key to success lies in keen observation; you can't look at your subject too much in a sitting.

Sorting these teething problems will give you a very sound foundation on which to build your image. Our next consideration will be the observation and representation of shadows and the type of shading that works for the skin folds around the eyes. With shading, start out cross-hatched and scribbly, then aim for smooth and soft on top. This is achievable with the right pencil leads. Start out with a correctable H and enrich the midtones later with a B or HB. A final dark contrast can be added with a 2B and even a 6B for the pupil or eyelashes. To draw an eye accurately is said to be one of the hardest aspects to perfect, and therefore one of the most satisfying to master. By following these tips and the step-by-step, stage-by-stage process from start to finish, you really will enjoy this challenge.

Free reference photos for all
Practise your drawing skills with the CD reference files

SOURCE FILE ON THE CD!

All in proportion

Avoid your subject looking cross-eyed

It is more than likely that you will be drawing a portrait to accompany your eyes so here are a few pointers about accurate proportions. Plot the eyes just above the horizontal halfway mark on the face. The eyebrows are just under a third of the way down the face – bear in mind that the density of the eyebrows can transform the look of a face. The eyeline now needs to be divided up into five. The eyes can then be drawn with an almond shape into the two spaces that are neither at the side nor in the middle. This means that the space that the nose occupies is the same size as the width of one eye.

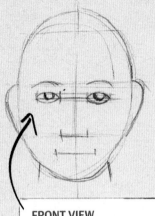

FRONT VIEW
The eyes ought to be slightly above halfway on the face, with the eyebrows roughly in line with the tip of the ears

SIDE VIEW
Common mistakes when drawing the eyes include placing them on the face's edge or too near the ears

Dimensions

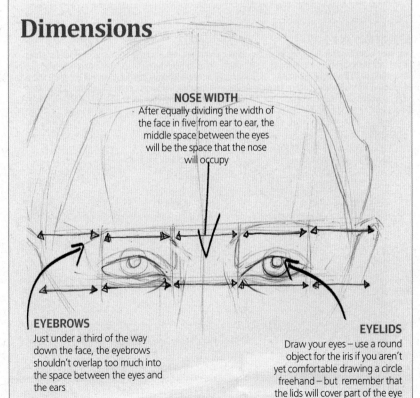

NOSE WIDTH
After equally dividing the width of the face in five from ear to ear, the middle space between the eyes will be the space that the nose will occupy

EYEBROWS
Just under a third of the way down the face, the eyebrows shouldn't overlap too much into the space between the eyes and the ears

EYELIDS
Draw your eyes – use a round object for the iris if you aren't yet comfortable drawing a circle freehand – but remember that the lids will cover part of the eye

Different eye shapes

What works and what doesn't

HOODED EYES
With careful observation you will notice that these eyes are half-covered by the top lid. Half the pupil is visible beneath and there is lots of white. Draw an egg shape and a circle at one end for the eyeball and pupil; divide this in half to denote the lid. Subtly build the shadows on the lids to create form.

SMALL EYES
Looking at small eyes, you will notice that they are long like a fat banana rather than an almond, and you can see almost all of the iris. Draw an egg shape once again, but this time the lids will encase it on either side. A slimline eyelid and short, stubby eyelashes accompany this elegant and understated type of eye.

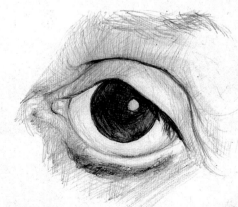

ROUND EYES
This one has a large round shape for the eyeball, just covered by a rounded lid that sits in a round socket. The sunken socket and large iris exaggerates the pupil size and shape of the eyeball. Capturing the perfect circle for the iris is nearly impossible freehand. When you start out, use a appropriately shaped object like a coin to build your confidence, then back to freehand.

Seeing is believing

Beauty is in the eye of the beholder – literally, in this case, so make sure you do it justice by perfecting your drawing skills

This tutorial needs careful consideration over the quality of your paper – cartridge is best – and a really good source to draw from. We used a large black-and-white photograph, a clean rubber and a range of pencils from 2H to 6B. You will need to set aside about three or four hours to follow this tutorial, as it should take you the best part of an afternoon. Take your time to look at your source material and tweak your drawing constantly. Don't get put off if you make any mistakes; keep trying as you will improve enormously with practise.

Guidelines for your eyelines

Blink and you'll miss it

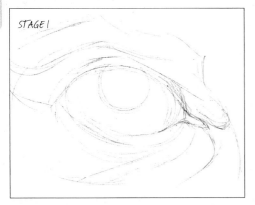

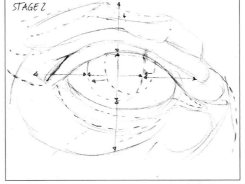

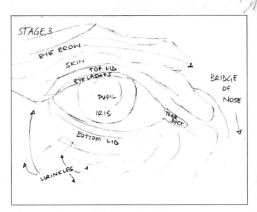

MAPPING THE MAIN SHAPE
Draw expressively and freely for a few minutes, to sketch out the general shapes that make up the different parts of the eye. You can afford to hold your H pencil loosely and make a curvaceous and soft sketch. The sketch's most important function is to show you how much paper the eye will occupy.

CHECKING YOUR MEASUREMENTS
Now to double-check that your sketch is accurate. You may find that when you observe the relationships between the different parts, you see that you have initially drawn the pupil in the wrong place; just move it to the right place. Use the pupil as your starting point and work out how many pupil widths make up the width and height of your image.

FIRMING UP THE FIRST SKETCH
You should now feel confident that your outline is correct and you can convey that confidence in your drawing. Rub out sketchy lines and, firmly but lightly, draw the most important descriptive lines. If you are in any doubt about what goes where, label the different parts so you don't get lost without the tones to guide you.

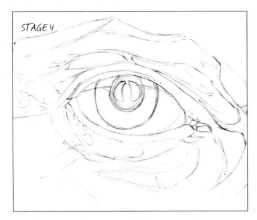

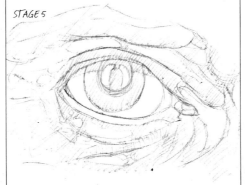

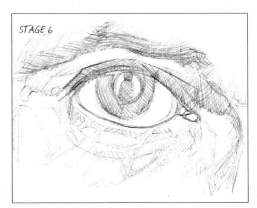

DETAILING THE TONES
Here is where your keen powers of observation will really help. You have to look carefully at the shape and relationships that the shadows take. Where are they deepest? Where are they subtle? Where are they delicate? Outline them all with confident H pencil lines once again.

THE FIRST TONES
Remove any labels, trust your outlines and begin to colour or shade in the shadows and dark areas. The lightest parts are the whites of the eye and the reflection in the pupil. But you may decide to leave a few other areas as white paper. Shade very loosely and quickly, making sure you shade in one direction.

THE SECOND LAYER OF TONES
Your first layer of shading should include all shadows very lightly in the middle of the tonal range. Carefully observing the darkest areas and shading them in the opposite direction can enrich this. You should now have a sound working sketch that can be easily changed if you still feel some areas aren't quite working.

STAGE 7

THE NEXT DOUBLE CHECK
At this stage, even if you think it is all going smoothly, take a good long look at your drawing as you may notice a few mistakes; possibly the too-round shape of the tear duct or the line of the bottom lid may be too sharp as it lies against the eyeball. The bottom lid is unprotected and moist, so it will pick up highlights without even trying and needs very little definition.

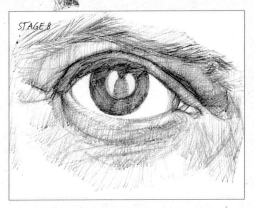

STAGE 8

MAKING MARKS – THE FUN BIT
The next focus is on the skin texture, folds and contours of the lids, wrinkles and brow. You can really go for it at this stage, scribbling and cross-hatching to your heart's content. Consider the curve of the folds and cross-hatch in the direction of the curves. This will help you get a real sense of the movement of the folds and creases.

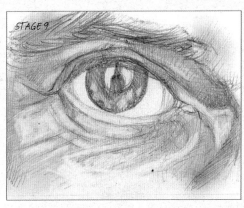

STAGE 9

SMUDGING – THE NEXT FUN BIT
Now we are working on the tones and highlights of the skin only. To enhance the smoothness of the skin, smudge your H pencil scribbles firmly with your finger. You should feel that the drawing is not set in stone from the start to finish, giving you plenty of room to correct mistakes. Finally, take a clean rubber and rub out the smudges to create highlights.

STAGE 10

THE EYEBROWS
Time to define. So far we have done all the work with an H pencil. Pick up your HB pencil and go crazy on the eyebrows. Look carefully to see the direction of the individual hairs and do your best to capture this direction with swift, short marks. These marks start heavily and tail off like a hair; you may need to do them back to front to suggest a softer edge.

STAGE 11

THE EYELIDS
Use your B pencil to pick out the defining lines surrounding the lids. Use a sharp lead for the top ones. The bottom lid needs a much softer line so use the blunt edge of your pencil to define it before you add with a rather sharper lead, small and subtle eyelashes on the bottom lid. The top lid will also require darker definition, especially at the edges of the lid.

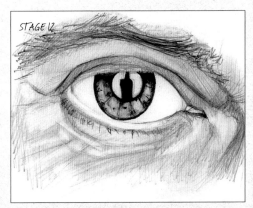

STAGE 12

THE IRIS AND PUPIL
Pick up your 2B pencil and your rubber. Look deep into the eye. You'll see speckles, blotches, a dark circle around the very edge and a massive reflection right in the centre. Recording the tones and the reflection brings the eye to life. Draw exactly what you see and don't worry if it looks wrong, it will all fit together when it's complete.

STAGE 13

THE TOP LASHES
Aim once again to make your marks in the correct direction that the real eyelashes follow. Use a B pencil once again or a HB. Layer upon layer with no curls, unless they are there. Then allow the dark shading you use here to creep down towards the tear duct.

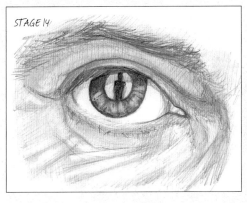

STAGE 14

LAST MINUTE HIGHLIGHTS AND LOWLIGHTS
The reflection brings the eye to life but don't forget to add realism to the eye with the all important eyeball shadows. The lashes cast a shadow over the very top of the eyeball and this continues down to the corners of the eye. Use an H pencil to create a subtle shadow.

STAGE 15

THE FINAL TOUCHES
Just a few reminders to polish it off. Check your wrinkles are still well picked out with your rubber. Smudge any areas that look too cross-hatched. Finally pick up your darkest pencil and give a final layer of darkness onto the eyelashes, the top half of the eye and the middle, lower section of the eyebrows. Finally, have a close look to check all is in order.

Art study | How to paint sunlight

How to...
Paint sunlight

If the colour palette is the soul of a
painting, then light must be its pulse and its life!

Unsuccessful ✗

Successful

SPLASHES THAT DON'T MAKE MUCH OF A SPLASH
This is basically the same painting as below, but we left
the sky sort of bland, no area of light source and not much
highlighting in the tree. The atmosphere here is completely
different, even a bit overcast and stormy. Notice that your view
wanders around, trying to decide on a focal point.

TIMID HIGHLIGHTS
We did add some
highlights and tiny splashy
strokes in the unsuccessful
image, but they're hardly
noticeable and definitely
not exciting. Wherever
you decide to place your
highlights, they will boost
the energy of the image
and add to its painterly
quality. In this one here,
the highlights on the
waves spring forth.

HIGHLIGHTS THROUGHOUT
Highlights and sparkles in the
water don't just happen in
isolation. We have to set the
entire stage by introducing
a light source, then highlight
all the other elements we've
painted into our scene.
Without actually painting
a sun, we brightened
the upper-right corner to
represent the light source.

SPLASHES THAT SPARKLE
Water highlights can be achieved with various brushes, from Leaky Pen
to FX brushes. Try them all and have fun! Splashes are mainly white,
but vary the opacity and brush size, thinking 'watery' as you work.
Splashes will sometimes have a darker shade of blue beneath them.

Water highlights

Have you ever spent idyllic hours, maybe an entire afternoon, happily painting
away, sure this was going to be your finest hour? Only to discover after you'd
done your final save that your painting was a bit of a disappointment? Maybe it
just didn't have that certain something. Chances are you were too sparing with
your lighting. Painting highlights and shadows is not at all difficult. In fact, it can
be the most fun part of painting. It just requires thinking in terms of making your
highlights the focal point – the star of the show.

In this art study we will take a closer look at adding light throughout the
painting, not just a sprinkling of highlights here and there. We'll consider which
colour palettes might be more effective for painting light at various times of day
(especially when we're going for a more painterly and less realistic look), how
to paint direct, hazy and dappled light, and we'll discuss painting shadows in
various lighting situations.

66.62%

Sunlight in different surroundings

For this segment we decided to explore the challenges of painting three lighting situations: Direct, Hazy and Dappled.

Again, none of what we've done is difficult – it simply requires that we think about our light source and how we want it to behave within the painted image. This applies whether we're painting in watercolours, oils, charcoal or acrylics, and is usually just as important in painting abstracted landscapes and scenes as it is in depicting very realistically rendered images.

The paintings we're asked about that don't quite satisfy the painter usually have less to do with the artist's talent and more to do with them not paying enough attention to lighting, highlights and shadows. And it's something we all forget at times, whether we've just begun painting or have been splashing on the paint for years.

So let's have a good look at the examples on this page…

Direct light

Direct light applied to your image can be the most powerful and arguably the most interesting form of all lighting, as it creates an echo-like image beyond everything it touches. And of course the more realistically you're painting, the more painstakingly you'll need to define this secondary image.

SHADOW AS AN IMPORTANT PLAYER
This shadow becomes second in importance as a focal point, only to the scraggly old paintbrush itself. We took liberties with the shadow colours, adding in touches of amethyst and sapphire tones to rescue it from being a blob of black.

JEWEL TONES TO PASTELS
The progression of colour from vibrant to pastel provides a push/pull effect, and adds energy to the painting. Here we're concentrating more on shadow than on highlights.

Hazy light

The scene before us takes on a romantic atmosphere as we gaze across the meadow through early morning or late evening haze that rises from the moist earth. The farther into the distance we can see, the heavier the haze becomes – much like depth of field in photography.

Dappled light

There are many ways to paint dappled light, one being to paint the image somewhat realistically and then overlay it with a mottled layer (set to one of the Screening blend modes). We chose another route, and painted this one abstractly in a colour palette that speaks of dappled light and shadow.

Different times of the day

For this segment we divided the image into three sections to form a triptych, and painted the first one as early dawn, the middle one as midday and the third one as late evening. Definitely not your typical triptych, but it was great fun to do! And because we can envision the sun beginning on one side, swinging overhead and ending on the other, it serves as a good example of how to deal with sunlight in your paintings.

It's important to consider the time of day when painting, especially with landscape scenes. Each segment has a definite mood, and you can exploit this once you understand which one is most relevant. Dawn and dusk are the more mysterious times of day, with midday offering harsh light and little shadow. Dusk tends to be hazier than dawn, especially in cities, as the pollution has built up over the day.

 ### Dawn

The sunlight is coming from the top-left corner, and as it spills down it creates shadows beneath the tree branches. You can see the progression of light from bottom to top of this panel, and the colours go from drab greens to yellow-greens bursting with life. Then we thought about how light would filter through the pine needles to highlight surfaces below, and brushed on lighter colours.

 ### Midday

At midday with the sun overhead the colours are harder, as are the divisions between highlight and shadow. The light reads as white, and you can almost feel the warmth as it reflects from horizontal surfaces. Compared with the other two panels, these colours might even seem washed-out. The story we're telling is still about light and the shadow shapes it carves below the images where it comes to rest.

 ### Evening

In the final panel we exercised our artistic licence with the colours, opting for cool blues and purples with just a few rays of golden light peeking through from the right side, softly touching a scattering of surfaces. Deciding where it will touch is the most fun part of all. The result of this exaggerated colour palette is an atmosphere of a summer evening, quietly waiting for nightfall to descend.

Painting with shadows

Just as light provides the focal point in paintings, the shadows map out the shapes and are no less essential in helping a viewer work out the forms in your scene and move around the canvas.

In the following examples we painted the entire images, but then desaturated half of each one to show just how perfectly the shadows and highlights map the image elements – providing a map of where to paint light colours or white, and where to paint deep colours that advance to black. This is a great trick for complex scenes or if you aren't feeling confident with applying the shadows and highlights freehand.

It's also a good way to make sure your image is tonally interesting. When you're in doubt about whether your painting contains enough highlight and shadow, make a copy of it, desaturate, and then squint your eyes as you look at it. If you see a nice pattern of darks and lights, then you have succeeded. If it seems flat, boost things up!

Shadows in the snow

This cabin in the snow painting was created in a limited palette, but when the image is desaturated we see even more clearly where the major shapes are. Because we painted it with a Wide Impasto brush, the brush strokes themselves provide interesting shapes within the image.

Bell tones

The little bell shapes in this pretty, white hyacinth painting create a playful, somewhat delicate vertical pattern, with shadows of the petals describing secondary areas of interest. Notice that the desaturated side takes on a somewhat sombre appearance, while the coloured side looks light and airy because our minds respond to colour.

Chalk patterns

This bright painting of ordinary pieces of chalk actually becomes a study in cylindrical shapes as the shadow map describes those large, dark areas. Notice that the medium greys were painted with medium colour values, the light greys with light colours and so on. A useful tool for when you're painting with light.

Size: 20.0   Opacity: 100%   Resat: 8%   Bleed: 100%   Feature: 2.7

How to...
paint still water

Introducing water into your landscape paintings will add life and sparkle to the final image. Here's a roundup of the best techniques for painting calm water, ensuring tranquil results every time

What works and what doesn't

Sometimes we stop short of painting water because it presents its own set of challenges. We will discuss how to paint calm, quiet waters, sometimes motionless, at other times softly rippling. You will see how to describe this seemingly clear liquid on a digital canvas and how to indicate its gentle movements, how to paint its edges and what colours to choose.

Successful ✓

'SNOW BLUE IN THIS SKY...
We usually think of using blue for water, but the blue we see in nature's water is, of course, the blue reflected from the sky. This painting is of an overcast, snowy day, and there's no blue in the sky so the colours seen in the water are shades of charcoal.

REFLECT ON THIS
Because we're facing the snow bank on the far side of the water, you would expect more reflections there.

SEEN IT? USE IT!
It's tempting to grab a blue hue and start painting that pool of water. Whatever colour you choose for the water should be one you pull from the surrounding scene. That way, the whole thing is cohesive and the pool looks as if it belongs in the painting.

CAREFUL BLEND
Here we used the Just Add Water blender. It's very useful in painting water, but in this example we went way too far and blended out all the character. It's opaque, boring and featureless.

Unsuccessful ✗

ADD PRESENCE
And how to describe the water's edges? Shadows were applied to anchor objects to the piece.

COLOUR CONTROL
Calm water may be smooth, but a painting with great expanses of one hue without textures just doesn't work. .

◼ Reflections

Everyone is at least a little mesmerised by reflections in the water, and they add so much to our paintings. When painting a photograph, it's easy to paint an existing reflection and just as easy to add them where there were none. Let's get started!

CURRENT AFFAIRS
Even if there are none, imagine deep, gentle currents in the water, and these will guide you in distorting your reflections. Paint with a broad brush and resist the urge to fiddle around with details.

MIRROR SHIMMER
In this, the surface of the water acts as a mirror of the entire scene. Remember that it's not a perfect mirror image; everything within it will be slightly softened, distorted or rounded as the water undulates beneath it. Take the water's movement into account.

REFLECTION SELECTIONS
Your reflections needn't be scientifically verifiable. We're more concerned with composition, so if your cloud needs to be larger to balance out a space, then make it larger. Not sure those trees would cast a reflection? It's your painting. You decide.

Step-by-step

Create realistic reflections by selecting areas of your photograph and applying them to the water, so that you get a true mirror image that you can then paint and distort as much or as little as you want

01 First, take a deep breath and step back from your image and consider where there might be reflections in the water or where they might enhance your composition. Choose the Lasso tool and loosely select an area of the painting. By selecting loosely, you're leaving yourself room to decide later what to keep and what to brush away.

02 Now copy and paste, and it appears on its own layer ready to move into position. Choose Layer Adjuster and hover the cursor over your selection while right-clicking, then select Free Transform. Now to move it into the water; drag top to bottom and reverse the image. Hold down Ctrl/Cmd and you can rotate the selection by dragging on the handles.

03 Once it's in position, right-click again and choose Commit Transform. Find a soft Eraser and begin removing the unwanted edges. Now drop the layer, and the selection is part of your canvas and ready to be painted. Repeat the process for other areas you want to convert to reflections and paint them all at once for a better flow.

◼ Reflecting on puddles

Puddles are great for a suggestion of water but mean you haven't got to paint great expanses. The priciples are the same as any water – take colours from the sky and keep things soft. Use shadows at the edge to give a sense of weight.

The puddles in the first image have formed in asphalt tire ruts and form the basis of an abstract image. We can see the sky reflected in the puddle closest to us, but the ones nearer the sun reflect only light.

The leaves lying in the water and the ones reflected from overhead make a beautiful mosaic in the third puddle.

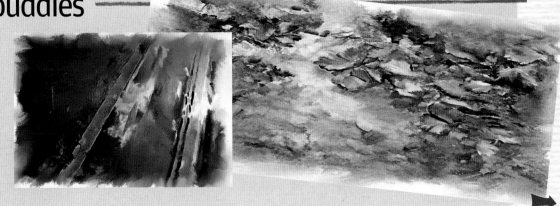

Size: 20.0 Opacity: 100% Resat: 8% Bleed: 100% Feature: 2.7

Art study

Painting ripples

Even still water has the suggestion of movement and so ripples are an important skill to master. They aren't complicated but there are fundamental rules. For the most part, our process of painting water digitally is the reverse of painting it traditionally. In a traditional painting, we would save the white areas and paint around them, but in digital painting we paint medium values first and then paint darks and lights over those.

Step-by-step

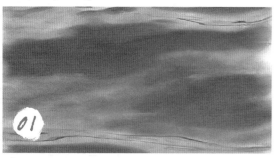

The Airbrushes set to less than 50 per cent Opacity are a great way to begin painting water ripples, glazing layers as you go in sweeping horizontal strokes. Brushstrokes and textures can be added later. Using medium value hues, begin describing watery ripples, keeping them smooth; think of painting satin as you go.

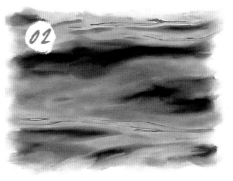

Now you'll begin to see the shapes forming into ripples where darker hues will add depth. Drop Airbrush Opacity to less than 30 per cent and begin defining those darker areas that will be the depths of your ripples, always keeping in mind the direction of your light source.

Time now to brush on the highlights, areas where the sunlight, moonlight or even harbour lights would touch the tops of the ripples with white. You may want to stop here or you might want to add bristle brushstrokes or some harder lines with the Pens or Pencils to indicate smaller ripples.

Painting water over rocks

For this, take a rock painting and then use transparent layers and the Gel composite method to introduce the water feel. In these examples, the water looks slightly green and grows more opaque where the water is deeper (you might choose blue or yellow ochre).

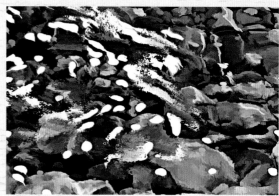

Patches of pale blue suggest the sky peeking through tree branches and add shimmer to the surface; exaggerated shadows between the stones add dimension and interest to our watery scene.

We can add more depth by painting floating flower petals, leaves or foam above the stones. Here, the white and blue pattern flicks on top of the water as an interesting element, as they define the water's current, leading our attention into the painting.

Painting water at sunset

Let's see what happens when water takes on vibrant colours not generally associated with water. We decided to paint a sunset reference photo with even more vivid colours. However realistic or abstract we go, the images in a sunset more or less become symbols, because of extreme lights and darks.

Where water meets the shore

It just takes a few straight, imperfect lines to suggest the water's edge. If that edge is in shadow, then paint a dark line, but if it would catch sparkles of sunlight, make it white. For this edge, we used the F-X Fairy Dust brush, set to a very small size, and painted loosely on a separate layer.

Step-by-step

01 Abstract art We began with an abstract of random brushstrokes, using various brushes from Acrylic Captured Bristle to Watercolor Wet Wash, preparing for the sun and its rays on the water. Take your time; even if you later paint most of it away, it remains the most painterly part. While we're laying colours in the appropriate areas, we don't want them completely segregated.

02 Fence The fence adds interest, so we kept it in our painting. Because the sun's rays are so concentrated, the fence becomes little more than a silhouette, so we don't even have to worry about describing depth in the boards. We began painting in the rectangle that will be the sun's rays across the water, starting with palest yellow near the horizon and going darker near the lower edge of the painting.

03 Sparkle The rays of the setting sun would sparkle on the water, and we've brought out the F-X Fairy Dust brush for this. Our brush size is very small, about five, and the Opacity is less than 50 per cent so it remains somewhat transparent. Choosing colours from the rest of the image, we brushed Fairy Dust in randomly horizontal strokes, painting onto an empty layer so that we could play with opacity and blending modes.

04 Final details We liked the sparkle of the Fairy Dust so much that we added light touches of it to the sun, the fence and the horizon. This is where we decided to say our painting was finished, but you could take it further and bring in more touches of realism if you like. The vibrant colours work well with either style because they're not really exaggerated.

Art study

How to paint...
Meadows and fields

Bring the outside in, with **Cat Bounds'** guide to painting rolling hilly vistas and soft meadows filled with summer flowers

ADD SOME VERTICALS
To counterbalance the horizontal shapes, I made sure I worked in some verticals in the form of tree trunks, blades of grass, flower stems and paint strokes

BANDS OF COLOUR
It seems meadows are usually about horizontal bands of colour, and I exaggerated that point when I splashed on the foreground, middle ground and trees in the background

AND A FOCAL POINT
We'll discuss this more later on, but for my focal point I decided to make mine really big, and sort of in your face, in the form of these very large, colourful Coneflowers

A SPRINKLING OF FLOWERS
Any self-respecting meadow needs at least a few wildflowers. Some of these can be simply a sprinkling of flower colours, while others need to be more realistically described

In this Art Study, we will get to explore some exciting colour palettes. After all, the sky isn't always a cerulean blue, the grass isn't always an emerald green, and sometimes it's just more satisfying to play around with the colours and step outside of your comfort zone. In addition to colour, we will be looking at two fabulous subjects to paint. Fields often have no dominate focal point but can still make amazing artwork. We will show you the tricks of the trade, but will first see how meadows give artists a host of things to consider, but an even greater amount of creative possibilities.

Meadows

Colours of meadows and skies

As you paint, imagine walking across a meadow with your sketchbook, and dipping your stylus into the colours you find there. There is an immediacy to nature that we each try to capture. Success depends on our original intent; I enjoy colour palettes that relate to the scene but inspire just an instant of surprise, and then recognition.

Skies

Meadows

Growing wild

I can't think of many things more enjoyable than painting a mass of wildflowers, because just about anything works. They can be seriously photo-realistic or abstracted to within an inch of their lives, and still, they're all beautiful!

01 **Wildflower source image** This source image from Stock Xchng (**http://www.sxc.hu/browse. phtml?f=view&id=750288**) is almost a painting already. The photographer has a good eye for composition, and I didn't see any need to crop anything or make any serious colour changes.

02 **Wildflowers in waiting** I began by softly painting the background using soft bristle brushes and the Just Add Water blender. I pasted in a few more flowers to fill empty places in the foreground composition, and painted them in a splashy fashion. At this stage I'm feeling my way into the painting.

03 **Growing wild** Now for some colour decisions as I bring in my own colours, like the golds that work better than the red-oranges, and a more vibrant green for the grass. I'm happy with the overall effect of softness and splashes of colour.

Art study

Fields

What works and what doesn't

Fields rarely have focal points, so it's up to you as an artist, to add these. Look at the examples below. The unsuccessful image pretty much copies the photo and results in a lot of nothing. The successful image has a tighter crop and flowers have been added for interest.

Fields of colour

On p64 we discussed painting seasonal landscapes, so we're not going to go into seasonal colours here, but of course that's a large part of the colour palette selection process — and in any of the seasons the colours can run the gamut from earth tones to vibrant tones.

Successful

Unsuccessful

Directional flow

How the viewer's gaze enters and travels through a painting can make or break it. Movement denotes life, and even in a painting of static elements, we can still create the essence of directional flow. I wanted this painting to be about the tall grass in the foreground, but also about the angles in the fields and the sky.

Step-by-step

01 **Step into my painting** This deep, dark area on the lower right is possibly the most obvious place to enter this painting. And then of course we'll be led upward, towards the tree and towards the light.

02 **Flowing grasses** As soon as we enter the painting, our gaze is drawn upward by the grass, towards the upper fields, and finally to the sky. I used several pen brushes and acrylic brush variants to describe the grass, remembering to include highlights and shadow areas.

03 **Following the angles** From the left side of the painting where the tree resides, our gaze continues to rise, this time swinging back toward the right and still following the angles of the fields.

04 **Into the clouds** Finally, we are swept back up towards the left of the painting, as we follow the clouds, and then back the way we came. This is a slightly exaggerated example, but it illustrates how every painting benefits from a visual path to lead us into it and through it.

Adding livestock

One more way to add life to our field painting is to add some livestock. Sheep are for me the easiest to paint because they're basically puffs of off-white wool with black faces, standing on small black legs. Paint animals on an empty layer above your field painting so as not to disturb the background, and so you can play with its size and positioning. Begin with some rough brush strokes and then refine the shape.

So, that's our Field and Meadow art study. We hope it's inspired you to try your own!

Art study

How to paint
realistic buildings

Employ a few traditional techniques and you can give your
building paintings a solid foundation

Making plans

When attempting a painting of a building, you need to decide on a few things before you make a start. Buildings are hefty objects, and to look convincing they need to feel as though they are a solid construct. So allow yourself some planning permission as you need to work out the correct perspective for the edges of the building. Draw some perspective guides and then sketch out your building. Once you have the outline and the colour filled in, you need to add shadows. These are what will make your building really take on a three-dimensional shape, so decide on your light source and apply shadows accordingly. You will feel like some of the shadows are too harsh, but stick with it and you'll be surprised at how well it all ties together.

To help you get a feel for the kind of considerations needed, we've approached this photo as if we were going to paint it, and written what sorts of things we would take into account.

01 PERSPECTIVE
Perspective represents an image as it is seen by the eye. Objects are drawn smaller as their distance from the observer increases. There are several types of perspective: one point, two points, three points and five points, depending on the viewpoint. Some angles will give a different impression on the viewer.

02 LIGHT SOURCE
The light source is important for the shading. It will dictate how dark the shadows will be, how the contours will be, where they will be placed, in which parts of the building, etc.

03 SHADOWS
Depending on the light source and the time of the day, we will have different shadows. Some of them are cast from other features of the building upon them.

04 STYLE OF THE BUILDING
When painting a building, you need to think about the style of it and what materials were used to build it. Is it wood, is it bricks, is it stone? How is the roof shaped? Does it have ornaments? How are the windows shaped?

05 HISTORY
As the building will be your centre of attention, it will be treated as having a personality. It's always good to think of location or the people who live there. A building with a story will make it far more interesting than a building with no meaning.

Working with perspective

After you have spent a bit of time looking at your building, it's time to start the sketching. The first thing you need to decide is the perspective of the viewer, as this will decide on the angles of the building. Here's a look at three of the most useful viewpoints.

One-point perspective

This refers to a single point converging on a plane. In other words, if you look down a road or a field, you will notice the rows of the field (which, in actual fact, are parallel to each other and level with the ground) seem to meet at the same point in the distant horizon. When you draw a cube or a room in one-point perspective, all of the lines that recede away from you will appear to converge on this point. This is called the vanishing point and always occurs on the horizon. One-point perspective is typically used for buildings where the front directly faces the viewer.

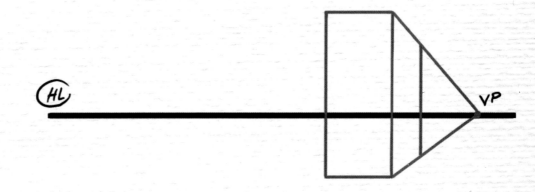

Two-point perspective

With the two-point perspective, we still have one horizon but now we have two vanishing points. Instead of looking at an object from straight on, we are looking at it from an angle. The corner of the cube in perspective is the point closest to us. In one-point perspective, the horizontal lines are parallel and the vertical lines are parallel. With two-point perspective, only the vertical lines are parallel to the edge of the page and each other. One of the most common errors is the distortion resulting from having both vanishing points within the field of vision, or too close to the subject. It's important to make sure your two vanishing points are far apart, otherwise you get forced, warped views.

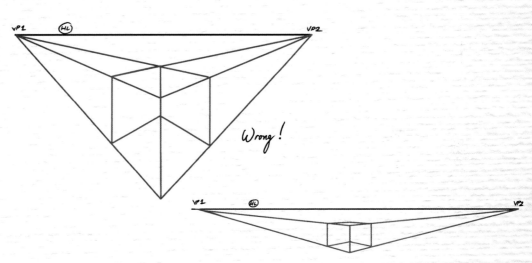

Three-point perspective

Three-point perspective is used to create dramatic camera angles – the upshot and the downshot. We have to start with the original two-point perspective setup – the horizon line is very high or low. Where the third point goes is entirely up to you, depending upon the type of shot you want to create (up or down). In very extreme compositions, the third point is a lot closer to the object and the shot becomes basically one-point perspective. If you are not going for extreme shots, make sure your third vanishing point is very, very far away from the object. Otherwise, like in two-point perspective, you may find some distortion due to the short distance between the vanishing points.

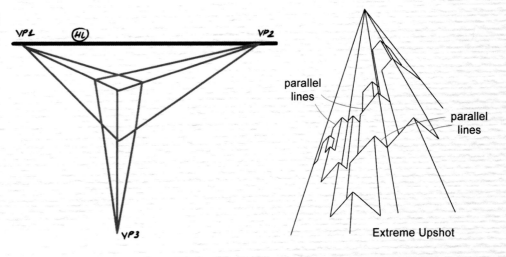

Start the painting

Now that we have taken into account all the considerations, we can start painting a building. Here, we show you the progression from initial perspective sketch through to final creation.

Art study

Building a house

01 Thumbnails and designs A thumbnail sketch is a quick way of seeing if something works or not. You have to think about composition and camera placement when doing a thumbnail. It may take several of these to get the right shot for your background and building. You may want to move the horizon line, play with the angle of the camera and all sorts of different compositional ideas.

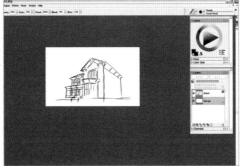

02 Use perspective A horizon line and vanishing points need to be established to draw objects in relationship to one another. Use horizontal lines parallel for the horizon, and depth guidelines to the vanishing point to draw the house. By using the vanishing points, we draw windows and doors. Draw diagonal lines from corner to corner. Where they cross is the centre of the square.

03 Drop in the base colours Now that our technical issues are solved, it's time to drop in the first colours. Never start with a flat white background. Choose your background colours, as they will lead the overall mood and atmosphere of your building. Rough out the sky, the street or the trees, for instance. Don't be too detailed. Just drop in the basic colours in blocks, using a big covering brush. We are more interested in the overall shape that in the details.

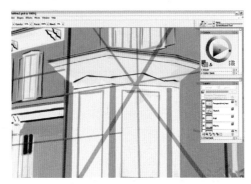

04 Start with details Add details to make the windows, doors and other elements pop out from the basic shapes, using your sketch and perspective lines layers in a low Opacity level as guides. Use a smaller covering brush and straight lines when necessary, with slight lower Opacity. You can do it on the same layer or create a new one. Do not add the shading yet.

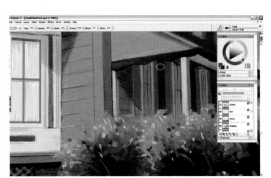

05 Shading and further details Until now, the house looked lifeless, and that was because of the absence of shading. There are many different brushes to use to make your house look traditional. In this case, we used the Square Chalk and the Scratchboard Tool pen for details on another layer. Feel free to use as many layers as you may need. Using the Color Wheel, make sure to pick colours that are not only darker, but have interesting hues.

66.62%

◼ Adding shadows

Shading depicts levels of darkness on the surface by applying media with a darker shade for darker areas, and lighter shade for lighter areas. As basic as this definition goes, shading is what makes the difference between a flat painting and a painting with a three-dimensional feeling. With shadows, we can create the illusion of depth by making any lifeless object look more realistic, dramatic and interesting to the eye.

01 ROOF
The roof casts a shadow underneath, but due to the position of the sun, it is not long enough to cover part of the wall.

02 WALLS
As the wall is made of wood panels, you can make them look three-dimensional by placing a cast shadow from the window upon it in a wedge shape, slightly noticeable. This may also apply to bricks, stones, etc.

03 WINDOW TOP
This time, the window top casts a shadow that not only covers the underneath part,

but also reaches onto the wall next to it, making a rhomboid sort of shape

04 WINDOWS
Windows can have a three-dimensional feel to them easily, simply given by a darker line where the sun doesn't hit.

05 PORCH
Sometimes the cast shadows can be in gradients. In this case, as the wall is far enough from the bottom roof, the shadow cast doesn't have a defined contour, but it's rather blurred.

◼ Simplify a scene

You don't have to paint every single brick or roof tile to create a successful painting of a building – in fact, you can get more impact by simplifying areas. Remember: you are creating an artistic representation of a structure. You only need to include the key visual elements and not everything that was needed to build it!

Windows

Although everyone knows a window is not just a hole in a wall, we don't need to draw every 3D shape of it. As with the bricks, just suggest the main structure lines to give form. The trick here is to accentuate the shapes using darker or lighter lines in the correct places to bring out the 3D shapes.

Brickwork

It is not necessary to paint or draw every single brick. Just suggest them, always using perspective. Change colours on some of them to add variety, avoiding the impression of them being the same. Also take in mind 3D shapes, highlighting some contours receiving light (and shading contours not receiving it). Also you can add some texture for more painterly effects. For this example, we used the Soft Oil Pastel and Just Add Water blender, and it took few minutes. Seen from far away, they will look convincing enough.

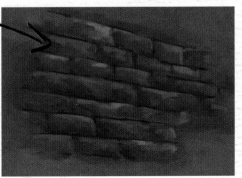

On the CD
PC and Mac

All you need to start using Corel Painter to create art

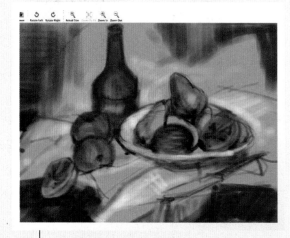

➟ Tutorial resource files

Look out for the 'On the CD' references in the tutorials. Whenever you see one of these, you can head over to the Tutorials section on the disc to download and use the source files. You'll find all sorts in here, from photos to sketches.

➟ Using Corel Painter X

In addition to the source files, you'll also find resources like patterns, stock photos and examples of final images to help you get to grips with digital art techniques, brushes and much more.

Sorry, content is only for non-commercial use.